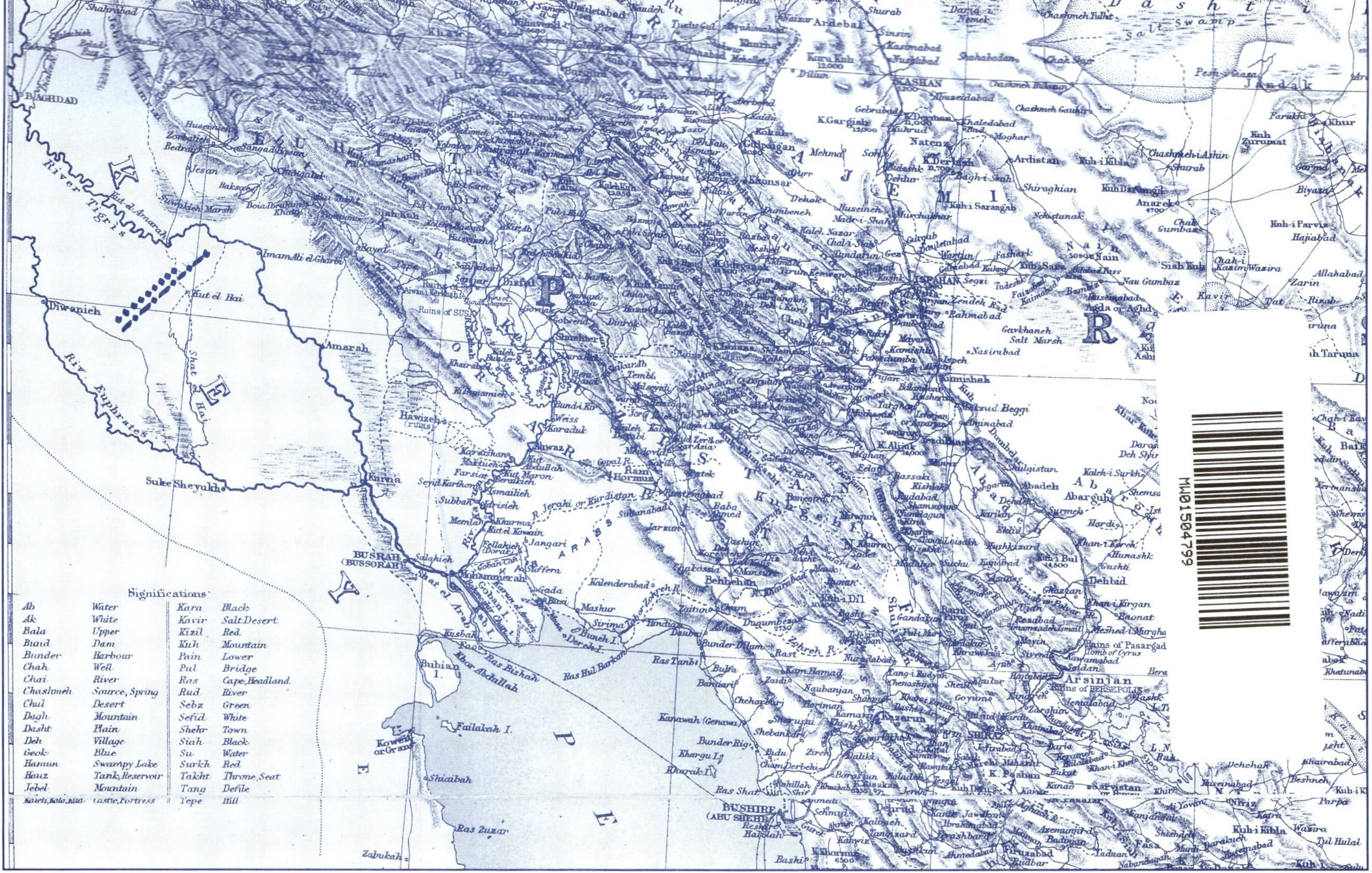
Significations
Ab Water
Ak White
Bala Upper
Bund Dam
Bunder Harbour
Chah Well
Chai River
Chashmeh Source, Spring
Chul Desert
Dagh Mountain
Dasht Plain
Deh Village
Geok Blue
Hamun Swampy Lake
Hauz Tank, Reservoir
Jebel Mountain
Kara Black
Kavir Salt Desert
Kizil Red
Kuh Mountain
Pain Lower
Pul Bridge
Ras Cape, Headland
Rud River
Sebz Green
Sefid White
Shehr Town
Siah Black
Su Water
Surkh Red
Takht Throne, Seat
Tang Defile
Tepe Hill
BAGHDAD
River Tigris
Riv. Euphrates
Diwanieh
Kut el Hai
Shat el Hai
Amarah
Kurna
Suke Sheyukh
BUSRAH (BUSSORAH)
Shat el Arab
Mohammerah
Failakah I.
Bubian I.
Ras Bishah
Ras Zuzar
Zabukah
BUSHIRE (ABU SHEHR)
Ras Shat
Kharag I.
Bunder Dilam
Ras Tanb
Behbehan
Kazerun
Arsinjan
Ruins of PERSEPOLIS
Ruins of Pasargad
Tomb of Cyrus
Abadeh
ISPAHAN
KASHAN
Natenz
Ardistan
Nain
Yezd-i-Khast
Kumisheh
Gavkhaneh Salt Marsh
Ruins of SUS
Ahwaz
Hawizeh
Kut el Amarah
Imam Ali el Gharbi
Salt Swamp
Jandak
Ruins of Pasargad

ROBE OF LIGHT

The Persian Years of the Supreme Prophet Bahá'u'lláh 1817–1853

David S. Ruhe

'Drape thyself . . . and put on, in the name of the All-Glorious, the broidered Robe of Light. Hear, then, the sweet, the wondrous accent of the Voice that cometh from the Throne of Thy Lord, the Inaccessible, the Most High.'

BAHÁ'U'LLÁH

GEORGE RONALD
OXFORD

GEORGE RONALD, Publisher
46 High Street, Kidlington, Oxford, OX5 2DN

ISBN 0–85398–355–0
A Cataloguing-in-Publication entry is available
from the British Library

Printed and bound in Great Britain by
Biddles Ltd, Guildford and King's Lynn

Table of Contents

List of Illustrations

Preface and Acknowledgements

Bahá'u'lláh lived a long and creative life. From the days when He was a 'young man with a faculty of speech like a rushing torrent' to His mellow wisdom and Revelation of 'Akká and Bahjí days in Turkish–Syrian Palestine, there was a great outflow of His Message. Bahá'u'lláh Himself reports many of the events of the nascent Bahá'í Faith as a contemporary reporter, as eyewitness, as participant. Often He brings forth recollections to illustrate points of teaching, or makes historical allusions in prayers and Tablets. Many, hopefully most, of these precious Writings are preserved in the International Bahá'í Archives in Haifa, but to the westerner these historic records pose three problems of access: their sheer volume, the similarity of certain passages to each other, and their languages of origin. There are more than 21,000 Tablets and letters of Bahá'u'lláh held in the Bahá'í Archives. These messages and many Bahá'í materials in the Persian and Arabic languages have been inaccessible to many western students who have not mastered the intricacies of the languages of the original Teachings. Until accurate English translations are made, and then always with the shortcomings of translations, these must be presumed to contain precious information which should have been included, and which will appear in later biographies.

Early chronicles of the Cause are singularly informative. Nabíl's Narrative, *The Dawn-Breakers*,* is of primary importance, particularly because Bahá'u'lláh Himself reviewed and apparently approved

* Although Nabíl's collection of materials began long years before, the actual composition of *The Dawn-Breakers* commenced in 1887, when he worked with Mírzá Músá, and was completed about two years later, within Bahá'u'lláh's lifetime.

parts of the manuscript, as attested by Shoghi Effendi, and 'Abdu'l-Bahá approved other portions; thus the quotations from Nabíl should be given a special weighting for a high level of authenticity. Since the Guardian, Shoghi Effendi, edited Nabíl's manuscript and translated chosen selections for publication in English, a further critical judgment has been added. However, in a number of passages in this book it has seemed useful to paraphrase dialogues and

Mullá Muḥammad-'Alí of Zarand, entitled Nabíl-i-A'ẓam, the Most Noble One, historian of the Bahá'í Faith in Bahá'u'lláh's time and author of The Dawn-Breakers.

descriptions by Nabíl based on interviews with participants in the historic events, in order to avoid a thicket of quotation marks.* Nabíl-i-A'ẓam is the primary source of the materials in this book. In his *The Dawn-Breakers* there are many direct quotations from Bahá'u'lláh and these are used in the text verbatim, with occasional slight changes marked. Nabíl gives various orders of information, ranging from quotations by sundry Bábís or Bahá'ís in whose veracity he had confidence to material which he has generalized. But he is not immune to the predictable effects of his ever-increasing respect and admiration for Bahá'u'lláh in becoming the contemporary biographer of the Greatest Soul. In company with Nabíl, the present author has inevitably conveyed his overwhelming feeling for the Supreme Prophet. But in toto this small book is a tribute to Nabíl, the great historian of the Bahá'í Cause.

'Abdu'l-Bahá's *A Traveler's Narrative: The Episode of the Báb*, and Shoghi Effendi's *God Passes By* are indispensable sources of information. And there are many collections of stories and data in Persian by Ishráq-i-Khávarí, 'Alí-Akbar Furútan and others, some of which have come to be available in English translation. In recent times Adib Taherzadeh's excellent four-volume study, *The Revelation of Bahá'u'lláh*, brings together a very large aggregation of data; similarly Hasan Balyuzi's *Bahá'u'lláh, The King of Glory* is at present the definitive biography in English. Moojan Momen's persistent and thorough scholarship has added very significantly to the stores of published information available to inquirers and scholars. R. Mehrabkhani's recent book on Mullá Ḥusayn has provided much background information. The high points of the Great Life seem quite clear, yet much pertinent authentic detail remains to be unearthed for ever-more-informative studies.

The Format of the Study

Chapter headings divide these early years of the life of a High Prophet into nine convenient segments. A Glossary translates and partially explains the Persian names and titles found in the text; in a few cases those Persian or Arabic names frequently used today are

* A note on quotations within the text. There are many of these, and many quotations inside quotations. Their precise nature and sources are given in the Bibliography. Where Bahá'u'lláh's and the Báb's own Words are given, the quotations are rendered in italics to set them uniquely apart from all other sources, but not to interfere seriously with smooth reading.

given their modern English spellings. However, the system of transliteration generally used is one adopted by a conference of orientalists at Geneva which was recommended and used by the Guardian of the Bahá'í Faith, hence has become the standard for Bahá'ís (see Note 1).

In this first portion of the life of Bahá'u'lláh several steps have been taken to achieve a certain consistency of narrative and a level of historical reality. Until Bahá'u'lláh first took unto Himself His title of Bahá (The Glorious One) at Badasht in 1848, He is called Mírzá Ḥusayn-'Alí Núrí (of Núr). After Badasht until His Declaration in Baghdad, the title Jináb-i-Bahá (the Honorable, the Glorious One) is used, often in the simple form of Bahá, after the usage of the martyr Ḥájí Mírzá Jání, earliest historian of the Faith. From Riḍván (21 April to 2 May) 1863* onward, as His Mission to channel the Message of God to mankind was increasingly visible, the noble title, Bahá'u'lláh, the Glory of God, is used for the High Prophet; generally this title occurs only in the Introduction and Notes.

A further comment on titles is necessary. In light of the attitude of Christians toward the Prophets of the Old Testament in the Torah, Neviim and Ketubim (the Law, the Prophets and the Writings), the word Manifestation is used for Bahá'u'lláh in many allusions from the Bahá'í Writings to Him who will be manifested by God, a Channel of God's Voice for an age in man's evolution, a Supreme Soul for the greatest of missions, the Father figure for a new age. Thus a Manifestation is far above the minor prophets of the Jewish Scriptures, but equivalent to the highest appellations for Jesus or Muḥammad.

As for titles of the distinguished personages of this chapter of Bábí-Bahá'í history, those frequently referred to are introduced by their full names, but thereafter by the given names or titles by which they are known to history, i.e. Mullá Muḥammad-'Alí of Bárfurúsh is called Quddús; Mullá Muḥammad-'Alí of Zanján is called Ḥujjat.

The historiographer's one privilege, taken with caution and full appreciation of its hazards, is always to provide pertinent details of settings and of historical personalities. There is no invented dialogue

---

* All dates have been converted to AD years of the Christian solar calendar, although Muslim calendar dates may sometimes also be given. But for those who wish to know the equivalent of a Gregorian date in the Muslim calendar, it is easy to deduct 622 (the year of Muḥammad's flight from Mecca to Medina, the Hejira) from the solar year, which will give an approximate result, bearing in mind that the Muslim lunar year is eleven days shorter than the solar year. Islamic lunar calendar dates can readily be found in library sources.

herein, nor added personal scenes, but informative materials from non-Bahá'í historians and travelers are supplied, such that this chronicle of the Great Soul emerges within the ambience of His times.

Notes and Appendices

There is a considerable accumulation of notes, many of general interest, at page bottoms. Indeed, for the serious student, many of the notes are truly a part of the text, excluded only to permit a reasonable flow of ideas. Notes of greater scope, in volume or in topic, are assembled as a separate section; and there are three Appendices.

The autobiographical details available through Bahá'u'lláh's many passages of recollection suggest that it is often important to provide complete quotations where only a selected portion has been included in the main narrative. In addition, there may be more than one quotation by Bahá'u'lláh on essentially the same subject, yet the apparently duplicative materials usually offer some useful details, hence are included in the notes. Further, every crumb of autobiographical material is here included, for the sheer interest of such precious items.

Second, the reader's encounter with a life lived in the Persian Islamic culture of the nineteenth century requires a measure of explanation of terms, customs, history and lore. Such notes may be helpful in their relations to otherwise confusing or strange elements of the text.

Third, in the case of the poetess Ṭáhirih it seems essential to give a greater taste of her genius, even if only in pale translation, hence a special Appendix item.

Fourth, there is commentary based upon the special knowledge and experience of the author and others, along with observations and data now available at this interval of about one hundred and fifty years from the happenings of that still feudal time before the effusion of modern science. Thus there is the inclusion of certain medical data, the prison soliloquy, geographical details from travels in Persia, items on the flora and fauna of the Middle East, and miscellaneous contents which may add to the reality of the land and the people of Iran of that time.

It should be very clear that this volume does not seek to present a story of the Bábí Faith throughout the days of its dramatic beginning and bloody travail, nor is there any attempt to describe in any detail its impact on Persia, the influences upon its adherents and contemporaries; this is left to others, scholars analyzing that time in history. Rather, the text is meager in Bábí historical data, giving only what is deemed to be necessary to create the proper setting for the incidents of Bahá'u'lláh's eventful life as these are clear from His own words.

Collaborators and Sources

A large number of people have assisted in the assembly of the facts here presented; others have aided in the enrichment of the volume. The Research Department of the Bahá'í World Centre has contributed accurate data and translations whenever requested. Dr. Vaḥíd Ra'fatí and Mrs. Bahárieh Ma'ání are particularly acknowledged for their helpfulness, the latter for her work on the Glossary. The Bahá'í World Centre Library has supplied the map of Persia used by Lord Curzon in a publication of 1891, and has been helpful in many details; Miss Louise Mould is to be thanked for her services. Mr. Daoud Ani has aided greatly through his special knowledge of Iraq and his personal experience in retracing the exile journey of Bahá'u-'lláh from Teheran to Baghdad. Dr. Amin Banani in 1975, during his sabbatical months in Iran, himself followed the Afchih-Tákur track so often ridden by Bahá'u'lláh; moreover, he documented this exciting traverse with color photographs and commentary. The distinguished artist-architect Hushang Seyhoun, dean of Persian Bahá'í architects, has consented to the use of a number of his extraordinary line drawings of Iran's unique sites and landscapes.

No gratitude is sufficient for the selfless and expert services of Mrs. Shirley Ross Macias, who not only undertook the task of converting cluttered pages to clean typescript over many drafts, but also checked references, and provided essential criticisms. The late Jan Conley typed the first crude draft in 1962. Beyond these two good friends, the long gestational period from 1949 to this date was borne with patience by a very knowledgeable, supportive and understanding wife, Margaret Kunz Ruhe, to whom this volume is dedicated in gratitude and loving tribute.

Introduction: The Great Soul and His Hour

There is properly no history;
there is only biography.
Ralph Waldo Emerson

Nothing is more important than to explore the Great Lives which periodically have released man from each grand new dilemma produced by his own social evolution. In any age the Supreme Souls born among mankind provide man's essential understanding of himself and of his relation to God. Through the different expressions of spiritual genius of each Manifestation of God, man's primary and innate needs are perceived and the profound ideas required for the creation of a new age, with growth into another great cycle of human progress, are put forth with divine power. Particularly do these architects of human evolution show how man can live in proper relationships with his human and material environments, so that he may thereby win his only true salvation.

The role of a Supreme Manifestation is indispensable, for He is the unique source of a new intuitive knowledge from God regarding human behavior. As He Himself tells it: '*A divine Mine only can yield the gems of divine knowledge, and the fragrance of the mystic Flower can be inhaled only in the ideal Garden, and the lilies of ancient wisdom can blossom nowhere except in the city of a stainless heart.*'[1]

He declares further: '*Know thou that they who are truly wise have likened the world unto the human temple. As the body of man needeth a garment to clothe it, so the body of mankind must needs be adorned with the mantle of justice and wisdom. Its robe is the Revelation vouchsafed unto it by God. Whenever this robe hath fulfilled its purpose, the Almighty will assuredly renew it. For every age requireth a fresh measure of the light of God. Every Divine Revelation hath been sent down in a manner that befitted the circumstances of the age in which it hath appeared.*'[2]

And He identifies certain key aims for His Message in this day of international organization. '. . . *it is Our purpose, through the loving providence of God – exalted be His glory – and His surpassing mercy, to abolish, through the force of Our utterance, all disputes, war, and bloodshed, from the face of the earth.*'[3]

His name was Mírzá Ḥusayn-'Alí, and He came from Núr in the mountains of northern Persia. His title was Bahá'u'lláh, the Glory of God. He lived from 1817 in Iran to His ascension in Syrian-Turkish Palestine in 1892. This biography of the first dramatic years of His life, told as fully as possible in His own words, seeks to relate the beginning of an epic tale, one retold roughly each thousand years of man's development.

The cast of characters

For this newest Revelation the dramatis personae can seem quite unfamiliar to people of the West, for they live and act in their Middle Eastern modes, names and dress. Such unfamiliarity was once true also of Jesus the Christ giving His Revelation of the East to the long-ago Greeks and Romans. Today's Bahá'í protagonists are very familiar in their generic identities. Moreover, the Bahá'í Faith has not one 'Suffering Servant', but two, each a layman and not a cleric. Each is a reformer and leader, building upon the Messages of His Predecessors, becoming the spirit of an era now upon us.

Mírzá Ḥusayn-'Alí early revealed his powers, first as a leader of the followers of the Báb in Iran, then taking the title of Bahá, the Glorious One. In exile in Iraq, all His great fellow Bábí disciples martyred, He declared His Mission and became known by the ultimate title of Bahá'u'lláh, the Glory of God. During further exile to Constantinople and Adrianople in Turkey His written Message became ever more world-embracing. Finally, an exile for life, He was consigned to prison in 'Akká in Syrian Palestine, thereby to fulfill Jewish and Christian Biblical expectations, to complete His Revelation, and to establish the World Centre of His Faith in the Holy Land of Jews and Christians.

Leadership and character of Mírzá Ḥusayn-'Alí, Bahá'u'lláh

It is essential to observe the emergence of spiritual leadership, here shown stage by stage in Bahá'u'lláh's life, wherein He displays His role as Supreme Prophet and as Channel and Mouthpiece of God. Because of the tumultuous events during the birthpangs of the new religion and the dissensions of the early believers, with many derogators, outright liars and fact-manipulators among the unfaithful and the enemies, the critical element of Bahá'u'lláh's consistency of highest character must be emphasized. Bahá'u'lláh's consistent supernal character is a pervading theme in this biography of a Supreme Soul, seen clearly first when He is 'Father of the Poor', then as organizer of the Bábí religious reform movement, then as architect of a new society growing from the innate nobility and magnanimity of the Blessed Beauty of a new Faith, Who brings the era of the Most Great Peace. Thus truth-telling in His own words is the indispensable core of this chronicle which seeks to be as autobiographical as presently available sources permit.

There are dishonest historians, those who write to please an official point of view, to justify unjustifiable acts, or to favor other motivations. However, for the judgments needed in essaying a history of a Great Spirit, a reliable guideline is plainly visible.

The High Prophet tells the truth, for that is His very Mission. Moreover, with His mind and memory of spiritual genius, His penetration of the true character of those about Him, His foresight sometimes carried to the level of prophecy, and His powers of speech, healing, and physical decisiveness – all these give Him a great surety without need for deception, least of all in what He leaves to posterity: His Message to mankind. Thus, the entire corpus of His written thought, ideas and guidance is the repository of truth, but one which must be seen through the lens of His troubled times (see Note 2).

The truth which He brings is the very substance of the spiritual evolution which He is creating. Since physical evolution of the brain and body cannot advance rapidly enough to meet the needs of mankind, the mind and spirit have been given the capacity to adapt speedily to meet the needs of an 'ever-advancing civilization'. Precisely at this time of critical demand for a quantum leap in social evolution has come Bahá'u'lláh with His Message: a great system of belief and of fundamental guidance.

Perspective on a Supernal Soul for the truth-seeker

Each seeker must be warned against himself. He must not permit the idealized, often mythologized images of other Supreme Souls to interpose themselves between himself as an independent inquirer and his search for a new High Prophet. The seeker must not fail to achieve true knowledge of Bahá'u'lláh, Who is the Great Spirit for this day. Nor should the myopic religionist who walks one road to God disallow those Others of different times and places, nor think that Revelation will not be vouchsafed in the future through the thrust of a timely new and original Supreme Prophet. There is an inevitable evolutionary volcanism created by God's certain Will for mankind.

Bahá'u'lláh has identified well the disease of religious finality, saying: '. . . *know of a certainty that the people in every age, clinging to a verse of the Book, have uttered such vain and absurd sayings, contending that no Prophet should again be made manifest to the world. Even as the Christian divines . . . have sought to explain that the law of the Gospel shall at no time be annulled, and that no independent Prophet shall again be made manifest, unless He confirmeth the law of the Gospel. Most of the people have become afflicted with the same spiritual disease.*'[4]

Man's religion of present and future is and will be fundamentally the same as that of the past, for man is still *Homo sapiens*. But his religion must be more challenging, wider in outlook, and also different in certain fundamental details. Mankind will continue to graduate from simple religious schooling to complex religious demands made by one interdependent world. For all this a great religious Liberator has come. He Himself has said: '*We, verily, have not fallen short of Our duty to exhort men, and to deliver that whereunto I was bidden by God, the Almighty, the All-Praised . . . Is there any excuse left for any one in this Revelation? No, by God, the Lord of the Mighty Throne! My signs have encompassed the earth, and my power enveloped all mankind.*'[5]

As a man, husband, father and suffering servant, Bahá'u'lláh was a genius at the least. As a Supreme Prophet emergent on the world stage, He was a phenomenon of dimensions befitting His time frame of at least a thousand years. As the Channel of God's Voice and Will, He was supernal, never God incarnate, but God's Instrument, His Voice of summons from Mount Carmel. One cannot separate these personae, for we are discovering for our time a new God Voice, High Prophet and human genius. He is plainly visible and He welcomes analysis. His Teachings compel investigation.

To the student and seeker

It is impossible for a Westerner to truly enter the thought world of nineteenth-century Persian culture, for that world had scarcely touched the age of science, then suffering its birthpangs in the West. Furthermore, the long centuries of influences brought by varied cultures from Asia and Europe had wrapped the Iranians in visible and invisible coils.

Every new book of serious intent and important scope requires something more of the student than to produce exciting stimuli. While this tale of the coming of the Supreme Mediator for our era is the greatest of all dramas, yet this fact is scarcely guaranteed to touch the person seeking only to rise above a sensate existence or one buried in fanaticism. However, from even an elementary sense of duty to his world during his brief life span, each person must fairly investigate the claim of Bahá'u'lláh, for so sweeping is His claim and so presumptuous is it if untrue that one is obligated to seek, properly and humbly, the truth of His claim to be the Great Teacher. Failure is easy. One may pass by, insensitive or inattentive. Ideally each person must, like an athlete for a contest, be prepared for a spiritual quest, for an adventure of the mind and soul alike. If the seeker be truly sincere, then God will choose to open the eyes of his perception. In the words of the so-called Tablet of the True Seeker: '*But, O my brother, when a true seeker determines to take the step of search in the path leading to the knowledge of the Ancient of Days, he must, before all else, cleanse and purify his heart, which is the seat of the revelation of the inner mysteries of God, from the obscuring dust of all acquired knowledge, and the allusions of the embodiments of satanic fancy . . . He must so cleanse his heart that no remnant of either love or hate may linger therein, lest that love blindly incline him to error, or that hate repel him away from the truth . . . That seeker must at all times put his trust in God, must renounce the peoples of the earth, detach himself from the world of dust, and cleave unto Him Who is the Lord of Lords.*'[6]

It is not mere goal-seeking, it is life-seeking. We dare not train our bodies to physical and mental powers alone. We must hone our intellects against the fine minds of today's most educated and literate society in all history, for much will be asked of every true seeker. And we dare not be passive in our search, even in the face of our obvious cosmic insignificance as individual humans. That search is the way of the spirit, of prayer and meditation, for only on that path will we reach the peaks of life's development for the individual and so achieve the best the human race can know in the farthest reaches of its capacities for this day. As Bahá'u'lláh asks of us all:

> *O my brother! Take thou the step of the spirit, so that, swift as the twinkling of an eye, thou mayest flash through the wilds of remoteness and bereavement, attain the Riḍván [Paradise] of ever-lasting reunion, and in one breath commune with the heavenly Spirits. For with human feet thou canst never hope to traverse these immeasurable distances, nor attain thy goal. Peace be upon him whom the light of truth guideth unto all truth, and who, in the name of God, standeth in the path of His Cause, upon the shore of true understanding.*[7]

Karbilá, Holy City of Iraq, site of the martyrdom of the Imám Ḥusayn in October 680 AD. The shrine of the Imám, with its three minarets, dominates the town.

I First Glimmerings

. . . there appeared on earth Aḥmad and Káẓim, those twin resplendent lights . . .[1]

Bahá'u'lláh

The nineteenth century was soul-shakingly different, for during that century dawned the true age of science which brought great emancipations, a profound understanding of the natural world, and new life-ways. More important to many, there dawned the age of universal religion, the fulfillment of the millennial spiritual expectations of those sensitive to the tides of moral thought and to the renewal of man's relationship with his Creator, whatever His name and whatever that human connection was conceived to be. In the world-mind of nineteenth-century man there was a mysterious restlessness of thought, groping to be formulated, a low and diffuse excitation as yet unfocused, a kind of ethereal music not quite heard. It was as though there had come a dim summons from the unfathomed reaches of the mass brain of mankind or from the cosmos itself. It was a summons ineptly felt by a scattered few, but heard precisely by two men, Shaykh Aḥmad and Siyyid Káẓim, born in far lands in the second decade of that century.

This worldwide phenomenon could much later be reported from its assembled evidences. It was a grand messianic movement, far-reaching and extremely varied, usually radically suspect, its leaders commonly ridiculed and persecuted, in the West its common theme a spiritual rebirth associated with Judaeo-Christian prophecies. In Britain there was Sir Edward Irving, in Germany Leonard H. Kelber and J. A. Bengel of the Society of the Temple. In North America it was Joseph Smith and his Mormons, the Latter-Day Saints; and it was also Mary Baker Eddy and her Christian Scientists; but it was Rev. William Miller in Pennsylvania who presented by far the most dramatic scenario for, primarily on the basis of his Biblical studies of a prophecy of Daniel, he predicted that the early 1840s would witness the Second Coming of Christ, with the Judgment Day and the Day of Resurrection. In a later decade his disappointed Millerites were salvaged to become the Seventh Day Adventists.* But the spiritual expectancy was far wider in scope for, true to form, the Middle Eastern cradle of Faiths was also hearkening to the subtle calls of the spirit.

As the nineteenth century was born in the Middle East there was the usual flurry of tribal conflicts, small and large, which have perennially bled out the hopes and happiness of the Levant. At the same time the great valleys of the Tigris and Euphrates rivers in Iraq were witnessing a significant renewal of the messianic hopes of Shi'ite Islám (see Note 3), hopes which were the unique stamp of that lesser branch of Islám which persisted strongly in Persia and Iraq after the sanguinary early breach which brought to dominance the Sunnát†, the law of the Prophet Muḥammad as recorded in the traditions and as espoused by a large majority of Muslims. Over the previous millennium the Shi'ite hopes of the advent of the Qá'im had been for them a binding continuity. Through these hopes Iraq and Iran had become an oddly appropriate setting for both Judaeo-Christian and certain Islamic prophetic fulfillments.

The eastern and northern portions of the Fertile Crescent, and particularly Mesopotamia, the land between the two rivers, have seen auspicious chapters of mankind's spiritual evolution. Two are told in the myths of Adam and Eve in the Garden of Eden, and of the Flood of Noah the Hebrew and of his myth-brother Utapishtim the Sumerian. There is also the well-authenticated chronicle of the migration of the patriarch Abraham and his tribe of Hebrews from Haran in the kingdom of Mari in northwestern Mesopotamia to the land of Canaan far southward. Twenty-seven long and tragic centuries thereafter lacerated the lands of the Crescent in the major social surgery of armies shaping new empires for temporarily dominant peoples: Hittites, Assyrians, Babylonians, Persians, Greeks, Romans, Byzantines. And finally in the seventh century that pain-racked land between the two rivers was overrun by the armies

* During the messianic period of the first half of the nineteenth century in the United States, the distinguished poet James Russell Lowell wrote a famous poem which became a popular hymn when set to music by Ton-y-Botel. Its date of composition is eerie, for in its second verse it reflects consummately well the challenge of the Millerites then, of the Báb and Bahá'u'lláh now. That verse of the 1844 poem: 'Once to every man and nation comes the moment to decide, / In the strife of truth with falsehood for the good or evil side. / Some great Cause, God's new Messiah, offering each the bloom or blight, / And the choice goes by forever, 'twixt that darkness and that light'. And the millennial fever was felt far and wide in the music, the arts, the thought of that time.

† The Sunná is the sum of Islamic law, i.e. the practices and traditions variously attributed to Muḥammad's guidance.

of Islám. The conquest by Semitic peoples asserting allegiance to the new Book of God, the Qur'án, brought not peace but fitful warfare and savage feuds between groups holding to contending loyalties, even though the protagonists may seemingly have been bonded by Islám. And in such internecine strife Iraq recurrently became a spoil of war. Despite a further thirteen bloody centuries of Parthians, Seljuks, Khorasmians, Mongols, Mamelukes and Ottomans, the enduring ideology in Iraq was yet an expectant one, however splintered by the endless dissonances of theologians locked in futile verbal combat. Then, as the nineteenth century began, a new voice was heard in Karbilá, the very place where the Imám Ḥusayn had lost his decisive battle and his life in October 680 AD. In his tomb-city some few heard the message of Shaykh Aḥmad of Aḥsá.

Populous Karbilá was a befitting place for such teachings as were his, for it was a place of pilgrimage and homage to the Shi'ite Islám of the Twelve Imáms. It was a place akin to Calvary of the Christians because of the death of the great Imám. Located fifty-five miles southwest of Baghdad, just beyond the muddy Euphrates River, Karbilá cherished lines of palm trees stingily greening the river banks before the desert gripped the vast rolling Iraqi grassland all about, those sunburned plains once so enormously productive before centuries of irrigation had salted the soil and raised the water table. The huge tumbled mud-brick tumulus of ancient Babylon lay nearby, of no concern save to archaeologists. Karbilá itself was a crowded haphazard of two- and three-storey dust-brown houses punctuated by cupola-crowned buildings marking the centers of sundry religious groups. Dominating the town was the mosque of the Imám Ḥusayn, the Prince of Martyrs, with its two slender minarets and its dominant but dissimilar third minaret, its wide court and airy porches framed by slender columns; it was a building which welcomed the Shi'ite pilgrim faithful. Across the city were scattered the domes of lesser mosques, in the southeast section a shrine of the Imám's brother, 'Abbás.

In his late maturity, after twenty-five years of religious study, Shaykh Aḥmad had left Aḥsá, an insignificant spot on the low sandy coast of Bahrain in the middle Persian Gulf, for drab Karbilá. There he developed a system of esoteric and mystical Islamic religious thought, wrote extensively, and gathered around himself eager disciples in training for the hair-splitting controversialism of that place and time. A Muslim among Muslims, pitting his Qur'ánic and philosophical knowledge against their agile and subtle minds, he perceived all too clearly that 'no reform, however drastic, within the

Faith of Islám, could achieve the regeneration of this perverse people', the Shi'ite fundamentalists of that hour. And this conviction was at least equally true of the Sunnís of the larger Muslim world as analyzed by others who dared to question the concept that Muḥammad, the Seal of the Prophets, was the end of all Revelation. Cautiously, Shaykh Aḥmad made clear to his students his conviction that 'nothing short of a new and independent Revelation . . . could revive the fortunes and restore the purity of that decadent Faith',[2] Islám. Further, although wary of the acute dangers which in that fanatical society confronted him because of his views, he warned his disciples of the coming of 'Him Who must needs be made manifest in the fullness of time'. In short, he predicted the coming of the promised Qá'im, the first One awaited by all Shi'ite faithful.

In 1817, after achieving scholarly distinction and winning a corps of followers, soon called Shaykhís after their master, he set forth on a long journey over a number of years, but first to visit the walled holy city of Najaf downriver. There the pointed dome and sharp minarets of the Shrine of the first Imám, 'Alí, cousin and successor to Muḥammad, dominated the town's monotonous jumble of low buildings. He paused to pay his respects to the Imám and to pray for the enlightenment of his fellow scholars. En route thereafter to pray at the Shrine of the Imám Riḍá in far-off Mashhad in Iran, Shaykh Aḥmad's first destination was Shíráz in the south of that country. In that city he visited the mosque of Vakíl, the preeminent mosque of the city where Friday prayers were conducted by the chief priest of Shíráz. There, with great prescience, he declared:

'Verily, this house of God betokens such signs as only those who are endowed with understanding can perceive. Methinks he who conceived and built it was inspired of God.' He admonished his fellow travelers, amazed at these words of high praise, to 'wonder not, for ere long the secret of my words will be made manifest to you. Among you there shall be a number who will live to behold the glory of a Day which the prophets of old have yearned to witness.'[3]*

From Shíráz the road to Yazd through the barren mountains of central Iran was dreary, hot, dusty. Early the party passed close to the imposing ruins of Persepolis, once Persia's capital city. Now it was only a crumbling monument to the powerful Achaemenian monarchs who had first brought Persia onto the then world stage as

* Bahá'u'lláh said, reflectively: '*The followers of Shaykh-i-Aḥsá'í* [Shaykh Aḥmad] *have, by the aid of God, apprehended that which was veiled from the comprehension of others, and of which they remained deprived.*' (*Epistle to the Son of the Wolf*, p. 120.)

conquerors and civilizers, roles abrogated over the centuries. Then, skirting 14,600-foot Mount Bul on the edge of the vast sweep of the Zagros Mountains, Shaykh Aḥmad proceeded through Dehbíd northeastward to Yazd, an essentially Zoroastrian city. For some months he paused to strengthen the Shaykhís of the city and to write many tracts. In Yazd he predicted to one 'Abdu'l-Vaḥháb that 'Ere long will the earth be turned into a paradise. Ere long will Persia be made the shrine round which will encircle the peoples of the earth.'[4] It was an unbelievable prediction even for the most optimistic of those who lived in that appallingly decadent land.

While he was yet in that city of covered streets, shadowed markets, and roofs everywhere guarding against the implacable sun, a city of ingenious wind towers cooling the houses, there arrived a brilliant young man, son of a silk merchant of the port town of Rasht in far Gílán province on the Caspian Sea. A youth of grave mien and deep-set eyes, recognized from his boyhood as a prodigy, he had

A bazaar street in Yazd, with arched roofs against the blazing sun of middle Persia. (H. Seyhoun)

been led by a vision to come to Yazd to enroll as Shaykh Aḥmad's disciple. And such were his powers of mind and spirit, so great his religious scholarship, so illumined his spiritual character, that after a few scant weeks with the master, the twenty-two-year-old Siyyid Káẓim won the accolade of chief apostleship from the sixty-four-year-old Shaykh at the time when he prepared to continue his journey northeastward to Mashhad in Khurásán province. Shaykh Aḥmad confidently gave Káẓim assurance of his capacity to lead the group of disciples left behind, saying:

'You will, through the knowledge which the Lord your God has bestowed upon you, resolve their problems and tranquilize their hearts. By the power of your utterance you will help to revive the sorely neglected Faith of Muḥammad, your illustrious ancestor.'[5]

Mashhad lay north and east across the forbidding inner desert lands where men survived through pure endurance, remarkable inventiveness, and back-breaking labor. There the need to transport water protected from evaporation had produced the incredible underground qanats, tunnels which brought the indispensable water long distances from the mountain watershed aquifers to the bone-dry towns and cities. Also, farmers at the mouths of the mountain valleys – treeless and even brushless because of the browsing sheep and goats – caught for their uses the meltwater of the scant snows of winter, storing it in cisterns to make possible a marginal agriculture wholly dependent upon those catchments. The overwhelming reality of that tremendous area of desert, with its salt sinks and evanescent marshes deriving from the intermittent interior streams, was the sun; the sun tolerated few clouds and rare rains, so far was it from the Caspian Sea with its barrier Alborz ranges, so distant from the Persian Gulf with the torrid coastal mountains blocking any hope of significant rainfall in the interior. Traveling the edge of this hard land through Káshán, the caravan of devout men on their mules and donkeys plodded onward in easy stages of perhaps fifteen to twenty miles per day, stopping at village and town way stations for rest and above all for water. Finally, in the far north of Teheran the road intersected the highway to Mashhad yet some six hundred miles eastward. After the long last stage of the overland desert trek, Shaykh Aḥmad arrived at Mashhad with its gold-covered dome of the Shrine of the Imám Riḍá. Fatigued, but in fulfillment of his heart's wish, he performed his acts of homage to the memory of the Shí'ite founders.

During his brief sojourn in Mashhad in 1817 Shaykh Aḥmad accepted the official invitation of Fatḥ-'Alí, the Sháh, to visit

Teheran, then a walled city large for its time. At the zenith of his eminence as a theologian, he proceeded to the capital to receive a royal welcome. On the occasion of a personal audience, the Sháh eulogized him as 'the glory of his nation and an ornament to his people',[6] a tribute honorably won through the merit of his seeking to clarify Shi'ite doctrine on major and minor issues.

How significant that during those very days in the capital city, at dawn on 12 November, a boy was born to an ancient and noble family of Mázindarán; his father was Mírzá 'Abbás of Núr, his mother Khadíjih Khánum, and the child was named Ḥusayn-'Alí, the very names of both Expected Ones. Long years later the adult Mírzá Ḥusayn-'Alí would give His own birth its true significance. '*Say, this is a Dawn in which the Most Mighty Tree hath been planted, and hath brought forth rare and peerless fruits . . .*' And again: '*All honour to this Dawn which hath appeared in truth above the Dayspring of effulgent glory . . .*' and '*All joy unto the Dwellers of the Realm on High for the appearance of this glorious, this wondrous Spirit.*' Despite the Shaykh's frequent allusions to a promised Ḥusayn, his powers as a seer were not sufficient to reach into the cradle of that infant of great destiny, although he spoke of strong intimations felt by him.[7]

Shaykh Aḥmad tarried only briefly in Teheran, leaving soon for Kirmánsháh in the southwestern mountains in acceptance of the invitation of its governor, Prince Muḥammad-'Alí, who frankly avowed adherence to his teachings. In instructing his most receptive followers of that city the Shaykh focused upon the theme of the coming of the Promised One, frequently using the honored names of Ḥusayn and 'Alí. In his profuse writings over the course of a four-year stay which ended in 1821 upon the death of the prince-patron, many were his allusions to the signs which would portend that long-awaited Coming. Among them was his assertion that 'the mystery of this Cause must needs be made manifest, and the secret of this Message must needs be divulged. I can say no more, I can appoint no time. His Cause will be made known after Ḥín [68].'[8*]

He even declared that 'soon you will know him in a certain fashion'. And he made another curious statement: 'If any among you live to that time (of discovery), he will see strange things between the years 60 and 67 (1845 to 1852).' During this time of predictions,

* The numerical value of letters is given mystical significance in Judaic, Islamic and related literature. Thus the year 68 in the abjad notation is 1268 AH or 1851 AD, when Bahá'u'lláh was in Karbilá, and the year before the Síyáh-Chál, 1852 (See Chapter Eight).

again the Shaykh's intimations failed to pinpoint, on 20 October 1819 in Shíráz, the birth of an infant to parents descended from the Imám Ḥusayn; the child 'Alí-Muḥammad was a mystery then, his time also appointed by God.

During these latter years from Teheran to Kirmánsháh and onwards, Siyyid Káẓim rejoined Shaykh Aḥmad, steadily gaining greater eminence among the Shaykhís and clearly validating the choice of the master. On the eve of their return to Karbilá in Iraq, Shaykh Aḥmad defined the mission of his successor, exhorting Siyyid Káẓim:

'You have no time to lose. Every fleeting hour should be fully and wisely utilized . . . For verily I say, the Hour is drawing nigh, the Hour I have besought God to spare me from witnessing, for the earthquake of the Last Hour will be tremendous. You should pray to God to be spared the overpowering trials of that Day, for neither of us is capable of withstanding its sweeping force. Others, of greater endurance and power, have been destined to bear this stupendous weight, men whose hearts are sanctified from all earthly things, and whose strength is reinforced by the potency of His power.'[9]

Karbilá had not altered one whit during Shaykh Aḥmad's years of absence, for it was yet the arena par excellence of Shi'ite theological gladiators expending their lives in expounding their controversial theses. But the sore-needed drastic reform of Islám lay in the near future. Now, his mission ended, his fatigue deep, Shaykh Aḥmad set himself to make a life-ending pilgrimage to Mecca and Medina in Arabia. The coastal voyage along the shores of the Persian Gulf and Arabian Sea, with its stops en route, was the last opportunity for the great teacher to spread his ideas and pay his final homage to the Founder of Islám.* A befitting finale followed his visit to the Ka'bih: he passed away in Medina in 1826 at the age of eighty-three and was buried in the Baqí cemetery close to the tomb of the revered Fáṭimih, daughter of Muḥammad.

With the passing of the master, Siyyid Káẓim zealously propagated the teaching work, exciting thereby much jealousy, criticism and hostility from the fanatical among the many religionists of Karbilá. Said they:

'For forty years we have suffered the pretentious teachings of Shaykh Aḥmad to be spread with no opposition whatever on our part. We no longer can tolerate similar pretensions on the part of his

* Copies are extant of Shaykh Aḥmad's principal works. His long and productive life extended from 1743 to 1826.

successor, who rejects the belief in the resurrection of the body, who repudiates the literal interpretation of the Mi'ráj [the "Ascent"]*, who regards the signs of the coming Day as allegorical, and who preaches a doctrine heretical in character and subversive of the best tenets of orthodox Islám.'[10]

But through missions undertaken by his best disciple Mullá Ḥusayn of Bus͟hrúyih, Siyyid Káẓim obtained support from outstanding ecclesiastical personages in Iṣfahán and Mas͟hhad, blunting the opposition in Karbilá even as his S͟hayk͟hí zealots shaped themselves into a new group; among them was the extraordinary young man who had so well demonstrated his courage, eloquence and great talents on those special missions. Now, intensifying his admonitions and building upon those of his predecessor, Siyyid Káẓim foreshadowed the approach of the imminent hour of spiritual challenge, replying to the insistent questioning of his followers by describing the signs of the Messenger Who was soon to reveal Himself:

'He is of noble lineage. He is a descendant of the Prophet of God, of the family of Hás͟him.† He is young in age, and is possessed of innate knowledge. His learning is derived, not from the teachings of S͟hayk͟h Aḥmad, but from God. My knowledge is but a drop compared with the immensity of His knowledge, my attainments a speck of dust in the face of the wonders of His grace and power. Nay, immeasurable is the difference. He is of medium height, abstains from smoking, and is of extreme devoutness and piety.'

He even hinted that He was in their very midst, unidentified, and chided them, saying:

'You behold Him with your own eyes, and yet recognize Him not!'[11]

His preparation of a chosen few disciples continued apace, punctuated by singular events. One morning in early 1842, an elderly disciple of particular spiritual sensitivity, S͟hayk͟h Ḥasan of Zunúz, was awakened at dawn and summoned to Siyyid Káẓim's presence, finding him dressed and ready for departure. Said Siyyid Káẓim:

'A highly esteemed and distinguished Person has arrived. I feel it incumbent upon us both to visit him.'

Walking some distance through the narrow and tortuous streets of Karbilá, they reached a simple house before which, expectant, stood

* Muḥammad's dream of His night 'ascent' to Heaven (see Note 4.)

† A Háshimite in Islamic parlance means a descendant of the Prophet Muḥammad, a Siyyid, from the tribal group of Hás͟him in southern Arabia.

a slender young man tastefully garbed in clothing of subtle color and design, and wearing the green turban of a siyyid. Warmly embracing each of his visitors in the customary way, the youth turned through the doorway and led them to an upper room, clean, bare of furnishings, but redolent of a gentle perfume and graced with flowers. Seated in these simple quarters, he shared with his guests the contents of a silver cup, uttering as a grace the Qur'ánic salutation, '*A drink of a pure beverage shall their Lord give them.*'[12] There ensued a time of deep silence of astonishing intensity, until the young man concluded the brief encounter by rising and escorting them to the street. All had transpired in an atmosphere of the deepest reverence, but to Shaykh Ḥasan, his mentor Siyyid Káẓim proffered no explanation of the interlude's meaning.

Three days later on Friday the youth arrived at the library of Siyyid Káẓim, where the savant was teaching his disciples. As he quietly took his seat with humility and dignity on the floor near the doorway, Siyyid Káẓim abruptly broke off his argument, to the amazement of his students, becoming silent. Urged to complete his thought, he declared:

'What more shall I say? Lo, the Truth is more manifest than the ray of light that has fallen upon that lap!' And he turned his face toward the youth, upon whom had fallen a spear of sunlight from the doorway.[13]

Others among the students of Siyyid Káẓim noted the luminous young man of such convincing piety, whose chanting of prayers was so moving, whose presence was so attractive that their curiosity at his identity was piqued, although they saw him only thrice at the gatherings. He revealed merely that he was a merchant of fabrics, a mercer from Shíráz and Búshihr. His stay was not a short one, about eleven months by his own account, but it was intensely private, a time of prayer and meditation. After a final visit to the Shrine of the Imám Ḥusayn, the young newcomer departed for Najaf to meet the obligation to pray at the Shrine of the Imám 'Alí. And from Iraq he returned to Persia.

Opposition to the Shaykhí movement continued to mount in priest-ridden Karbilá. Simultaneously civil rebellion was smoldering, to erupt in a revolt against the Turkish overlords touched off by eviction of the Ottoman representative from the city, with consequent siege by Turkish troops. Boldly seeking to mitigate the strife, Siyyid Káẓim encountered the same stiff-necked clerics who were his theological opponents. Despite his warnings to them of the grave consequences of their acts, he failed in his mission of mediation with the Governor Najíb Pá<u>sh</u>á. However, because these efforts were appreciated by the authorities, his home became the permitted sanctuary of the <u>Sh</u>ay<u>kh</u>ís in the city when, in January 1843, after twenty-four days of assault, the Turkish troops of the Pá<u>sh</u>á mercilessly crushed the rebellion in sanguinary fashion, massacring those who had not sought asylum in that house.

Time was running out, as Siyyid Káẓim deeply felt it. He was fearful of the hour too, knowing its mortal hazards. Yet he also knew its glory and reward, saying:

'I am spellbound by the vision. I am mute with wonder, and behold the world bereft of the power of hearing. I am powerless to divulge the mystery, and find the people incapable of bearing its weight.' Again and again, adverting to the Personage Who was to come, he would say: 'I see him as the rising sun.' And many times he would describe Him: 'He who is destined to be made manifest after me is of pure lineage, of illustrious descent, of the seed of Fáṭimih.* He is of medium height, and is free from bodily deficiency.' Then, feeling his life's end drawing close, his sense of urgency deepened as he passionately exhorted his companions to fulfill the extraordinary mission for which he was preparing them: a holy search for not one but two Manifestations of God.

'O my beloved companions!' he cried. 'Beware, beware, lest after me the world's fleeting vanities beguile you. Beware lest you wax haughty and forgetful of God. It is incumbent upon you to renounce all comfort, all earthly possessions and kindred, in your quest of Him who is the Desire of your hearts and of mine. Scatter far and wide, detach yourselves from all earthly things, and humbly and prayerfully beseech your Lord to sustain and guide you. Never relax in your determination to seek and find Him who is concealed behind the veils of glory. Persevere till the time when He, who is your true Guide and Master, will graciously aid you and enable you to recognize Him . . . Well is it with every one of you who will quaff the cup of martyrdom in His path. Those of you whom God, in His wisdom, will preserve and keep to witness the setting of the Star of Divine guidance, that Harbinger of the Sun of Divine Revelation, must needs be patient, must remain assured and steadfast . . . For soon after the first trumpet-blast which is to smite the earth with extermination and death, there shall be sounded again yet another

---

* Fáṭimih, the daughter of the Prophet Muḥammad and wife of the first Imám, 'Alí, the greatest woman of Islamic tradition, is considered by Muslims to be the symbol of chastity and womanly virtue.

call, at which all things will be quickened and revived . . . Verily I say, after the Qá'im the Qayyúm will be made manifest.* For when the star of the Former has set, the sun of the beauty of Ḥusayn will rise and illuminate the whole world . . .'[14]

Foreshadowing that millennial hour soon to be known, and perhaps subtly directing their search toward Persia, he projected its brilliance to his students:

'To have attained unto that Day of days is to have attained unto the crowning glory of past generations, and one goodly deed performed in that age is equal to the pious worship of countless centuries . . .

'O my beloved companions! How great, how very great, is the Cause! How exalted the station to which I summon you! How great the mission for which I have trained and prepared you! Gird up the loins of endeavor, and fix your gaze upon His promise. I pray to God graciously to assist you to weather the storms of tests and trials which must needs beset you, to enable you to emerge, unscathed and triumphant, from their midst, and to lead you to your high destiny.'[15]

It was Siyyid Káẓim's custom each year to visit Káẓimayn on the west bank of the Tigris River close above Baghdad, site of the shrine-tombs of the seventh and ninth Imáms, Músá Káẓim and Muḥammad-Taqí. It was a brown town of sun-dried brick buildings set among a sea of date palm groves; its claim to beauty and significance lay in the two domed shrines, each with its pencil minaret. In November 1843 he left Karbilá for Baghdad accompanied by faithful Shaykhí disciples. Outside of Káẓimayn at the mosque of Baráthá, during the noonday prayer with his companions, he was accosted by an unknown shepherd who related details of a startling vision wherein the Prophet Muḥammad had bade him convey His loving greetings and bear tidings of import to Siyyid Káẓim when they should meet:

'Rejoice,' the Prophet had said for Siyyid Káẓim's ears, 'for the hour of your departure is at hand!' He had then foretold that three days after the Siyyid's return to Karbilá, 'you will wing your flight to Me. Soon after shall He who is the Truth be made manifest. Then shall the world be illumined by the light of His face.'[16]

To the shepherd, after his delivery of the unexpected message, Káẓim said: 'Of the truth of the dream you have dreamt there is no doubt.'

* Qá'im: The Great One who shall arise. Qayyúm: the Self-Subsisting, Self-Existent, All-Compelling.

And to his disciples, mourning at this death notice, he exhorted them, saying: 'Is not your love for me for the sake of that True One whose advent we all await? Would you not wish me to die, that the promised One may be revealed?'[17]

Calmly accepting the warning and unafraid, even welcoming his own demise since the promise was that the Qá'im would then arise, Siyyid Káẓim completed his prayerful pilgrimage to Káẓimayn and returned to Karbilá. As predicted, on the day of his arrival home he fell sick. And on 31 December 1843, he passed away in his sixtieth year, leaving behind some three hundred written works as testimony to his industry and theological insights. Infinitely more important, he left behind a cadre of trained visionaries inspired by his guidance, impelled by a great urgency, and fortified by his promise of their success in the greatest of missions: the discovery of two Manifestations sent by God to man for this new Age in travail.

> For verily I say, the Hour is drawing nigh, the Hour I have besought God to spare me from witnessing, for the earthquake of the Last Hour will be tremendous.[18]
>
> **Shaykh Aḥmad**

Najaf (l.) downriver from Karbilá along the Euphrates, is one of the two holiest shrine cities of Shí'ite Islám in Iraq. The mosque of the First Imám, 'Alí, Successor to the Prophet Muḥammad, dominates the drab town. Here lived many Shí'ite scholars with their students. Kaẓimayn (r.) lies on the Tigris just above Baghdad, and is the Holy City of the Seventh and Ninth Imáms, Musá Kaẓim and Muḥammad-Táqí Kaẓim; the place of Siyyid Kaẓim's last pilgrimage.

Inscription by Mírzá 'Abbás Buzurg on the gate lintel of Tákur Mansion. Removed at the time of new construction, it was installed in Tákur Mosque; there it has been preserved in his memory and as an example of classic calligraphy.

The village of Tákur in Núr district, Mázindarán province, looking northward to the rugged barren mountains hemming in the Núr River valley, home of the spirit for Mírzá Ḥusayn-'Alí as he grew to manhood among his family and kindred. (Seyhoun)

2 The Celestial Tree Grows

When thou enterest the sacred abode of the Beloved say:
'I am at thy command.
This is the home of Love; enter with reverence.
This is holy ground; remove thy shoes when thou enterest here.'

Inscription on the lintel of the gateway to the Mansion of Mírzá 'Abbás Buzurg in Tákur, Núr.

'*My name is Bahá'u'lláh, and my country is Núr.*'[1] Thus simply did Mírzá Ḥusayn-'Alí give his spiritual title, the Glory of God, and identify his true home as the Núr region, the place of light, in Iran. And, like all great events of human evolution, his coming as a man of destiny was essentially unseen, unheard, unnoticed.

In the fall of 1817 during the time when Shaykh Aḥmad visited Teheran by invitation of Fatḥ-'Alí Sháh, near day-break on the twelfth day of November a son was born to a noble family of Núr in Mázindarán province.* The infant Ḥusayn-'Alí first opened his eyes in that family mansion in Teheran where he was to live a large part of his childhood, youth and early manhood. His father, Mírzá 'Abbás, was a nobleman of great capacity and promise, while his mother, the lady Khadíjih, was 'Abbás's second wife and paternal cousin.[2] The boy's ancestry could be traced back across eventful centuries to the Sassanian dynasty of kings and to the Persian Prophet Zoroaster but also, crucial to his genetic heritage, to the sons of Abraham through his third wife Katurah.† During some four millennia these blood-lines had diverged from their origins in the nomads and townsmen of the eastern Fertile Crescent who were then generating the peoples

* In a later Tablet Bahá'u'lláh spoke of the supernal significance of His own birth, saying: '*Blessed is indeed this Holy Tree, which is raised up through the power of truth, that all the people of the world may seek the shelter of its shadow.*' (unpublished Tablet; see also p. 14.)

† In support of this statement, there is the elucidation by the Universal House of Justice (July 1985) that 'Abraham had other sons than Isaac and Ishmael, who in those days migrated to Persia and Afghanistan, and the Blessed Beauty (Ḥusayn-'Alí) is one of their descendants.' See also Mírzá Abu'l-Faḍl, *Herald of the South*, June 1969, p. 8. In *God Passes By*, p. 94, it is simply stated that 'He derived His descent . . . from Abraham . . .'

destined to uplift the world through their concepts of God and His Will for mankind. Significantly, these genetic traces, termed '*this mighty Stock*,'[3] carried down through the generations a potential for that unique quality: spiritual eminence. And with his birth Teheran was blessed, as he himself declared in later days: '*Let nothing grieve thee, O Land of Ṭá* [Teheran] . . . *for God hath made thee "the Dayspring of His light", inasmuch as within thee was born the Manifestation of His Glory. Be thou glad for this name that hath been conferred upon thee – a name through which . . . both earth and heaven have been illumined.*'[4]

The child's ancestral roots were planted deep in the towering Alborz range which dominated Mázindarán province north of the capital.* There he perennially spent his summers in the village of Tákur, in the mountains which were the home of his spirit. That mountainous province between the Iranian Plateau and the Caspian Sea had played its part in Iran's war-bedeviled history, but also from ancient times had been a place of retirement, of prayer and meditation for mystics and holy men, including the Prophet Zoroaster as tradition has it. One of the many legends of Mázindarán predicted the growth of a celestial tree whose branches would reach to heaven, and whose fruit would be for the life of the nations; many had sought this fabled tree. Another legend of expectation and hope predicted that the king of war and hatred would be imprisoned in one of its high mountains.[5]

But more important to the child than mythology, whatever its latent truths and his future fulfillment of them, were the dominant ideas and forces which permeated his people: the Zoroastrian concept of the struggle between good and evil; the Messianic Shi'ite Muslim expectation of two Mighty Ones, the Qá'im and the return of the Imám Ḥusayn; and the powerful creativity of Persian culture which had tenaciously survived and absorbed conquests, tyrannies, Islamic fanaticism and recurrent foreign imperialisms. To these ideas and forces the hypersensitive child was exposed in a uniquely Persian thought-world. Moreover, in a land of poverty, insecurity and violence the child's lot was one of affluence, safety and peace. And in a land corrupt almost beyond description,[6] Mírzá Ḥusayn-'Alí was the son of an upright and generous father, a man of high motives of

* The region now called Núr district extends from above the Shimírán range eastward to include a large portion of Mázindarán province. Balade-i-Núr was the center of the district in early times, and holds the tomb-shrine of the scholar-saint Shaykh Aḥmad, disciple of the Imám Ḥasan 'Askarí from the early years of Shi'ite

service, considered a genius by his friends. Further, in a day when lack of education was almost universal in Persia, from his birth the boy was bathed in the rich and stimulating atmosphere of the learning of that time, both in his mountain home and in the highest social levels of the capital city.

The household of Mírzá 'Abbás was a large one, for Islamic law permitted up to four wives, a challenge which usually only wealthy men could seek to meet. Mírzá 'Abbás's father, Riḍá-Qulí Big, arranged his son's first marriage with a family relative, Khán-Nanih; their two children were Áqá and Muḥammad-Ḥasan.[7] After 'Abbás had moved to live primarily in Teheran when he sought his fortune in government service, he took as his second wife his cousin the lady Khadíjih, a widow with a son, Muḥammad-'Alí, and two daughters, Sakínih and Ṣughrá. In the ancestry of lady Khadíjih was the Prophet Zoroaster, a supreme heritage. To 'Abbás she bore a daughter Sárih, a son Mihdí (destined for an early death), then Ḥusayn-'Alí, another son Músá, and lastly a daughter Nisá. Kulthúm, his third wife, and his three legal concubines were mothers of another eight surviving children over several decades.* Sixteen children born to Mírzá 'Abbás are known, thus producing a huge and typically complex Persian family of the nobility, but one given a measure of coherence and integrity through the strength of character of Mírzá 'Abbás himself.

The family estates in Núr district were extensive, including lands and a mansion at Tákur village in the Núr valley and another property at Dárkalá not far from the Caspian shores. The many land-bonded serfs and the city servants were dealt with in the customary feudal ways of that hour, and were pawns of a difficult period when new imperial powers from the north and west were threatening their inept and corrupt rulers. In Teheran the interconnected cluster of seven great mansions of the family was situated in the old Shimírán Gate quarter close to the imperial compound. In 1824 Mírzá 'Abbás had purchased a mansion, thereafter building the complex, including the great house which became its center, on the large scale befitting his position, resources and needs, and those of his close relatives. In

---

Islám. The title 'Núr' was given to the district because the illumined Aḥmad was said to display light around him when he spoke. (Source: Yaḥyá Núrí, *Bahá'í Studies Bulletin*, Vol.3, No.1, fn.1, p. 94–95.)

* Sárih was simply called 'Ukht', sister, by Mírzá Ḥusayn-'Alí, and was usually known by this affectionate name. Kulthúm's children were Sháh-Sulṭán, Taqí, Riḍa-Qulí, Ibrahim (who died in his youth) and Fáṭimih-Ṣulṭán. The three concubines of Mírzá 'Abbás were Kúchik, mother of Ḥusníyyih. It is not clear whether other children born to 'Abbás died in infancy or childhood.

the homes there were carpeted rooms of state, family and service rooms for all needs and luxurious private baths of great beauty. Cool rooms below ground connected with the wind towers looming above the roof lines, towers whose air circulation system ameliorated the fierce heat of Teheran summers.

The old city of Teheran in which they lived had six gates and eighteen towers, the enclosing walls extending over a four-mile circumference, and had become the capital of the Qájárs in 1788; its population was something over one hundred and sixty thousand persons living within or close to the city walls. It was generally unpretentious, a jumble of one-, two- or rarely three-storey buildings set along erratic streets or blind lanes; in the more affluent city quarters the mud streets were sometimes even paved with brick, and high blank walls fenced the passageways, shutting out prying and possible dangerous intruders from those who lived inside the heavy barred doors. Beyond the blind barriers lay houses which prized large to tiny courtyards bringing flowering greenery and also the needful pleasure of pools or fountains into what was often dusty, drab, limited and crowded housing.

The boy genius, growing up as a child in his varied and surely tumultuous family aggregation, lived principally in the capital city, in the national channel which opened into the exciting nineteenth century of international commerce and conquest by western imperialists, a century witnessing the dawn of the age of science whose dynamic forces were felt even in backwater Persia. But also he summered in the barren northern ranges among the rough hillmen who were his kin and subjects, in the countryside which he repeatedly termed '*the place of the spirit!*' He swam in the intellectual and emotional currents of his time, but with his spiritual roots in the mountains, even as he felt the powerful inner stirrings of a unique destiny.

From his very infancy the child Ḥusayn-'Alí was different.

'This child never cries,' said his mother, amazed. 'He is so unlike other babies who cry and scream and are forever restless while in the nursing stage . . .'[8]

And from his earliest childhood he was singled out among his siblings by relatives and family friends, whose composite opinion was that the child had extraordinary powers of intellect, wisdom and innate knowledge, and was superior to others of his age and class. A common prediction applied to the little Ḥusayn-'Alí in that superstitious age of high child mortality was that 'such a precocious child will not survive!',[9] for it was anticipated that child prodigies were

The northern suburbs in Shimírán district, in the foothills of the Alborz Range, were the retreats of the privileged of Teheran; high walls enclosed the palaces, mansions and estates of the nobility and ambassadorial units, these including residences of the Núrí nobles of Mírzá Buzurg's extended family.

especially fated to suffer early doom. All who encountered him in those years of boyhood admitted that he was gifted in every way, and in addition was adorned with a rare purity and nobility.[10]

During his childhood and youth he witnessed the rise of his father in the rough and dangerous world of the Sháh's court, where royal favor extended to Mírzá 'Abbás meant a succession of posts culminating in the governorship of the mountainous western province of Luristán, with its capital city Burújird. During this arduous period he showed great skill and courage in dealing with the turbulent and rebellious Lur and Bakhtíyárí tribesmen, famed for their warlike traditions and frequent banditry. As a nobleman's son in Teheran during this period, the boy breathed the gossipy air filled with the machinations and intrigues of the Sháh and his ministers. Typical of the vanity of the Sháh was his notice, even in that society of bearded and mustached men, of Vazír 'Abbás's particularly long and luxurious beard, one which offered competition to the royal appendage, hence he ordered 'Abbás to cut it shorter or pay a fine. The bold 'Abbás accepted this challenge, paid the fine, and kept his facial hair.[11] Beard dimensions in hirsute men are meaningless, but the power behind the whimsical order well illustrates what the testimony of historians makes clear, that there was no better education in the often terrifying politics of absolute power in a feudal state than in the domain of the Qájárs, the dynasty then ruling Iran.

Omens of the boy's future came through dreams, which in that time and culture were given great credence. Two of the dreams were such as to call for interpretation by soothsayers.

At the age of five or six Ḥusayn-'Alí had dreams which he related to his father, describing a desert garden in which huge birds were attacking him from every side but without harming him; and he told also of swimming in waters where birds of the air and fishes of the sea were attacking him while he remained unscathed. The Vazír called upon a famous seer who explained the visions as indicating that the child would become the founder of a great cause and that, despite the attacks of the leaders and learnèd of the world, the birds and the fishes of the dream, no harm would come to him but rather that he would be victorious over all.[12]

At another time, Mírzá 'Abbás himself dreamed that the boy 'appeared to him swimming in a vast, limitless ocean. His body shone upon the waters with a radiance that illumined the sea. Around his head, which could distinctly be seen above the waters, there radiated, in all directions, his long, jet-black locks, floating in great profusion above the waves . . . a multitude of fishes gathered round him, each holding fast to the extremity of one hair. Fascinated by the effulgence of his face, they followed him in whatever direction he swam. Great as was their number, and however firmly they clung to his locks, not one single hair seemed to have been detached from his head, nor did the least injury affect his person. Free and unrestrained, he moved above the waters and they all followed him.'

The Vazír again consulted a famous soothsayer and asked for an interpretation. The man declared:

'The limitless ocean that you have seen in your dream, O Vazír, is none other than the world of being. Single-handed and alone, your son will achieve supreme ascendancy over it . . . No one will resist his march, no one will hinder his progress. The multitude of fishes signifies the turmoil he will arouse amidst the peoples and kindreds of the earth. Around him they will gather, and to him will they cling. Assured of the unfailing protection of the Almighty, this tumult will never harm his person, nor will his loneliness upon the sea of life endanger his safety.'

Taken to see the small boy of the symbolic dreams of future eminence, the soothsayer looked intently upon his face, carefully examining his features. Charmed by his appearance, he extolled every trait observable in his countenance. So profuse was his praise of the child that from that day forward the Vazír became even more devoted to this son. 'Like Jacob, he desired only to ensure the welfare of his beloved Joseph, and to surround him with his loving protection.'[13]*

One day when Ḥusayn-'Alí was seven years old, his parents were watching him as he walked nearby. His mother, deeply fond of her extraordinary child, remarked that he was rather short of stature, but his father reacted strongly, saying:

'That matters not. Do you not know how great his intelligence, how wonderful his mind? Are you not aware of his capacity and abilities? Of his great perception? He is as a flame of fire. Even at this young age he surpasses mature men.'[14] Perhaps his mother wished for a large body to house the giant intellect and supernal spirit of her son; such a thought felt by him would have created a sadness within the perceptive child as he matured.

Noble families educated their sons in the lore of their society through tutors who taught them letters, manners, the Qu'rán and the classical poets, and also martial arts, and who perhaps gave to the young men the rudiments of a broader learning if the tutors were able and perhaps even learnèd. Ḥusayn-'Alí was beyond the best efforts of the nameless tutors who served 'Abbás's household; yet he so greatly respected the role of the teacher and particularly the teacher who brought spiritual and moral values, that later he recommended allocation of a portion of inheritances from the deceased to their influential teachers. And he avoided the classes in the religious schools which in that day posed as education, being unwilling to be taught by any such teachers, later testifying that:

'*We have not entered any school, nor read any of your dissertations. Incline your ears to the words of this unlettered One, . . .*'[15]† of this youth

---

* Both dreams are suspiciously similar; the first dream purportedly by Ḥusayn-'Alí (per Mírzá Abu'l-Faḍl), the second experienced by Mírzá Buzurg (per Nabíl). Perhaps they are the same dream, recalled erroneously by one or the other reporter.

† The full quotation: '*We have not entered any school, nor read any of your dissertations. Incline your ears to the words of this unlettered One, wherewith He summoneth you unto God, the Ever-Abiding. Better is this for you than all the treasures of the earth, could ye but comprehend it . . .*'

who needed no formal learning, who avoided the wholly inadequate education of his day and place, and especially the false so-called sciences, mere constructs of words and systems which later he sharply condemned. But with his absorptive mind and intuitive spirit he perceived the dynamic world about him and fathomed the good and the evil, the ethics and the sciences. At another time he asserted that, '*The learning current among men I studied not; their schools I entered not. Ask of the city wherein I dwelt, that thou mayest be well assured that I am not of them who speak falsely.*' '*This Wronged One hath frequented no school, neither hath he attended the controversies of the learnèd.*'[16]

'From childhood he was extremely kind and generous. He was a great lover of outdoor life, most of his time being spent in the garden or the fields. He had an extraordinary power of attraction, which was felt by all. People always crowded around him. Ministers and people of the court would surround him, and the children were also devoted to him.'[17]

From childhood he was also pointed out as remarkable for sagacity, and held in high regard by the wise, and from his earliest adolescence he was celebrated for single-mindedness among those of the ministerial class, both relatives and strangers. 'His extreme aptitude was admitted by all, and his excessive acuteness and intelligence were universally avowed. In the eyes of the common folk he enjoyed a wonderful esteem, and in all gatherings and assemblies he had a marvelous speech and delivery.'[18]

Once in his boyhood he overheard two divines, vain in their huge turbans, giving theological lessons to two women who sat concealed behind a screen, thus to assure the men's separation from the women. A question put forward by one priest to the two students was whether the angel Gabriel had a higher station than the devoted Qanbar, slave of the first Imám, 'Alí. Before any reply could be made, the boy respectfully expressed his astonishment at the illogical question, for he pointed out that Gabriel was the one in the Qu'rán through whom the Holy Spirit descended upon the heart of the Apostle of God, Muḥammad. Therefore, not even 'Alí himself could reach the station of Gabriel, how much less Qanbar the slave.[19]

Such tilting with the pretentious divines may well have recurred during the boy's years of maturation. And to add to his innate shrewd appraisals of men and their motives came sage advice from others about the ubiquitous priests of Shi'ite Islám. Once the head shepherd of the family flocks which ranged the mountains commented candidly on the priestly corruption of that day, saying:

'My Lord! I have one piece of advice to give unto you. Never trust the 'ulamás!'[20]

Over the years there was a rich and complicated sibling interplay. The growing to maturity of the many children of Mírzá 'Abbás meant a stream of marriages arranged among the noble families for their many purposes of power, prestige and wealth, although surely romance sometimes intervened as a factor to confuse and confound the matchmaking. So it was that Mírzá Áqá,* the elder half-brother born of Khán-Nanih, came of age and his marriage took place in Teheran. According to the custom of the country there was feasting for seven days and nights. The program on the last day of entertainment for the guests was a puppet play dramatizing and mocking the great Ottoman Sulṭán Salím. The ministers, the grandees and officials of the city were there in a great throng and, as Mírzá Ḥusayn-'Alí recounts in his recollections: '. . . *I ascended to one of the upper rooms of the building where I sat down to observe the scene. Presently a tent was pitched in the courtyard, and before long some small figures in human form, each of which seemed no more than about a handspan in height, came out of the tent, and raised the call "The Sulṭán is coming! Set out the chairs!" Other figures then emerged, some of whom were seen to be engaged in sweeping, others in sprinkling water, and thereafter another character, who was pronounced to be the chief herald, raised up his voice and bade the people assemble for an audience with the king. Next, three groups of figures made their appearance and took their places, the first group attired in hats and cummerbunds after the Persian fashion, the second wielding battle-axes, and the third comprising a number of serjeants-at-arms and executioners bearing clubs and canes. Finally a splendid figure, arrayed in regal majesty, wearing a kingly diadem upon his head, and bearing himself with the utmost haughtiness and grandeur – now advancing, now pausing in his progress – came strutting onto the scene and, with unparalleled solemnity, gravity, and sedateness, proceeded to seat himself upon a throne, whereupon a volley of shots was fired, a fanfare of trumpets was sounded, and the king and tent were enveloped in a pall of smoke.*

When the smoke had cleared, the king was seen to be ensconced upon his throne and surrounded by a suite of ministers, princes, and dignitaries of state who, having taken their places, were standing at attention in his presence. At this moment a captured thief was brought before the king, who gave the

* Unfortunately, Mírzá Áqá was destined for an early death. His young widow, a niece of Mírzá Naṣru'lláh, Áqá Khán, forthwith was married to Áqá's brother, Mírzá Muḥammad-Ḥasan, later to become a loyal follower of his half-brother, Mírzá Ḥusayn-'Alí, Bahá'u'lláh. See Balyuzi, *Bahá'u'lláh, The King of Glory*, p. 13.

order that the offender should be beheaded. Without a moment's delay the chief executioner proceeded to execute upon him the royal sentence, whereupon a red-coloured liquid resembling blood came trickling from his headless torso. This done, the king fell into conversation with those in attendance, and while he was thus engaged, intelligence arrived that rebellion had broken out on such and such a frontier. Thereupon the king reviewed his troops and despatched several regiments supported by units of artillery to quell the uprising. A few minutes later cannons were heard booming from behind the tent, and it was announced that the king's troops were at that moment engaged in battle with the insurgents.

I was greatly perplexed and bewildered to conceive the nature of this spectacle. When the show was over, the curtain of the tent was drawn. Then, after some twenty minutes, a man emerged from behind the tent carrying a box under his arm.

"What is this box?" I asked him, "and what was the nature of this display?"

"All these lavish trappings," he replied, "the king, the princes, and the ministers, their pomp and glory, their might and power, everything you saw, are all now contained within this box."

I swear by My Lord Who hath brought into being all things through a single word from Him that, ever since that day, all the trappings of the world have seemed in the eyes of this Youth akin to that same spectacle. They have never been, nor will ever be, possessed of any weight, though it be to the extent of a grain of mustard seed. How greatly I used to marvel that men would pride themselves upon such vanities, whilst those possessed of insight, ere they witness any evidence of human glory, perceive with certainty the inevitability of its waning. "Never have I looked upon any thing save that I have seen extinction before it; and God, verily, is a sufficient witness."

It behoveth everyone to traverse this brief span of life with sincerity and fairness. Should one fail to attain unto the recognition of Him Who is the Eternal Truth, let him at least comport himself with reason and justice. Erelong these outward trappings, these heaped-up treasures, these earthly vanities, these amassed battalions, this gorgeous finery, these proud and overweening souls – all shall pass into the confines of the grave, as though into that box. In the eyes of those possessed of insight, all this conflict, dissention and vainglory hath been, and will ever be, like unto the sport of children. Take thou good heed, and be not of those who see and yet deny.'[21]

How descriptive was this puppetry of the sham and cruelties, the crudity and injustices of the Sháh's court and of Persia, although it was meant to make a laughing-stock of the Turkish rivals of Persia. All the manifest treasures, all the familiar pomp and honors were already felt by the boy to be as child's play, having no value to a person of insight. In a later passage he expressed again the feeling of the puppet show: '*Neither the pomp of the mighty, nor the wealth of the rich, nor even the ascendancy of the ungodly will endure. All will perish, at a word from Him.*' And again, '*The days of your life flee away as a breath of wind, and all your pomp and glory shall be folded up as were the pomp and glory of those gone before you.*'[22]

When he was only thirteen or fourteen years old he became renowned for his learning. He would converse on any subject and solve any problem presented to him. In large gatherings he would discuss matters with the 'ulamá, the leading mullás, and would explain intricate religious questions. All of them listened to him with the greatest interest.[23]

There were many happy experiences and observations. As a boy and youth Mírzá Ḥusayn-'Alí repeatedly savored the sixty-mile rides over the mountains from Tákur to Afchih en route to Teheran.* Starting at dawn or in the pre-dawn if possible, he and his companions would follow the Núr River westward through familiar villages to Balade-i-Núr. They then would ride southward up the tributary Yál River to the stone and brick village of the same name, Yálrúd, site of the convergence of other mountain streams, and often a first stop in the journey. All along the narrow valleys were the hard-won small fields, the willow and plane tree copses and the poplar windbreaks guarding humble stone peasant huts mud-plastered against the mountain winds and the snows. Down every ravine came clear small streams singing and chuckling and grumbling to become, ultimately, the great river Haráz emptying into the Caspian Sea. In the early dawn the company would climb the treacherous rocky path cut by Sháh 'Abbás† along the edge of the 500-foot deep Yal River Gorge, walking their horses along the steep trail, with chukar partridges booming away from under foot. Mírzá Ḥusayn-'Alí could exult in the thin cold air constricting his lungs, the moist rock faces glinting in his eyes, the clouds designing shadow graphics on the brushy hillsides as they climbed to the 9,000-foot Kushak Pass. Everywhere was evidence of centuries of gnawing goats, sheep and cattle competing for forage with the great Persian fallow deer, the gazelles and ibex already almost hunted to extinction,

* In 1975 Dr Amin Banani, distinguished orientalist and professor at the University of California at Los Angeles, made the traverse afoot and with horse and donkey from Afchih to Yalrúd and Tákur along the trail made historic by the rides of the young Mírzá Ḥusayn-'Alí of Núr. His photographs and chronicle form the basis for this passage.

† The Safavid Sháh Ábbás the Great (1588–1630 AD).

their aggregate teeth obliterating the regrowth of the once great Alborz forests cut down for man's purposes.

Then, a rider among riders, he with his companions would pass through Kushak and over the 10,000-foot Kabúd Pass with its splendid view of volcanic snowy 19,000-foot Mount Damávand, its crater yellow-edged with sulfur in summer. And so into the valley of the Sifídáb River with its refreshing small cataract where horses and men paused to drink; here he and his company could make camp in the flower-sprinkled herbs and grasses. In the early morning another hard climb out of the Lar River Valley and over the Marghe Sar Pass before an end-of-the-day test of endurance over the Afchih Vashm Pass, pressing the steeds hard in the last light or in the early darkness to reach fire and hospitality in Afchih. Typically for the young nobleman it was late dinner and a bed in the hillside mansion of a Núri neighbor, Mírzá Naṣru'lláh, Áqá Khán, who owned the village. In the handsome two-storeyed brick and plaster mansion above Afchih's orchards and poplars he could be sure of a warm welcome and a soft sleep free of rocks and cold dew. Tomorrow's long forty-mile ride southwestward through the rough country of the Lavásán district, across the river Taj into Shimírán, would bring him to Teheran.

Yálrúd was a considerable stone and brick village in Núr district, situated in the beautiful side valley which was the customary route from Tákur to Afchih. The young Mírzá Ḥusayn-'Alí passed through it frequently whenever in Teheran he felt the need for refreshment in the mountains of home or was required to return from Núr to the moiling capital city. Also, in Yálrúd lived his married elder sister, the well-loved young Sárih with her husband Maḥmúd. Here also the scholar Shaykh Muḥammad-Taqí, a distant relative, conducted a religious school of some distinction, its popularity attracting hundreds of students aspiring to knowledge of Qu'ránic lore, youths who also were escaping the numbing labors endured by their parents. On one visit to Yálrúd the youth Mírzá Ḥusayn-'Alí sat among the students in the bare classroom, cross-legged on the floor mats, respectfully attending to the dialogue. A riddle had been propounded, thrown out to them by the Shaykh to test their reasoning processes, who related an Islamic tradition which states that 'Fáṭimih is the best of women, but for the one born of Mary.' But since Mary, the mother of Jesus, had no daughter, what did this mean? The students failed to reply satisfactorily. Then Mírzá Ḥusayn-'Alí pointed out that the initial statement emphasized the impossibility of any alternative, since there could be no woman

Afchih in Lavasán district, the mansion of Mírzá 'Aqá Khán of Núr, Ṣadr-i-A'ẓám, the second Prime Minister of Náṣiri'd-Dín Sháh. A mansion frequently visited by Mírzá Ḥusayn-'Alí, Bahá'u'lláh, when en route to or from Teheran and Tákur, and acquired by the Bahá'ís in later years.

comparable to Fáṭimih. The reply silenced all. And, on another occasion, when the Shaykh was seeking to clarify an abstruse tradition of metaphysical nature, the youth Mírzá Ḥusayn-'Alí, passing by and pausing to listen to the class discussion, offered a clear explanation of the idea propounded.

The next day Shaykh Muḥammad-Taqí scolded his students for failing the test, saying, 'For years I have been instructing you and have patiently striven to instill into your minds the profoundest truths and the noblest principles of the Faith. And yet you allow, after all these years of persistent study, this youth, a wearer of the kuláh,* who has had no share in scholarly training, and who is entirely unfamiliar with your academic learning, to demonstrate his superiority over you!'[24]

When Mírzá Ḥusayn-'Alí had departed, Shaykh Muḥammad-Taqí

* The kuláh was the lambskin cap worn by members of the laity.

related to his disciples two of his recent dreams, the details of which he believed were of utmost significance.

'In my first dream,' he began, 'I was standing in the midst of a vast concourse of people, all of whom seemed to be pointing to a certain house in which they said the [Lord of the Age] dwelt. Frantic with joy, I hastened in my dream to attain His presence. When I reached the house, I was, to my great surprise, refused admittance. "The promised Qá'im", I was informed, "is engaged in private conversation with another person. Access to them is strictly forbidden." From the guards who were standing beside the door, I gathered that that person was none other than [Ḥusayn-'Alí].'[25]

Of the second dream the Shaykh recounted that he came upon a room filled with chests which, he was told, belonged to Mírzá Ḥusayn-'Alí. On opening one, he found it packed with books, all of whose lines were studded with gems, their brilliance awakening him.[26]

The students doubtless cared little for the meaning of the dreams, but another person was vitally concerned, for the school of Shaykh Muḥammad-Taqí was scarcely Mírzá Ḥusayn-'Alí's principal interest in Yálrúd. The village was owned by the wealthy Vazír Ismá'íl whose son, Mírzá Maḥmúd, was the young husband of the lady Sárih; she had contrived an engagement between her brother Ḥusayn-'Alí, and her husband's young sister Ásíyih. The marriage was to occur as soon as the girl came of age; and surely this engagement was quickly noised about in that small village. Thus when Ásíyih's mother visited the house of the priest one dawn to attend morning prayers, he told her that he had excellent news for her, forthwith telling her his dream of the chest full of Mírzá Ḥusayn-'Alí's books, each page gem-studded. He himself was puzzled at the meaning of this surprising distinction given to the young man of no visible achievement, hence in his conceit interpreted it to the woman as referring to the youth's relationship to him and his publications.[27] On hearing the theologian's interpretation later repeated by him, one listener reacted cannily to this palpably erroneous deduction, saying: 'But you yourself did not have permission to enter.'[28]

To the wise and thoughtful of the nineteenth century, dreams meant clues for conduct, even prophetic glimpses of the future, while today they are interpreted as the hieroglyphs of the primitive unconscious or traces of usually analyzable memories. Shaykh Muḥammad-Taqí was not to live to see his dreams fulfilled, his young man of the lambskin cap the author of gem-studded volumes of religious and social thought and guidance. But the times were writing their premonitions upon the sensitive and the susceptible, including even the egotistical priest. And for the youth Mírzá Ḥusayn-'Alí, who can now know of his flashes of illumination, his growing inner sense of a noble destiny during those years of human maturation?

Hear Me, ye mortal birds! In the Rose Garden of changeless splendor a Flower hath begun to bloom, compared to which every other flower is but a thorn, and before the brightness of Whose glory the very essence of beauty must pale and wither.[29]

Bahá'u'lláh

The south face of Tákur Mansion as restored in late years following the great damages of flood and military action. The room of state was entered by the stairs on the right; an extensive garden surrounded the mansion; the village extends up the valley and mountain slopes beyond the building.

Landscapes for the spirit of the Prophet: two great upland plane trees enduring the winter winds and snows; a mountain stream cutting its raw valley through the Alborz rock masses, grinding its slow path to the mother Caspian Sea. (Seyhoun)

Dramatic mountainscapes in the Alborz range, well revealing the hardihood of the Mázindaráni mountaineers, hill people who survive and shape the mountains to their labors and wills, defying the elements, seeing God in His Creation all about them. (Seyhoun)

Mount Aurang and the ruins of Mírzá Buzurg's fine mansion at Tákur. (Seyhoun)

Afchih in Lavasán district, an orchard village, property of Mírzá 'Aqá Khán of Núr and end of the mountain track of Núr Valley and Tákur; riders came down the valley at upper right, passing through the village en route to Teheran 40 miles southwest.

3 Father of the Poor

Be generous in prosperity, and thankful in adversity. Be worthy of the trust of thy neighbor, and look upon him with a bright and friendly face. Be a treasure to the poor, an admonisher to the rich, an answerer to the cry of the needy, a preserver of the sanctity of thy pledge . . .[1]

Bahá'u'lláh

The imprint of the mountains was upon the young Mírzá Ḥusayn-'Alí. Although city-born at the southern edge of the great Alborz Mountains rippling eastward across the top of Persia, the youth always felt his true home to be the long green valleys between the denuded razorback ridges of the mountain district of Myavand in Núr, place of the family estates. How potent the stimulus of such an environment upon a nascent spiritual genius!

Iran stretches endless semi-arid and desert miles from Iraq and Turkey in the west to Baluchistan and Afghanistan in the east, from the inhospitable and waterless south coast bordering the Persian Gulf and Gulf of Oman to the northern ranges at the Caspian Sea and Turkestan border. The emptiness of deserts has ever encouraged contemplation among those seeking inward vision, while mountains have gripped man's outward sight with the grandeur of earth forms and the forces of God's creation, lifting man's horizontal gaze to the heavens. Where better for a spiritual leader to strengthen his thews of spirit through prayer and meditation in silence and solitude than at the upper edge of the high desert plateau of Persia where immense mountains leap skyward to the cosmos? How better to free the spiritual growth of a Channel from God than to destine Him to be born where every sight and thought would elicit profound feelings of the insignificance but also the wondrous capacities of man! For the young Mírzá Ḥusayn-'Alí, whose microclimates alternated between Teheran and provincial highland Núr, there was a year-round rich variety of experiences to expand his sensitivities. The consummate human harp, its thousand thousand strings already genetically tuned by God's Fingers, properly began its every-thousand-year song* in settings befitting the preparation of a Great Soul.

The small village of Tákur, then perhaps of forty to sixty families served by a simple mosque, straddled a brawling mountain stream draining a part of the tumbled range of raw mountains to the north. Each year when the winter snows melted, the brook became a dangerous torrent threatening alike the humble houses and the mansion of the lord of the countryside as it plunged into the deep valley of the Núr River. The village was of generally mean and uninviting stone and brick dwellings, flat-roofed, lying haphazardly along meandering rocky lanes which reached up into the valley notch and mounted the lower slopes of Mount Aurang. Occupying the best site where the brook valley met the river valley, on a fertile bench ending at the cliffs, the wall-enclosed property of Mírzá 'Abbás dominated the village. Its arched gateway owned a singular pious inscription of welcome, saying on the lintel: 'When thou enterest the sacred abode of the Beloved say: "I am at thy command. This is the home of Love; enter with reverence. This is holy ground; remove thy shoes when thou enterest here." '†, and it opened into extensive gardens surrounding a rectangular two-storeyed mansion of brick and stone. Paired doorways flanked the generous central hall with its splendid stained-glass windows and high ceiling. On each side of the hall and above lay rooms of habitation and service.

To the northwest Mount Aurang reared into the sky, a fellow peak at the northeast forming the other lip of the tributary valley; both presented great expanses of naked rock. Southward across the spring-angry Núr River, grinding its way eastward through a long canyon to the mother Haráz River, a sheer rock wall with sharp talus slopes at its bottom leapt upwards, a barrier steep even for goats.

The district of Núr extended north over the mountains into the

* The idea of thousand-year cycles of Divine Revelation is perhaps first clearly stated by Zoroaster, as noted by Nietzsche in *Thus Spake Zarathustra* (Zoroaster). And it is confirmed by Bahá'u'lláh that His primary span of influence as the Supreme Prophet for this 'Day' will be of at least a millennium's duration.

† These lines paraphrase what Moses heard on Mount Horev in Midian as He approached the Burning Bush. Balyuzi in *Bahá'u'lláh, The King of Glory*, p. 19, gives an alternative translation of the Tákur inscription: 'When thou reachest the threshold of the Beloved say "Aye", / For there neither "salám" nor " 'alayk" can find a way. / This is the vale of Love, hold thy steps; / This is holy ground, shed thy footgear.' The gate lintel now hangs in the small mosque of Tákur, having been salvaged at the time of construction of a road through the village which cut off the northern edge of the mansion property. It was written in the admirable calligraphic hand of Mírzá 'Abbás himself.

rain-drenched plain at the southern edge of the Caspian Sea, that huge inland lake some eighty feet below sea level which remained from the Ice Ages. Its receding shoreline had exposed the fertile alluvial benches and beaches of Mázindarán and Gílán. From the north and east the great watersheds of the Volga, Ural and Amu Darya Rivers fed its diminishing domain. From the Persian mountains fast-flowing rivers drained rain and meltwater northward into the sea, cutting great canyons across the grain of the ridges. Well-watered, its sturgeon fisheries productive, its surf mild and inviting, the Caspian shore was the most friendly and agreeable land in all Persia, with its narrow plain, its several bays and mantling heavy forests. Indeed, the entire province was later called 'the verdant isle' by the Báb because of its greenery and its beauty, famed too as it was throughout Persia for its bounteous displays of flowering plants, and for their fragrances in all seasons, even in winter with its diminutive ice flowers. It was exciting too, for the mountainous Caspian shore rich in game remembered the days when its fierce Hyrcanian tigers were captured for combats in Roman arenas; herds of hardy wild boars remained to offer dangerous hunting thrills.

During his growing years at Tákur, Mírzá Ḥusayn-'Alí learned to walk and ride in the silence and magnificence of the subalpine valleys. Here every peasant knew the boy as he grew into youth and manhood, for as chattels they were wary of, yet eager to see and know, the men of the dominant family which owned them, their loyalties, and their very hopes of whatever happiness was possible for them in that difficult time. Each villager and countryman in the fertile valleys of Mírzá 'Abbás's estates very likely had his tales of personal encounters and also his guesses about the future of the young rider with the startling mind and acute perceptions. More astonishing, perhaps, was the occasional realization that the youth's understanding of them included deep sympathy for each one, however humble. But there was one over-arching reason for the unhampered unfoldment of his capacities: his well-favored time of youth occurred under the eye and in the shadow of his estimable father, the Vazír 'Abbás, whom he, in utter respect, called by the title: Master.

In Mírzá Ḥusayn-'Alí's own word of honor: '. . . *my father enjoyed a most enviable position among his countrymen. His vast wealth, his noble ancestry, his artistic attainments, his unrivaled prestige and exalted rank made him the object of the admiration of all who knew him. For a period of over twenty years, no one among the wide circle of his family and kindred, which extended over Núr and Teheran, suffered distress, injury or illness.*

They enjoyed, during a long and uninterrupted period, rich and manifold blessings.'[2]

Indeed, Mírzá 'Abbás had won the favor of Fatḥ-'Alí Sháh during the latter portion of his reign, receiving from him ever greater responsibilities and finally, for a period, the governorship of Luristán based in its capital city of Burújird. Famed for his calligraphy, Mírzá 'Abbás so impressed the Sháh with his artistic prowess, political sagacity, courage and administrative talents that he was awarded the title of Buzurg, the Great One. As a token of honor he was given a robe worn by the king and his home village of Tákur was exempted from taxation. Sometime later, he was appointed Vazír to Imám Virdí, chief of the Qájár clan to which the royal family belonged. And then, during 1834 or early 1835, he undertook a close relationship with a daughter of the Sháh named Sháh Begum, Ḍíyá'u's-Salṭanih (Light of the Sultanate) (see Note 6). Perhaps her own artist-calligrapher skills first brought her close to Mírzá Buzurg, who then taught her new skills of a fine art; but possibly he was her agent in business matters.[3]* During this period, with the death of his sponsor Fatḥ-'Alí Sháh and the accession of Muḥammad Sháh to the throne in 1834, the good fortune of Vazír Buzurg began to change for the worse.

Early in his reign in June 1835 the new king executed his father's Prime Minister, the able and noble Mírzá Abu'l-Qásim of Faráhán,† Buzurg's esteemed friend. Then, in that same month, the Sháh brought into power as his new Prime Minister a ruthless elderly intriguer, Ḥájí Mírzá Áqásí, a Súfí.‡

However, in the days following the murder of Mírzá Abu'l-Qásim

* The relationship between Mírzá Buzurg and the Princess Sháh-Begum, Ḍíya'u's-Salṭanih, is unclear. Suffice it to say that perhaps he became her agent for various matter, and certainly he taught her new skills in calligraphy. Her relatives have recorded that her first marriage was to one Mírzá Mas'ud Anṣárí in April 1836, when already the court case against Buzurg had been unfavorably completed and he was in sorry debt. Her grand-daughter and other descendants came to have a very honorable history in the Faith. (See Momen, fn. p. 18, Balyuzi, *Bahá'u'lláh, The King of Glory*, rev. ed.)

† Several times in His Writings Bahá'u'lláh recalled the evil murder of Mírzá Abu'l-Qásim Faráhání, his admired friend, the associate of his father, and freely castigated the Sháh. In one of His Tablets (*Tablets of Bahá'u'lláh*, p. 65) He states: '*His Majesty Muḥammad Sháh, despite the excellence of his rank, committed two heinous deeds. One was the order to banish the Lord of the Realms of Grace and Bounty, and Primal Point* [to Máh-kú and Chihríq]; *and the other, the murder of the Prince of the City of Statesmanship and Literary Accomplishment.*', [i.e. Mírzá Abu'l-Qásim Faráhání, poet and scholar, Prime Minister of Persia 1821–1835].

‡ A Ṣúfí is one who espouses ideas usually identified as Muslim mysticism. The name derives from 'ṣúf', a simple woolen garment which exemplified the rough garb of some early non-materialistic devotees. (See Note 6.)

The upright Mírzá 'Abbás Buzurg and the corrupt intriguer who ruined him. The father of Mírzá Ḥusayn-'Alí, titled Buzurg, the Great One, by Fatḥ-'Alí Sháh, and his evil antagonist, the cunning and avaricious Ḥájí Mírzá Áqásí, Prime Minister of Muḥammad Sháh, who was largely responsible for the deterioration of Persia at that time.

Faráhání, a crime occurring with the strongly suspected complicity of the rumored new appointee, Áqásí, but before his confirmation as Prime Minister, Mírzá Buzurg had written to Prince Bahman, a stormy petrel of national politics, expressing his candid hope that:

'May this satyr be kept away from the Sháh.'[4]

The treacherous prince allowed the letter to come into the hand of Mírzá Áqásí after his appointment, thus exciting his quick and hostile reaction to the able Mírzá Buzurg. Because Buzurg was not in Teheran, but away serving the Crown in his governorship, Áqásí summoned the eighteen-year-old Mírzá Ḥusayn-'Alí, whom he deemed to be the most responsible of the Vazír's sons and for whom he had conceived a certain affection because of his recognized talents.

Calling the youth to his splendid chambers already echoing with ugly intrigues, there perhaps to probe him for additional suggestive information on his father Mírzá Buzurg, who must now be thought of as a dangerous and powerful potential enemy, he arranged the intimidating confrontation with his chamberlain Shafi' Khán as witness. Clad in his elegant robes and tall hat, the new Prime Minister, his long seamed fox face half scowling, his grizzled double-pointed thin beard accenting his words, flourished the critical letter before the youth, vehemently declaring:

'See this; I do not know what I have done to your father to deserve this.'

To the chamberlain's attempt to divert him from Mírzá Buzurg on the grounds that the letter could not have been written by him, Áqásí's retort was:

'Impossible! There is none who can produce such a beautiful specimen of calligraphy and such a wonderful piece of writing, such prose!'

Mírzá Ḥusayn-'Alí remained discreetly silent during the outburst, and the Prime Minister concluded by saying:

'What shall I, what can I do? He is your father. For your sake I will try to forget this and let bygones be bygones. But write to your father and advise him not to do it again.'[5]

During this time of gathering difficulties for the praiseworthy Mírzá Buzurg, a bright spot gladdened all who knew the two families of the neighbor Vazírs. The girl Ásíyih of Yálrúd had come of age and the long-awaited marriage to Ḥusayn-'Alí of Núr could be planned. In the earliest bloom of her maturity, the young girl was already noted for her beauty, her wisdom, intelligence and high-mindedness. She was slender, graceful, gentle but vivacious, her dark blue eyes a striking feature. Well bred by her estimable family, she was stamped with an unfailing courtesy, and from her warm heart came an extraordinary consideration for others. Thus when Mírzá Ḥusayn-'Alí was almost eighteen and the lady Ásíyih perhaps fifteen,* arrangements were finalized for the second marriage uniting the families of the Vazírs Mírzá Ismá'íl and Mírzá Buzurg, thus 'adding wealth to wealth', as it was said. The traditional lengthy preparations were set afoot: for six months before the marriage a jeweler worked at the bride's home preparing her rich court clothing, whose buttons were of gold set with precious stones. Prepared also were the many parental gifts which together constituted the bride's dowry, to be taken by the girl from her parents' home to that of her young husband at the time of the wedding. Thus when she set forth from Yalrúd, accompanied by forty mules loaded with her nuptial endowments, Ásíyih brought extensive possessions to her married life in Tákur.[6] The marriage ceremony occurred sometime between September 24 and October 22, 1835. And with marriage the young nobleman moved into a new world of responsibility and fulfillment. Before him was a lifetime of love and sharing with this noblewoman of a great destiny, known by her title Navváb, her Highness, her Excellency.†

The first hard blow upon Mírzá Buzurg came from nature. A flash flood arose, probably from heavy rains and snow meltwater, in the raw mountains north of Tákur. The floodwaters, sweeping down the narrow side valley in whose mouth the village lay, carried away most of the settlement and destroyed the Vazír's splendid mansion before dumping the wreckage into the brawling river Núr. 'The best part of that house, which had been known for the solidity of its foundations, was utterly wiped away by the fury of the roaring torrent. Its precious articles of furniture were destroyed, and its elaborate ornamentation irretrievably ruined.'[7]

Simultaneously, the Prime Minister in Teheran, despite his assertion of forgiveness, continued to fuel his smoldering anger at Mírzá Buzurg, taking revenge through vicious bites, shark-like. First he engineered the Vazír's dismissal from his governorship. Next he cancelled the generous allowance from the government which had been awarded to Mírzá Buzurg for his distinguished services. The

* In Islamic lands of that time the formal religiously ordained age of permission to marry was fifteen for boys and nine for girls. However, parents had their personal ideas of the proper time for marriage in the cases of their own children. Furúgh Arbáb, in her *Akhtarán-i-Tábán*, has given Ásíyih's age at marriage as fifteen.

† The title Navváb/Navábbih (fem.) was a title used for descendants of the Ṣafavíd and Qájár kings.

consequent financial squeeze forced the mortgaging of much of his extensive property, and included the sale of the great houses in Teheran in which he and his extended family lived. The houses were shortly bought back by Mírzá Ḥusayn-'Alí, but new economic attacks impended, for Mírzá Áqásí intrigued to bring financial ruin upon the worthy Mírzá Buzurg.

Exorbitant legal claims were made against Mírzá Buzurg, their bases not known. The court decision of 1836, which we may suppose was powerfully influenced, even dictated by the Prime Minister, was so large an exaction that Mírzá Buzurg could not readily meet the sum demanded in the decree, and forthwith was held under house arrest in his mansion at Tákur, there to be cruelly pressed by the collector sent to extort the money legally due. A daily witness to the insulting behavior and injustices forced upon his esteemed father, Mírzá Ḥusayn-'Alí finally could bear no longer the aggravation felt by the entire household. Riding the hard horseback miles to Teheran, he sought the dismissal of the unjust collector who had so misused his authority. Obtaining papers ordering the dismissal of the man, he returned to Tákur to remove this thorn from the side of his beloved father, thus ameliorating in some part these days of misfortune.[8]

During this troublous period the large property complex in Teheran, including the house of Buzurg himself, '*was sold at spurious auction for a negligible sum*' to two brother princes, Firaydún, entitled the Issuer of Edicts (Farmán-Farmá), and Sulṭán-Murád, entitled the Sword of the Sultanate (Ḥisámu's-Salṭanih), who '*divided the property between themselves*'. Following this conspiracy and fraud, Mírzá Ḥusayn-'Alí separated from his half-brother, the physician Mírzá Riḍá-Qulí who, with his mother Kulthúm, '*established his residence close to the entrance of the Mosque of the Sháh*'. He himself and a number of the family members '*lived near the Gate of Shimírán*' in a rented house not far from the mansion of his youth just stolen from them. To it he took his mother Khadíjih, his wife Ásíyih, his other stepmothers and a number of brothers and sisters, never again to occupy the great family mansion where he had been born.[9]* As effective

* It is helpful to quote in full from Bahá'u'lláh's *Epistle to the Son of the Wolf*, p. 170: '*In the early days we all lived in one house, which later on was sold at auction, for a negligible sum, and the two brothers, Farmán-Farmá and Ḥisámu's-Salṭanih, purchased it and divided it between themselves. After this occurred, We separated from Our brother. He established his residence close to the entrance of the Masjid-i-Sháh (Mosque of the Sháh), whilst We lived near the Gate of Shimírán.*'

head of the family, he assumed the care of many of the dependent persons among the relatives.

Áqásí's revenge upon Buzurg was wellnigh complete, the contemplated ruin nearly total. Yet, despite his grave change of fortune, the Vazír maintained his calm and dignity, and pursued within the restricted limits of his means his acts of benevolence and charity. And '*he continued to exercise towards his faithless associates that same courtesy and kindness that had characterized his dealings with his fellow-men*'.[10] He sought without success to regain his properties sold under illegal duress. Finally, he hoped to retire to Iraq, but died in 1839 before his wish could be realized. However, in fulfillment of his devout intention, his body was transported to Najaf, site of the tomb of the Imám 'Alí, near which he was buried with all honor.

Upon Mírzá Buzurg's passing, family friends wished Mírzá Ḥusayn-'Alí, his most promising son, to succeed to his father's place in the government, but he would not accept. Whereupon Prime

The Mansion of Mírzá Buzurg and Mírzá Ḥusayn-'Alí, Bahá'u'lláh, in old Teheran, built by Mírzá Buzurg and stolen by Qájár princes. The rooms of state look into the garden, and are entered through the door to the right. A wind tower crowns the roof, left. (Seyhoun)

Minister Áqásí, shrewd judge of men that he was, dismissed the issue, for through personal visits to Mírzá Ḥusayn-'Alí's home he had gained many observations of the young man's role in the Núrí family which he was engaged in destroying. Moreover, he was unwilling to bring this incorruptible into the seamy power structure of the government. And he had come to respect the young man, had shown him many marks of favor, hence wisely remarked:

'Leave him to himself. Such a position is unworthy of him. He has some higher aim in view. I cannot understand him, but I am convinced that he is destined for some lofty career. His thoughts are not like ours. Let him alone.'[11]

Despite the accuracy of his appraisal and his high opinion of Mírzá Ḥusayn-'Alí, the Grand Vazír lived in his world of feral power and absolute corruption and could not resist visiting a continuing retaliation upon the son of his derogator. Seeking to purchase an estate in the village of Qúch-Ḥiṣár owned by the family of Mírzá Buzurg, he summoned the young nobleman to him in order to effect an immediate purchase of the well-watered and beautiful property near Teheran. The young man demurred, saying: '*Had this property been exclusively mine own, I would willingly have complied with your desire. This transitory life, with all its sordid possessions, is worthy of no attachment in my eyes, how much less this small and insignificant estate. As a number of other people, both rich and poor, some of full age and some still minors, share with me the ownership of this property, I would request you to refer this matter to them, and to seek their consent.*'[12]

Dissatisfied with this response, the Grand Vazír sought to gain the property through fraudulent means. Whereupon Mírzá Ḥusayn-'Alí obtained the consent of all concerned, then sold the property to a sister of the Sháh who had repeatedly expressed her desire for its ownership. Informed by his sister of the circumstances of her acquisition of the estate, the Sháh's rebuke blunted the fury of the balked Áqásí. But the Prime Minister turned upon the youth who had dared to thwart his machinations, seeking now to discredit him with accusations of sedition. Calling Mírzá Ḥusayn-'Alí to his presence, knowing well his reputation for generosity and hospitality, he sought to provoke him, saying:

'What is the purpose of all this feasting and banqueting in which you seem to delight? I, who am the Prime Minister of the Sháhan-sháh of Persia, never receive the number and variety of guests that crowd around your table every night. Why all this extravagance and vanity? You surely must be meditating a plot against me.'

'Gracious God!' Mírzá Ḥusayn-'Alí exclaimed. *'Is the man who, out of the abundance of his heart, shares his bread with his fellow-men, to be accused of harboring criminal intentions?'*[13]

Recognizing, if unwillingly, the truth of the young man's high motivations, Áqásí broke off the fray. 'On a number of other occasions, [Ḥusayn-'Alí's] ascendancy over his opponents was likewise vindicated and recognized. These personal triumphs achieved by him served to enhance his position and spread abroad his fame.'[14] There were many who recognized the powers of the unique young man who, notwithstanding his lack of instruction and formal education, showed such keenness of penetration and readiness of 'apprehension that when, during his youthful prime, he appeared in assemblies where questions of divinity and points of metaphysics were being discussed, and, in the presence of a great concourse of doctors and scholars, loosed his tongue, all those present were amazed, accounting this as a sort of prodigy beyond the discernment natural to the human race. From his early years he was the hope of his kindred and the unique one of his family and race, nay, their refuge and shelter.'[15]

Uniquely perceptive was he, startling his associates by his penetration to the very marrow of an issue. Once one Naẓar-'Alí of Qazvín, a Ṣúfí esteemed by the Sháh, held forth in a gathering on the spiritual station attainable by a human being and gave himself as an example, saying:

'Should my servant come to me and say that Jesus Christ was at the door, asking for me, my detachment is such that I would express no wish to see Him.'

Mírzá Ḥusayn-'Alí boldly challenged this assertion, asking a counter question:

'You are close to the sovereign and he is devoted to you, but if the chief executioner with his men were to come to this door, telling you that the monarch wished to see you, would you be calm or perturbed?'

After a thoughtful pause, Naẓar-'Alí confessed:

'In truth, I would feel anxious.'

'In that case', replied Mírzá Ḥusayn-'Alí, *'you should not make such an assertion.'*[16] For how much greater his anxiety in coming face to face with a Supreme Prophet of God, standing before His all-perceiving Eye, and that without warning!

Later in his life, reflecting upon the *'thick clouds of oppression, which obscure the day-star of justice'*, hanging over his people, Mírzá Ḥusayn-'Alí identified the thick clouds as *'the exponents of idle fancies and vain imaginings, who are none other but the divines of Persia*'.[17] Further, contrasting his countrymen with the peoples of the West who were energetically but foolishly pursuing vain and materialistic goals at great cost of life and wealth, he sorrowed that '*the people of Persia . . . are dispirited and sunk in deep lethargy*'.[18]

In those years immediately following his father's death, despite his having a living elder half-brother Muḥammad-Ḥasan, and despite his having just entered his twenties, Mírzá Ḥusayn-'Alí had assumed the recognized leadership of the large family group of brothers, half-brothers and step-brothers, sisters, half-sisters, and step-sisters, plus their sundry widows and wives. Doubtless to some degree he also had influence upon the aunts and uncles and their numerous dependents. It was a huge and demanding family complex, typical of those feudal years of an Islamic polygamous nobility, with all the familiar potentials for every manner of personal frictions, of personality differences, of competing hopes and ambitions. To the emergent tasks of family leadership and care the young man brought that sagacity combined with benignity which had been his identified characteristics since childhood. These were fortified by his courage and willingness to seek to solve family problems in the best ways possible. Furthermore, he was a discreet person, avoiding discussion of his and other private lives, and was without ostentation or any seeking of adulation. Happily too, he loved humor and was of a sunny disposition. For himself and his young wife Ásíyih, who was bringing her notable charms and warmth to the new household near the Shimírán Gate, there was evolving a very special life pattern quite atypical of such noble families in the capital city.[19]

Northern Teheran, where they lived, held the great palace compound with its government buildings, and also contained the principal bazaars and shops of the craftsmen in metal, cloth and ceramics. By contrast, southern Teheran, both inside and outside the walls, was crowded, impoverished, its working people scarcely distinguishable from the many beggars, the sick and the handicapped. Its streets were malodorous, swarming with noisy people and scrawny domestic animals, and were littered with wastes. Workers could anticipate thoroughly hazardous and usually short lives, for they were hapless victims of a gravely flawed society. Perceiving the need beneath the tragedies, Mírzá Ḥusayn-'Alí and the lady Ásíyih set themselves to lives of service not only to the poor and troubled, but also to aid those of the upper classes so deeply requiring guidance. Their life pattern reflected in part their privileged origins, but their deeds sought to ameliorate the many social and economic wrongs afflicting their society.

The couple occupied their rented house near the old moat not far from the palace. During the summer months they might sojourn at Tákur, or occasionally at Dárkalá on the Caspian plain not far from Ámul, and once at Murgh-Mahallih, the 'abode of the birds', on a hill slope of the Shimírán suburb near Teheran. In this élite district north of Teheran the estates of the wealthy were found in the well-watered valleys draining the formidable mountains which northward rose to more than 12,000 feet. Groves of trees graced the picturesque rocky gorges in the places served by perennial springs, and from the hill bases emerged the underground qanats, thirty-four of them feeding water into thirsty Teheran. The family spent one summer in the Garden of Ḥájí Báqir in Shimírán, living in a three-storey dwelling overlooking a small lake, in the middle of which was a large platform of bedrock surrounded by vegetation. At times a tent was pitched on the little island for gatherings of up to one hundred and fifty friends.[20]

A property of Mírzá Buzurg's outside of Teheran had a garden park planted and designed by him. A central focus point permitted views down the four radial pathways between the flowering plants. When he and his family visited the site, Mírzá Ḥusayn-'Alí usually arose in the early morning and then, while the sun was rising above the eastern horizon, prepared and shared tea with them as they gathered about him. After the moment together, he would walk through the roses, pausing at intervals perhaps to contemplate the special beauties of a particular rose on its bush.

The life of the capital city was of little interest to the couple, and they took small part in the reciprocal social events, state functions and luxurious living of their peers. They wasted no thought on retrieving their material advantages, however diminished, from Mírzá Buzurg's former great wealth, preferring to devote themselves to charitable causes. Caring for the poor, the troubled and the unfortunate was their way of life. So recognized was this unusual life pattern that Mírzá Ḥusayn-'Alí became known by the title of 'Father of the Poor' while the gracious and good-hearted lady Ásíyih won the counterpart name of 'Mother of Consolation'. Their yet-considerable resources enabled them to aid many in that land of shameful wealth and grinding poverty. No one was turned away from their doors. The hospitality which had been challenged by the Prime Minister was the very hallmark of their home and their lives.

Murgh-Maḥallih, the 'abode of the birds' in Shimírán district, place of a summer interlude of the young family of Mírzá Ḥusayn-'Alí, Bahá'u'lláh.

Years afterward, their daughter Fáṭimih, then entitled Bahíyyih,* remembered her mother of those days, saying with deep feeling:

'. . . I always think of her in those earliest days of my memory as queenly in her dignity and loveliness, full of consideration for everybody, gentle, of a marvelous unselfishness, no action of hers ever failed to show the loving-kindness of her pure heart; her very presence seemed to make an atmosphere of love and happiness wherever she came, enfolding all comers in the fragrance of gentle courtesy.[21]

In the house near the Shimírán Gate the children of Mírzá Ḥusayn-'Alí and lady Ásíyih were born. So typical of that time of mortal danger for young children threatened by an array of grave childhood illnesses, the first two sons Káẓim and Ṣádiq were lost in their infancies and the fourth son, 'Alí-Muḥammad, died in child-

* Bahíyyih (the brilliant one, feminine of Bahá), the title later given to the girl Fáṭimih, is the name by which she is now known, or by her later title the Greatest Holy Leaf.

hood. At a night hour on 23 May 1844, was born another man-child, and he was named 'Abbás in honor of his distinguished grandfather.

As leader of the family of Buzurg, the spirited young man of Núr, Mírzá Ḥusayn-'Alí was being steadily tempered in the fires of Persian feudalism. For him no life of carpenter shop or caravan agent, nor yet of monastic isolation, but rather a hot-cold plunge into the real life of an authoritarian dynastic system of steel fang, golden claw and of befouled human relations inherent in that thoroughly corrupt social order. For him no fealty also to a Shi'ite priestly organization which in its way was quite as corrupt as the Sháh and his princelings, for its adherents persisted in their sterile '*sciences built upon words*', as later he termed their futile exercises. Moreover, he sensed that deep ferment in Persia which derived in part from the initial ideological penetration by the industrial and neo-scientific Christian West.

In the seething brew of Shi'ite Iran and nearby Iraq, the subject of religious prophecy was being fanned by a new breeze of that millennial expectancy so characteristic of the Islám of the Twelve Imáms, now hearing the anticipatory voices of Shaykh Aḥmad and Siyyid Káẓim. As 1844 began, lines of spiritual energy were converging upon unworthy Persia. The mild, courteous, yet hardy young layman of the kuláh, he who had a higher calling for his life, awaited his Mission.

> *Every Prophet Whom the Almighty and Peerless Creator hath purposed to send to the peoples of the world hath been entrusted with a Message, and charged to act in a manner that would best meet the requirements of the age in which He appeared.*[22]
>
> **Bahá'u'lláh**

The courtyard of the House of the Báb in Shíráz, with its pool and old orange tree, at the center the room of the Báb, and above the Room of the Declaration. (Seyhoun)

The upper room of the House of the Báb in Shíráz, wherein Mullá Ḥusayn of Bushrúyih, the first disciple, accepted the Declaration of the New Messenger of God on that momentous night of May 23, 1844, when began a new Age.

4 The First High Prophet

No sooner had mankind attained the state of maturity, than the Word revealed to men's eyes the latent energies with which it had been endowed – energies which manifested themselves in the plenitude of their glory when the Ancient Beauty appeared in the year sixty, in the person of 'Alí-Muḥammad, the Báb.[1]

Bahá'u'lláh

Shaykh Aḥmad and Siyyid Káẓim had seen the vision, had sown the seeds and prepared the soil for a pregnant hour in history. Their followers, spiritual revolutionaries rebelling from the sterile obfuscations of Shi'ite Islám, had been disciplined by the two great teachers for their dramatic roles. The year 1844 (1260 AH) had begun. It was the lunar year 'sixty' promised in Shi'ite prophecy for the return of the Twelfth Imám. And so, in the springtime, still mourning the death of Siyyid Káẓim, but mindful of his strong counsel, his visionaries led by the learnèd young clerics Mullá Ḥusayn of Bushrúyih and Mullá 'Alí of Basṭám were ready for their unique leap into the unknown, guided by the subtle compass of the spirit but doubtless also by hints from the prescient Káẓim. They were on a mighty quest: the search for a new High Prophet, the Qá'im, He Who shall arise, He who would be identified as the Mihdí, the One Who is guided, and also as the Ṣáḥibu'z-Zamán, He Who was the Lord of the Age, these prophetic titles deriving from the complex lore of Shi'ite Islám.

Their master dead but beckoning them onward, a group of sixteen ardent disciples doubtless remembered clues dropped by him which pointed to Iran, then sought further guidance through forty days of prayer at the old mosque of Kúfih where the Imám 'Alí had been struck down by a poisoned sword. Thereafter they set forth for Najaf in two parties. Mullá Ḥusayn with his younger brother and nephew then proceeded down the Euphrates, and took a boat from Baṣra across the upper Persian Gulf to the port of Búshihr, while Mullá 'Alí with the others traveled on foot overland to arrive later at the rendezvous in Shíráz. From the port town Mullá Ḥusayn's small party traversed the raw coastal lands and climbed through the three-thousand-foot jagged mountains of desiccated southern Persia to the town of Kázirún, then walked eastward to Shíráz. Arriving a few hours before sunset on 22 May, and sending his two companions to seek rooms at the Ílkhání Mosque, Mullá Ḥusayn was meditatively walking outside the western gate of the city when a radiant youth accosted him with an unexpected welcome. Not recognizing the erstwhile quiet visitor of Siyyid Káẓim's Karbilá classes, Mullá Ḥusayn was startled by the warmth of his greeting and puzzled by his invitation to refresh himself at his home, hence sought to excuse himself. But the youth overruled his plea to join his companions, saying:

'*Commit them to the care of God. He will surely protect and watch over them.*'[2]

The compelling presence of the young man induced Mullá Ḥusayn to accompany him through winding walled lanes to the door of a modest home, to which they were admitted by an Ethiopian servant, Mubárak.* As they passed the portal, the young host recited the ceremonial Qu'ránic verse: '*Enter therein in peace, secure!*',[3] a salutation felt by Mullá Ḥusayn to be an auspicious augury for this surprising encounter. Indeed, the household, and the very walls of the home, felt the oncoming spiritual impact of that impending night. Sleepless, the young man's wife intuitively knew the power to be released by the momentous meeting of two powerful spirits at an ignition point of religious experience.

Mounting to an upper chamber, carpeted, aromatic, the host Siyyid 'Alí-Muḥammad offered a beverage, then prepared tea for his guest; it was the first hour after sunset. They shared evening prayers, whereupon the young man demonstrated to his guest in dramatic fashion that in all particulars he fitted the description of the anticipated Great One of the House of Muḥammad given by Siyyid Káẓim, that 'He is of a pure lineage, is of illustrious descent, and of the seed of Fáṭimih. He is of medium height . . . and is free from bodily deficiency.'[4] It was then two hours and eleven minutes after sunset. He then speedily resolved certain cryptic allusions in the writings of their two teachers. And finally he launched into a commentary on the Qu'ránic Chapter (Súrih) of Joseph,[5] penning

* The Ethiopian servant Mubárak (the blessed one) was the able and loyal servant of the household of Siyyid 'Alí-Muḥammad, He Who was the Báb, the Gate. He accompanied the Báb to Mecca, and was with Him at the time of His arrest in the village of Dalaki (or Kinar-Takhtih). (See Abu'l-Qásim Afnán, *Black Pearls*, Kalimát Press, 1988.)

the first portion of that remarkable essay,* the Qayyúmu'l-Asmá', which predicts the coming of the Most Great One, the Qayyúm.

Throughout the night the newfound Master transfixed His first great disciple with words of wondrous power, His voice musically rising and falling in gentle intonation as he resolved all of Mullá Ḥusayn's doubts and made him '*the recipient of the effulgent glory of the Sun of divine Revelation*'.[6]

In its entirety this lengthy essay is rightly called the '*first, greatest and mightiest*'[7] of all the books of this lofty Spirit who identified Himself as the Gate, the Báb. Remarkably, the Báb in the opening passage of this first effusion of His ministry '. . . extols the virtues and anticipates the coming of . . . the "Most Great Master" . . .' In that essay is the astonishing passage: '*Do not say, 'How can He speak of God while in truth His age is no more than twenty-five?' Give ye ear unto Me. I swear by the Lord of the heavens and of the earth: I am verily a servant of God. I have been made the Bearer of irrefutable proofs from the presence of Him Who is the long-expected Remnant of God.*'[8]†

Further, He eulogizes '*the people of Bahá*', of Glory, calling them '*the Companions of the "ruby, crimson-colored" Ark*'.[9] And in that opening chapter He dwells upon the malice of the Biblical Joseph's envious brethren, thus predicting what the later Manifestation is destined to suffer at the hand of His own brother and kindred. He prophesies His own martyrdom in stating His fealty to Him Who would be made manifest, saying: '*O Thou Remnant of God! I have sacrificed Myself wholly for Thee; I have accepted curses for Thy sake; and have yearned for naught but martyrdom in the path of Thy love*'.[10] Thus dramatically, at the very moment of His own declaration of mission, He laid the foundation for a universal expansion of the newborn Faith through the Second Great Teacher soon to reveal Himself.‡

That night of 22–23 May 1844 was doubly blessed, for far to the north in Teheran Mírzá Ḥusayn-'Alí of Núr and his beloved wife Ásíyih Khánum were expecting a third child, their two first-born sons having perished as babes. In the young parents' hearts there must have been great anticipation of an heir, the hope that this child might be the son endowed to fulfill the family's noble name, to

* The title of the essay, the Qayyúmu'l-Asmá, means 'Names of the Self-Subsisting'.

† See note on the 'Remnant of God', p. oo (chapter 6).

‡ A remarkable echo of this memorable moment was heard halfway around the world, in the United States of America. There an inventor, Samuel F. B. Morse, inaugurated the era of mass communication media with his demonstration of the telegraph. On 24 May 1844, he sent the first telegraphic message: 'What hath God wrought.' Accounting for the global time differences, the concurrence was close.

expand its destiny, to continue the physical immortality of a precious genetic stock. So it was that God's spiritual timing brought the lady Ásíyih's delivery on that very evening of the declaration of a new Prophet. There was born a son who was healthy and whole and hope fulfilled, and he was named 'Abbás, the lion.*

During the forty days following the declaration of the Báb, in the midst of which Mullá 'Alí of Basṭám arrived with his twelve companions, seventeen more disciples espoused His Cause. Fáṭimih of Qazvín,† Qurratu'l-'Ayn, the sole woman of the group who had been students of Siyyid Káẓim in Karbilá, had predicted His discovery and sent a letter of homage via her brother-in-law, thus becoming the seventeenth disciple. The last to arrive in Shíráz, the eighteenth to declare his recognition, was an ardent youth of twenty, Mírzá Muḥammad-'Alí of Bárfurúsh in the Caspian north. All acknowledged the Báb's claim to be the Forerunner of a new Dispensation of God, and the prophetic fulfillment of Shi'ite Islám's teachings. These eighteen were the first 'unit' (Váhid), and were called the Letters of the Living‡ by the Báb; to each a letter was written. He Himself was the nineteenth of that spiritual company of the elect.[11]

The seventeen were not long allowed to bask in the spiritual aura of the new Master. Early in July, after a brief period of indoctrination, He sent them to their active teaching among the people with a most memorable charge, a command to perform an impossible task no less inclusive than the reformation of an age of mankind, beginning with decadent Persia with its tyrannical nobility and its fanatical priests. His call to heroic and self-sacrificing service is the timeless one of ideological renascence. '*O My beloved friends! You are the bearers of the name of God in this Day. You have been chosen as the repositories of His mystery. It behoves each one of you to manifest the attributes of God, and to exemplify by your deeds and words the signs of His righteousness, His power and glory. The very members of your body must bear witness to the loftiness of your purpose, the integrity of your life, the*

* The name 'Abbás originally meant a 'furious lion from whom all other lions flee', hence the characteristics of a lion are often adduced as the word's meaning, thus to mean 'stern, formidable, austere, of loud sound (roaring), stentorian'.

† See Note 8.

‡ The poetic title, Letters of the Living, was given to the eighteen first disciples of the Báb, each of whom independently, through visions and prayer, had discovered the Qa'ím as foreshadowed by Siyyid Káẓim. In the book *The Dawn-Breakers* are reproduced the original letters to each one in the beautiful script and format of the Báb's graphic handwriting.

reality of your faith, and the exalted character of your devotion. For verily I say, this is the Day spoken of by God in His Book . . .

You are the witnesses of the Dawn of the promised Day of God. You are the partakers of the mystic chalice of His Revelation . . .

Beseech the Lord your God to grant that no earthly entanglements, no worldly affections, no ephemeral pursuits, may tarnish the purity, or embitter the sweetness, of that grace which flows through you.

I am preparing you for the advent of a mighty Day . . . The secret of the Day that is to come is now concealed. It can neither be divulged nor estimated. The newly born babe of that Day excels the wisest and most venerable men of this time, and the lowliest and most unlearned of that period shall surpass in understanding the most erudite and accomplished divines of this age.

Scatter throughout the length and breadth of this land, and, with steadfast feet and sanctified hearts, prepare the way for His coming . . . Arise in His name, put your trust wholly in Him, and be assured of ultimate victory.'[12]*

One by one the Báb sent His disciples '*with steadfast feet and sanctified hearts*' to their perilous specific tasks of proclamation of the new Message. For Himself He determined to declare His role and Mission to the Custodian of the Ka'bih, the Sherif of Mecca, in that holiest spot of Islám. He requested that Mírzá Muḥammad-'Alí of Bárfurúsh accompany Him on this momentous pilgrimage to the Holy Places of Islám in Arabia. To the indomitable and learnèd Mullá 'Alí of Basṭám was given the exceedingly dangerous task of returning to Iraq, there to announce in Najaf and Karbilá, centers of Shi'ite Islám, the claim of the Báb to be the return of the hidden Imám.[13]† For the inspired and resolute Mullá Ḥusayn, there was a special summons and responsibility. Dispelling his disappointment in not being chosen to be His companion on pilgrimage, the Báb pointed him to the north, saying: '*Grieve not that you have not been chosen to accompany Me on My pilgrimage to Ḥijáz. I shall, instead, direct your steps to that city which enshrines a Mystery of such transcendent holiness as neither Ḥijáz nor Shíráz can hope to rival . . . Visit, on your way, Isfáhán, Káshán, Tihrán and Khurásán . . . The hosts of the invisible Kingdom, be assured, will sustain and reinforce your efforts. The essence of*

* The entire message to the Letters of the Living is one of the most stirring summons of service to God and man ever given by a Manifestation of God to His disciples. Its text in full is found in Nabíl's *The Dawn-Breakers* (pp. 93–94) and in Appendix 1. It could well be inscribed on the forehead of every sincere believer, whatever his faith.

† See fn pp. 98–9, on the Shi'ite tradition of the Hidden Imám. For the fate of Mullá 'Alí, see Note 7.

power is now dwelling in you, and the company of His chosen angels revolves around you. His almighty arms will surround you, and His unfailing Spirit will ever continue to guide your steps . . .'[14] And of his mission to Teheran, the Báb presented an exciting prospect, saying: '*A secret lies hidden in that city. When made manifest, it shall turn the earth into paradise. My hope is that you may partake of its grace and recognize its splendor.*'[15]

In accordance with these singular instructions of great promise, and carrying precious scrolls, Mullá Ḥusayn set off on this first mission for the Báb with his characteristically high spirit and persuasiveness, seeking out the Shaykhís en route. Iṣfahán, Káshán and Qum were essentially obdurate: in Iṣfahán he found only a youth, a sifter of wheat, and some five others destined for great service in the new Cause; in Káshán a single to-be-distinguished convert; in fanatical Qum none. But there was much planting of seeds along his route through his challenging words on the new Teachings.

Arriving in Teheran in late July or early August to discover the 'Mystery of transcendent holiness', Mullá Ḥusayn settled into a room in the religious college of Mírzá Ṣáliḥ,* not far from the Shimírán Gate. There Ḥájí Mírzá Muḥammad of Khurásán, leader of the Shaykhís of Teheran, welcomed his distinguished associate, but was skeptical of the new Teachings which contained such disturbingly convincing contents and were presented so vehemently. He even went so far as to rebuke Mullá Ḥusayn for his failure to fortify the Shaykhí community in its doctrines. But to a young Shaykhí, a favored disciple of the leader and a priest-tutor, one Mullá Muḥammad Mu'allim of Núr district, fell the signal honor of becoming the courier of Mullá Ḥusayn.

The youth's room in the college was adjacent to that of his master, and he overheard the equivocal conversation with Mullá Ḥusayn. Impressed by the great powers and passion of the visitor, he felt keenly the unsatisfactory behavior and cautious attitude of Ḥájí Mírzá Muḥammad; moreover, he was attracted by his fellow youth's vibrant personality. Awaiting an opportunity for private discussion, he knocked on Mullá Ḥusayn's door that midnight, found him awake and seated beside his lamp. He was welcomed with such heartfelt warmth that he was impelled to discharge his strong feelings.

* Known also as Páy-i-Minár, 'at the foot of the minaret' of the mosque.

'I can now see', said Mullá Ḥusayn, 'the reason why I have chosen to dwell in this place. Your teacher has contemptuously rejected this Message and despised its Author. My hope is that his pupil may, unlike his master, recognize its truth. What is your name, and which city is your home?' And upon his giving the answers, Mullá Ḥusayn continued the inquiry, mysteriously precise for one essentially unacquainted in Teheran, saying:

'Tell me, is there today among the family of the late Mírzá Buzurg of Núr, who was so renowned for his character, his charm and artistic and intellectual attainments, anyone who has proved himself capable of maintaining the high traditions of that illustrious house?'

'Yea,' replied the young priest. 'Among his sons now living, one has distinguished himself by the very traits which characterized his father. By his virtuous life, his high attainments, his loving-kindness and liberality, he has proved himself a noble descendant of a noble father.'

'What is his occupation?' asked Mullá Ḥusayn, to which Mullá Muḥammad replied: 'He cheers the disconsolate and feeds the hungry.'

'What of his rank and position?'

'He has none, apart from befriending the poor and the stranger.'

'What is his name?'

'Ḥusayn-'Alí.'

'How does he spend his time?'

'He roams the woods and delights in the beauties of the country-side.'

'What is his age?'

'Eight and twenty.'

To Mullá Muḥammad's surprise the questions were put forth with great eagerness, the answers received with sheer delight as the dialogue continued:

'I presume you often meet him?'

'I frequently visit his home.'

'Will you', Mullá Ḥusayn asked, 'deliver into his hands a trust from me?' Handing the young man a scroll* wrapped in cloth on which was written a portion of the Commentary on the Súrih of Joseph, with the request that it be handed to Mírzá Ḥusayn-'Alí at dawn, he added:

* In addition to the scroll containing a portion of the Qayyúmu'l-Asmá, Mullá Ḥusayn is said to have carried a copy of the Báb's instructions on visiting the Holy Shrines of the Imáms.

'Should he deign to answer me, will you be kind enough to acquaint me with his reply?'[16]

Since Mírzá Ḥusayn-'Alí and his brothers were living in rented homes in that same Shimírán Gate quarter, Mullá Muḥammad's walk was short through the empty streets for delivery of the scroll at the break of day, an hour when the poor often came to the gates of the wealthy seeking aid. To his surprise he found Mírzá Músá, brother of Mírzá Ḥusayn-'Alí, standing at the doorway as he approached, and to him he communicated his mission. Músá turned into the house, returning shortly to extend a message of welcome, and ushered Mullá Muḥammad into the courtyard, thence to the principal audience chamber. There he presented the scroll to Músá to lay it before Mírzá Ḥusayn-'Alí, who bade both be seated, unfolded the scroll, glanced at its contents and began to read aloud certain passages. Enraptured as they listened to the sound of his voice and the sweetness of its melodies, both were startled when, after his reading a single section of the scroll, Mírzá Ḥusayn-'Alí turned to his brother, saying:

'Músá, what have you to say? Verily I say, whoso believes in the Qu'rán and recognizes its divine origin, and yet hesitates, though it be for a moment, to admit that these soul-stirring words are endowed with the same regenerating power, has most assuredly erred in his judgment and has strayed far from the path of justice.'[17]

Dismissing the young priest, he charged him to take a loaf of Russian sugar and a package of fine tea* to Mullá Ḥusayn, such prized gifts conveying his appreciation and respect.

Hastening back to the college and the learned stranger, the youth delivered the gifts and message to Mullá Ḥusayn. Joyfully, exultantly, he accepted them with a surprising depth of feeling, kissing the gifts and, taking Mullá Muḥammad into his arms, kissed his eyes, saying:

'My dearly beloved friend! I pray that even as you have rejoiced my heart, God may grant you eternal felicity and fill your heart with imperishable gladness.'[18]

Mullá Ḥusayn's behavior was so amazing and unexpected that

* In Persia in the mid-nineteenth century sugar was a comparatively rare and valuable commodity. From Russia were imported handsome conical creations of crystalline sugar, a kind of rock candy, to be cracked off in small pieces for sweetening tea in the Persian manner, i.e. passing the hot tea over sugar crystals held under the tongue. The tea industry of Iran, essentially new in the country at that time, was centered in a growing area of the Caspian coast near Rasht. Tea was yet a precious product, especially valued when selected leaves were chosen and when there was optimal curing. A number of Bábís were producers of tea.

Mullá Muḥammad pondered the spontaneous bond between men who had never met, but for him the puzzle was not yet solved. Then, on the eve of Mullá Ḥusayn's departure for Khurásán without his having made personal contact with Mírzá Ḥusayn-'Alí, but having undertaken quiet daily missions and engaged in confidential interviews with inquirers, including attempts to acquaint the Sháh and his ministers with the Báb's Message, Mullá Ḥusayn said farewell, admonishing the young priest to extreme caution in relating his observations.

'Breathe not to anyone what you have heard and witnessed . . . Divulge not his name, for they who envy his position will arise to harm him. In your moments of meditation, pray that the Almighty may protect him, that through him He may exalt the downtrodden, enrich the poor, and redeem the fallen . . . Ours is the duty to raise the call of the New Day and to proclaim this Divine Message unto all people. Many a soul will, in this city, shed his blood in this path. That blood will water the Tree of God, will cause it to flourish and to overshadow all mankind.'[19]

To that scroll fragment of the Qayyúmu'l-Asmá' the hypersensitive Mírzá Ḥusayn-'Alí had responded as a chord plucked by the Divine Harpist. Cursorily acquainted as he probably was with the preparatory doctrines of Shaykh Aḥmad and Siyyid Káẓim, his immediate recognition of the Báb's spiritual authority aligned him with the new Cause. It was as though he were always a Bábí, so ready of spirit was he. And his perceptive brother Músá, hearing the reading of a single long passage, almost simultaneously identified with this newborn Truth. Certain religious conformists had earlier accused the young Ḥusayn-'Alí of 'religious pliability' and now their prognostications were fully confirmed. Indeed, his inherent readiness for the new Truth assured instant recognition of the Báb, and thus He became another primary Disciple of the new High Prophet. In that moment, too, he began his own Mission from God.

As ever, Mírzá Ḥusayn-'Alí proved himself to be that singular combination, a man of contemplation and of action. With his espousal of the Báb's Cause his life opened upon a sublime new chapter, for this calling by God was also directed to him. But first he must proclaim that a new, God-sent power was abroad in the land, a force for profound change in almost every aspect of life. Religious and social reforms were critically needed; therefore a reformer he must become, first proclaiming the cleansing Message of the young siyyid from Shíráz to whom he was spiritually attuned, and Whose Teachings he would amplify in God's set time.

The house of Núrí relatives in Teheran must have buzzed with the realization of the dramatic injection into their family of a potent new religious message now supported by the family leader and genius. Not surprising then that a half-brother, Mírzá Yaḥyá, fourteen at that moment of Mullá Ḥusayn's mission, should also have become a Bábí, following the lead of his older half-brothers. This youth had been taken under the special tutorship of Mírzá Ḥusayn-'Alí, becoming his ward upon the early passing of his mother Kúchik, and already had been under his brother's instruction from his early years. He was grave, silent, courteous, modest, a solitary who was fond of the poems of the mystics and was later termed 'an amiable child' by an older Bábí. And perhaps there were even then others of the family also willing quietly to follow the dangerous, unconservative Bábí ideas which were sure to lead to trouble with the mullás. Ultimately three other brothers and several sisters espoused the Faith.

It was probably late summer when Mírzá Ḥusayn-'Alí set out for Núr, first northeastward to Afchih, then over the ever-thrilling mountains through lady Ásíyih's Yálrúd village and so to Tákur on its little plateau above the murmurous Núr River so shrunken at that season. Arriving home to the warm embrace of the rebuilt mansion of Tákur there below the great looming barrier of Mount Aurang, he immediately set forth to declare the new Revelation to associates and relatives. He discovered that Mírzá Muḥammad-Taqí, his distant relative of the Yálrúd school and the dreamer of prophetic dreams about him, had passed away, to be succeeded by his ineffectual son Mullá Muḥammad, who found himself with a dwindling band of dispirited disciples. To inquiries from Núrí notables about affairs of the court, Mírzá Ḥusayn-'Alí turned disinterested answers, instead converting the questions into opportunities to present the Bábí Message in terms befitting each inquirer, while persuasively pointing to the immeasurable benefits which the new Faith would bestow upon them and upon Iran. That a young nobleman should be deeply concerned with religious matters was startling enough, but how surprising that no mullá was able successfully to challenge his theses, so ably did he expound the ideas of the new Cause. The Núrís were also compelled to reluctant admiration at his zeal but also at his self-effacement despite the depth of the thoughts presented with such verve.

Among the first converts of his salutary expositions of the Cause of the Báb were Mírzá Muḥammad-Ḥasan, his half-brother, and also Muḥammad-Taqí Khán, a close relative. But his uncle 'Azíz fiercely opposed these heretical new views; traveling to the village of Sa'ádat-

Ábád, he personally appealed for immediate intervention against his nephew by Mullá Muḥammad, the chief divine of the Núr district, saying:

'O vicegerent of the Prophet of God! Behold what has befallen the Faith. A youth, a layman, attired in the garb of nobility, has come to Núr, has invaded the strongholds of orthodoxy, and disrupted the holy Faith of Islám . . . Whoever attains his presence falls immediately under his spell, and is enthralled by the power of his utterance. I know not whether he is a sorcerer, or whether he mixes with his tea some mysterious substance that makes every man who drinks the tea fall a victim to its charm.'[20]

The Shaykh perceived how foolish were these assertions by the alarmist 'Azíz and put him off, but at the same time felt himself unable to confront the phenomenal young man whose 'speech was like a rushing torrent and whose clearness in exposition brought the most learnèd divines to his feet'.[21] He was not confident that he could muster the community's support to confound the young teacher, nor had he the moral integrity to travel over the mountains to fathom the truth of the reports. Instead, he sent two trusted envoys, his sons-in-law, Mullá 'Abbás and Mírzá Abu'l-Qásim, to challenge the man and the Message; and he pledged his unreserved endorsement of whatever conclusions they might reach. Since Mírzá Ḥusayn-'Alí was then at Dárkalá,* the winter home on the coastal plain near the Caspian Sea north of Tákur, they set out to meet him there. At his house, to which they were admitted with warm hospitality, they found him at the center of an assemblage 'engaged in revealing a commentary on the opening Súrih of the Qu'rán entitled "The Seven Verses of Repetition".' Sitting then on the floor among the others, listening to his melodic words, the lofty theme being presented so cogently and in a manner so gripping and electric, Mullá 'Abbás abruptly rose from his seat and walked to the door, standing there in reverence and submission. To Mírzá Abu'l-Qásim he confessed, his eyes tearful, that:

'You behold my condition. I am powerless to question Mírzá Ḥusayn-'Alí. The questions I had planned to ask him have vanished

---

* The wealthy families of the nobility owned multiple homes for their numerous members, and the clan of Mírzá Buzurg Núrí was such a typical family. Tákur mansion lay in the high central east-west-running valley of the Núr River, and in winter was often shut off from access routes. Dárkalá, another home of the family, by contrast lay north over several mountains in the lowlands of the old sea benches of the Caspian, and shared the milder, rainy weather of that area. Hence it was preferred for midwinter occupancy by those of the family who were not in Teheran or in houses near the capital city.

suddenly from my memory. You are free to proceed with your inquiry or to return alone to our teacher and inform him of the state in which I find myself. Tell him from me that 'Abbás can never again return to him. He can no longer forsake this threshold.'

But the second emissary, Abu'l-Qásim, had also been deeply moved and responded:

'I have ceased to recognize my teacher. This very moment I have vowed to God to dedicate the remaining days of my life to the service of Mírzá Ḥusayn-'Alí, my true and only master!'

Upon the two men's return home, the news of their abrupt and dramatic conversion and their abandonment of Mullá Muḥammad as their mentor roused the populace throughout the area. Ecclesiastics, officials, merchants hastened now to the home of the young nobleman in Dárkalá. When a number of these Núrís espoused the Bábí Cause, they put forth the suggestion that 'if Mullá Muḥammad, the chief priest, were also to join the new Faith, you would win all who are of substance in this countryside'.

To this Mírzá Ḥusayn-'Alí responded: '*I am come to Núr solely for the purpose of proclaiming the Cause of God. I cherish no other intention. If I were told that at a distance of a hundred leagues a seeker yearned for the Truth and was unable to meet me, I would, gladly and unhesitatingly, hasten to his abode, and would myself satisfy his hunger. Mullá Muḥammad, I am told, lives in Sa'ádat-Ábád, a village not far distant . . . It is my purpose to visit him and deliver to him the Message of God.*'[22] So declaring, Mírzá Ḥusayn-'Alí set forth for that village with a number of those who now had become followers of the Báb. There Mullá Muḥammad most ceremoniously received him in his home, showing the customary hospitality to one whom he knew as a former acquaintance.

Said Mírzá Ḥusayn-'Alí: '*I have not come to this place to pay you an official or formal visit. My purpose is to enlighten you regarding a new and wondrous Message, divinely inspired and fulfilling the promise given to Islám. Whosoever has inclined his ear to this Message has felt its irresistible power, and has been transformed by the potency of its grace. Tell me whatsoever perplexes your mind, or hinders you from recognizing the Truth.*'[23]

To this invitation to open his pores of search towards enlightenment, the high priest offered a qualifying proposal, saying: 'I take no action unless I first consult the Qu'rán. I have invariably, on such occasions, followed the practice of invoking the aid of God and His blessings by opening at random His sacred Book and consulting the first verse of the particular page upon which my eyes chance to fall.

From the nature of that verse I can judge the wisdom and advisability of my contemplated action.'

Mírzá Ḥusayn-'Alí had no objection to this procedure, whereupon the chief priest called for a copy of the Qu'rán, opened it, glanced therein, closed it and refused to reveal the nature of the verse thus summoned from the pages. He said no more than this, that 'I have consulted the Book of God, and deem it inadvisable to proceed with this matter,' thus tacitly admitting the poor augury for him of that fateful verse.

Plainly, the weak character of Mullá Muḥammad could not bear to admit the import of his plunge into the wisdom of the Qu'rán. And plainly the verse was one which somehow disturbed him deeply, perhaps arousing a fear of the spiritual forces loosed in the district, forces which were upsetting his precarious status as chief religious advisor of the people. Mírzá Ḥusayn-'Alí perceived his craven withdrawal from engagement and arising, graciously excused himself to depart forthwith for Dárkalá.

During this same period in northern Mázindarán there occurred an intriguing incident. In the course of a riding excursion into the countryside with companions, Mírzá Ḥusayn-'Alí saw a youth in dervish dress seated by the roadside at the bank of a brook. He had kindled a fire and was cooking and eating his food. Speaking from the saddle, Mírzá Ḥusayn-'Alí inquired:

'*Tell me, dervish, what is it that you are doing?*'

'I am eating God! I am cooking God and burning Him,' said he.

Upon this surprising reply given so directly and simply, Mírzá Ḥusayn-'Alí smiled and began to probe the young man's thoughts in kindly but penetrating manner while his fellows tarried, interested in the unexpected casual encounter. Within a short space of time Mírzá Ḥusayn-'Alí had completely swayed the young skeptic, enlightening him on the true nature of God, purging his mind of idle fancies and speculations, and permitting him to recognize the light now so unexpectedly illumining his very soul. The loving stranger discovered that the young dervish was a mendicant Súfí poet named Muṣṭafá Big of Sanandaj in Kurdistán. As the riders prepared to depart, the young man showed himself to be so attracted to the teachings and the teacher that, abandoning his cooking utensils, he straightway arose and followed them. On foot behind his master's horse, full of newborn enthusiasm, he joyously chanted verses of a love song, composed as he walked, and dedicated it to the stranger to whom his song paid homage: 'Thou art the Day-Star of guidance. Thou art the Light of Truth. / Unveil Thyself to men, O Revealer of the Truth.' and with the refrain: 'Tear asunder the veils . . . Tear asunder the veils!'

When in later years the poem was widely circulated, it became known that a Ṣúfí (see Note 6) with the dervish title of Majdhúb), the one attracted, had composed it without premeditation in praise of his newly found master. No one suspected the object of the poem, for the dervish alone had then recognized the high station of that unknown rider encountered on a country road.

Mírzá Ḥusayn-'Alí's return to his home countryside of Núr district in Mázindarán province, now as an inspired Bábí teacher, was the first effective expansion of the new Faith in Persia. In a single-hearted feat of persuasion made possible by his eloquence and singular learning, by his sure responses to difficult questions of theology or behavior, but particularly by that integrity of character and loving personality so empathetic to people of all kinds, he had quite won the hearts and spirits of his own people of Núr. However, beyond their esteem for him who was to be named the '*benevolent Counsellor*', they gave fealty to the Báb, He Who was the '*Voice of the Crier*'.[24] They were so energized that they continued the process of converting those unconvinced or others who had not been in contact with the dynamic young man so ardently determined to bring each one into the fold of God's new Message. As he said later: '*God knows that at no time did we attempt to conceal ourself or hide the Cause which we have been bidden to proclaim. Though not wearing the garb of the people of learning, we have again and again faced and reasoned with men of great scholarship in both Núr and Mázindarán, and have succeeded in persuading them of the truth of this Revelation. We never flinched in our determination; we never hesitated to accept the challenge from whatever direction it came. To whomsoever we spoke in those days, we found him receptive to our call and ready to identify himself with its precepts.*'[25]

When Mírzá Ḥusayn-'Alí found it necessary, perhaps as spring approached and travel was less hazardous, to return to his family and many concerns in Teheran, the new plant of faith had put down strong roots in many hearts. Indeed, Núr district became the first stronghold of the Bábí Teachings and was regularly enriched by visitors and messages from both Mírzá Ḥusayn-'Alí and the Báb Himself.

Mullá 'Alí of Basṭám, that lion-hearted second most talented disciple, had meanwhile returned to Iraq as instructed by the Báb, and by his open proclamation of the Báb's Teachings had created strong opposition in Kúfih, Najaf and Karbilá. During his stormy visit to Karbilá in August he had informed Fáṭimih of

Qazvín, Qurratu'l-'Ayn, of the precise identification of Siyyid 'Alí-Muḥammad as the Promised One, the Báb, thus confirming her intuitive letter of recognition. Sent to Baghdad by the Governor of the province, he was held in prison until his January trial by the bloodthirsty priests, eager for his death but unable to agree upon it. In April 1845 he was sent in chains to Constantinople to be consigned to hard labor in the naval yards, there to perish unsung for his selfless valor and devotion. (See Note 8.)

During this same period the Báb, with Mírzá Muḥammad-'Alí of Barfúrush (Quddús) as his secretary, and accompanied by the Ethiopian servant Mubárak, had set forth on their arduous pilgrimage to Mecca, departing from Búshihr on about 16 October 1844. He made a direct and open claim to be the Qá'im at the Ka'bih in Mecca, a claim which fell upon deaf ears, and returned in May or June 1845, after eleven lunar months out of Persia. The Báb then remained in Búshihr, while Quddús returned to face a storm of aroused reaction from the divines of Shíráz.[26] With two other Bábís he was arrested and viciously maltreated, and the three were expelled from the city.

Turning then to apprehend the Báb in Búshihr, Governor Ḥusayn Khán sent a company of horsemen from Shíráz to arrest the young Teacher. He, however, on 30 June 1845 met the troop at the village of Dalaki, forty miles from Búshihr, and so captivated them by His powers and presence that they courteously escorted Him to Shíráz, acting as His honor guard rather than His captors. In an early confrontation with the Governor, the Báb was irreverently and rudely dealt with, and was confined to His own home for a number of months during which the Bábí community of Shíráz was established through many conversions.

Controversy increased among the mullás, but was ameliorated by Shaykh Abú-Turáb, the kindly chief priest of Shíráz. The Báb was summoned to the Mosque of Vakíl* at the time of Friday prayer where, from the pulpit, the young Siyyid acknowledged the validity of Islám, then confounded those who challenged Him to state His Mission by eloquently addressing the assembled crowd in terms not yet understandable to them: '*O people! Know this well that I speak what My Grandfather, the Messenger of God* [Muḥammad], *spoke twelve hundred and sixty years ago, and I do not speak what My Grandfather did*

---

* The Mosque of Vakíl (the Regent) was named after the nineteenth-century ruler Karím Khán who, like Oliver Cromwell, chose not to seize the crown, but instead gave himself the title Vakíl, the Regent.

not. 'What Muḥammad made lawful remains lawful unto the Day of Resurrection and what He forbade remains forbidden unto the Day of Resurrection', and according to the Tradition that has come down from the Imáms, 'Whenever the Qa'ím arises, that will be the Day of Resurrection'.[27]

The Báb was telling the simple truth, for as a Siyyid His 'Grandfather' was Muḥammad, He Himself was the Qá'ím, and the long-awaited Judgment Day, the Day of Resurrection, was upon them all, little as they recognized it.*

Despite the restrictions placed upon Him, these months of winter into spring through summer were extremely fruitful, for a new company of disciples was found among the eager inquirers. As seekers or as Bábís, they received instruction and imbibed spiritual power, thus gaining a resolute dedication to pursue the thrilling but hazardous task of spreading the Faith to the people, the authorities, and the ecclesiastics of Persia.

The fire had been lit, but the flames were yet low. For the Báb and the Bábís, crisis upon crisis impended. And the conflict would be with entrenched Islamic traditions, the divines His prime enemies.†

> *Magnify Thou, O Lord my God, Him Who is the Primal Point, the Divine Mystery, the Unseen Essence, the Day-Spring of Divinity, and the Manifestation of Thy Lordship, through Whom all the knowledge of the past and all the knowledge of the future were made plain, through Whom the pearls of Thy hidden wisdom were uncovered, and the mystery of Thy treasured name disclosed, Whom Thou has appointed as the Announcer of the One through Whose name the letter B and the letter E have been joined and united . . .*[28]
>
> **Bahá'u'lláh**

* In a well-known tradition, the Imám Ṣádiq has said: 'When our Qá'im shall arise, the earth will shine with the light of her Lord.' (Bahá'u'lláh, *Epistle to the Son of the Wolf*, p. 112.)

† In the Book of Certitude, the *Kitáb-i-Íqán*, Bahá'u'lláh provides a pungent quotation from the traditions of Qu'ránic literature which states the prophetic prediction of the Báb's Coming: '*In the "Avalím", an authoritative and well-known book, it is recorded: "A youth from Baní-Háshim shall be made manifest, Who will reveal a new Book and promulgate a new law;" then follow these words: "Most of His enemies will be the divines." In another passage, it is related of Sádiq, son of Muḥammad, that he spoke the following: "There shall appear a Youth from Baní-Háshim, Who will bid the people plight fealty unto Him. His Book will be a new Book, unto which He shall summon the poeple to pledge their faith.*' (*Kitáb-i-Íqán*, p. 241.)

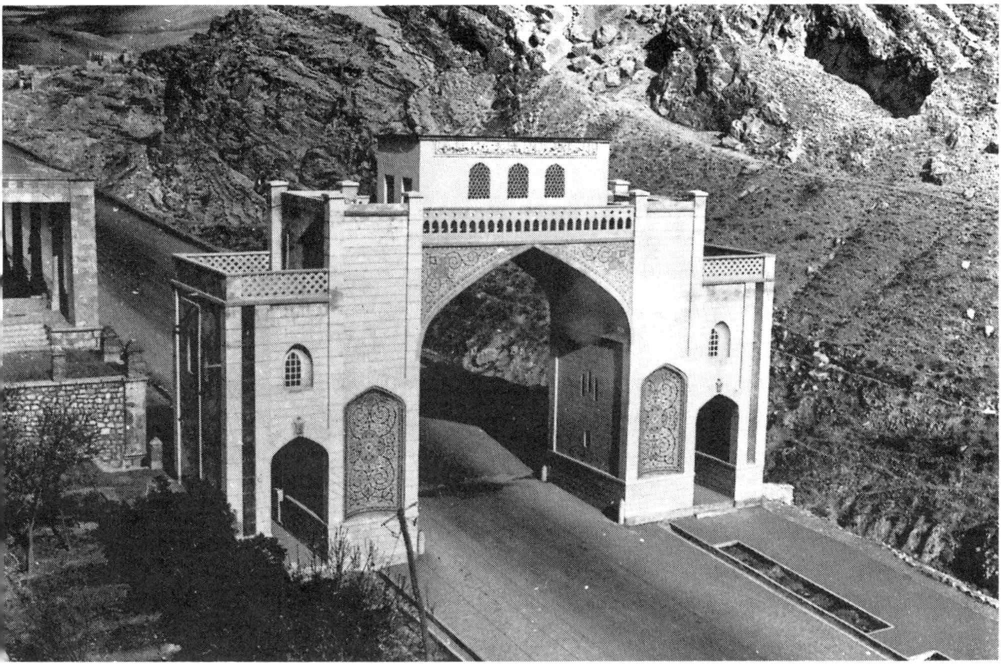

A modern view of the northern gate of Shíráz, through which the Báb had the last view of his home city as He was expelled to Iṣfahán. A modern road skirts the rocky gorge, passing through the monumental gate with its huge Qur'án held in the chamber overhead. Below: Chihríq in Persian Kurdistán, a prison-fortress near the Turkish and Iraqi borders which witnessed a further incarceration of the Báb. Now ruinous and abandoned, its location and demeanour yet suggest the Báb's name for it: 'the grievous mountain'.

Above: Máh-Kú, castle-fortress-prison under its great cliff near the Turkish and Armenian borders in far northwest Iran, place of the Báb's long incarceration and site of the Revelation of His Book, the Bayán. The buildings on the right include the site of the Báb's prison.

5 Epicenter of the Bábí Cause

I testify that no sooner had the First Word proceeded, through the potency of Thy will and purpose, out of His mouth, and the First Call gone forth from His lips than the whole creation was revolutionized, and all that are in the heavens and all that are on earth were stirred to the depths.[1]

Bahá'u'lláh

Word of the Báb's charismatic personality and intuitive knowledge was rapidly being noised abroad. His Teachings were spreading in the wake of His disciples as they fanned out by horse and foot across Persia and Iraq to expound the new Faith come to fulfill Shi'ite Islám. A claim so bold and sweeping, presented by men and women so zealous and of such convincing learning, began to generate the inevitable strong counter-reaction. The marketplace clamor and gossip swelled in volume and level, a predictable response in this land swarming with malcontents eager for change and titillated by controversy.

Soon after the Báb had returned to Shíráz following His pilgrimage to Mecca, fresh fuel was added to the fires of religious reformation. The Sháh's chosen agent, the supremely learnèd Siyyid Yaḥyá of Dáráb,* dispatched to investigate the validity of the claims of the new Teacher, became a follower of the Báb following potent interviews with his fellow Siyyid; worse, he abandoned his privileged position at the court and plunged into the gathering ideological fray. Alarmed, the newly appointed Governor of the province of Fars looked with jaundiced eyes upon the increasing enthusiasm of the Bábís, for the dangers of zealots who might ignite the passions of the mercurial Persians were well known to those who held the reins of so-called law and order. A ruthless man, jealous of his position and power after disastrous foreign assignments for the Sháh, Governor Ḥusayn Khán was eager to regain his standing by such acts as quashing a dangerous new group which conceivably might catch the

* Soon to be titled Vaḥíd (the unique, the peerless, the illustrious, the matchless one).

imagination of an inflammable Shírází public. Probably on the orders of Prime Minister Áqásí he sent his chief constable with police over the house-tops to snatch the Báb from His home in the middle of the night before His followers and sympathizers could intervene, possibly planning a secret murder to follow the abduction. This arrest occurred on or about 22 September 1846, just as the first victims of dread cholera* were dropping dead in the streets and perishing in their beds throughout Shíráz.

With characteristic explosiveness the plague began to strike down rich and poor alike, and its impact city-wide was reported to an apprehensive Governor. Was it the preemptive Hand of God preserving the young Siyyid for His short Ministry? Reading the grim omens of an explosive epidemic and hearing of the Báb's cure of the son of the chief constable in whose house He was confined, the Governor fearfully released his captive while commanding His departure for Iṣfahán. Forbidden to return home, the Báb immediately departed, never again to see His beloved wife Khadíjih or the city of His birth. It was the end of September 1846 as He passed through the northern Alláh-u-Akbar Gate in its rocky pass, doubtless pausing to look back at Shíráz in its beautiful bowl valley, with its rows of cypresses and azure-tiled domes, the Shíráz of poets Ḥáfiẓ and Sa'dí, the Shíráz now to be only a memory. As his party skirted the ruins of Persepolis, resounding yet with its echoes of an ancient imperial Persia so much in contrast with the decadent present, the Báb knew that it was the ending of the first phase of His meteoric mission.

In Iṣfahán He found asylum with the chief priest of the city, in whose splendidly artistic and luxurious home He remained for forty days until His persuasive dialogues with high-ranking priests aroused sharp antagonisms. Then, to avoid their overt hostile actions, He took secret refuge for four months in the house of the Governor of the city, Manúchihr Khán, who had become His devoted follower and patron.

His disciples were preaching actively when the untimely death of the Governor exposed the Báb's place of concealment to his vicious

---

* Outbreaks of cholera and bubonic plague were frequent during the 1830s in Persia, and claimed the lives of large numbers of victims; Amánat (p. 97) says that ninety percent of the population were stricken during the decade; these terrible epidemics were deemed to be signs of the coming apocalypse. Once introduced into areas of low sanitation, cholera can smolder for years, with periodic eruptions deriving from the many human carriers of the disease found in a population after the initial outbreak.

successor, Gurgín Khán, who speedily carried out an order of arrest with transfer to Teheran from the Sháh and Prime Minister Áqásí. In the custody of a contingent of Nuṣayrí* soldiery under one Muḥammad-Big, who quickly became devoted to Him, and accompanied by several Bábís, He was escorted first to Káshán, then through Qum-Rúd and Kinár-Gird to the village of Kulayn, a hamlet owned by Áqásí and situated some ten miles from the capital. From Kulayn the Báb then wrote to the Sháh requesting an audience.

On 1 April 1847, while the Báb's company of twelve cavalrymen with its captain were encamped outside the village, Mullá Mihdí of Kand with a companion arrived from the city bearing a sealed letter and gifts from Mírzá Ḥusayn-'Alí. When delivered into the Báb's hand, these tokens elicited expressions of delight and joyous gratitude, whereupon the sadness and frequent tears which had been His since the precipitate departure from Shíráz gave way to optimism and exultation. Mullá 'Abdu'l-Karím, one of His companions of the journey, recalled that 'a look of confidence settled upon His countenance; His words were invested with such transcendent power, that a feeling of profound reverence wrapped our very souls. No one dared to question Him as to the cause of so remarkable a change in His speech and demeanor. Nor did He Himself choose to allay our curiosity and wonder.'[2]

Moreover, there was the strange night incident when the Báb quietly left His tent, disappearing for many hours and returning to custody from the direction of Teheran, never explaining the interlude. There were those who suspected a secret tryst with Mírzá Ḥusayn-'Alí; he, however, later categorically stated that he had never met the Báb.

After twenty days at Kulayn – a time during which the Sháh, piqued as he was at the defection of Siyyid Yaḥyá, his most valued religious adviser, could readily have summoned Him for an interview to appraise the merit of His Message, and also to judge His virtues and great powers – a letter arrived from Prime Minister Áqásí. Politely worded, the order of 17 April 1846 called for the Báb's incarceration in the prison castle of Máh-kú in far northwestern Persian Azerbaijan, and promised in empty phrases a later summons to the court for the requested audience. Thus on or about 18 April 1846, the Báb with His now devoted military escort set forth on the long and rocky upland road to Tabríz, avoiding en route the large towns of Qum and Qazvín.

* The Nuṣayris of western Iran were a messianic community.

Hearing of the sentence of exile at his place of confinement in the Teheran house of Mayor Maḥmúd Khán, a redoubtable disciple of the Báb, Mullá Muḥammad-'Alí of Zanján, titled Ḥujjat (the Proof), clandestinely undertook to organize a rescue party of Zanjánís and others from Qazvín and Teheran which planned to overwhelm the guards somewhere beyond Zanján, deliver the Báb and spirit Him away to their mountains of Gílán. Since the escort soldiery numbered only a dozen Nuṣayrí horsemen who, through their sympathy for the Báb, were assumed not to be inclined to resist over-valiantly, the rescue party planned a bold tactic. Beyond Zanján, at a bivouac of the soldiers, the would-be rescuers swarmed at midnight upon the camp of the Báb with the guards fast asleep or pretending sleep. But the Báb refused to permit them to carry Him off to a time of freedom in hiding and sent them home unhappily, saying:

'*The mountains of Azerbaijan too have their claims.*'[3]

Arriving in Tabríz, that city of earthquakes which was the capital city of Sháh Ismá'íl, the Báb was held for forty days in a cell within the Ark, the massive citadel of the city. Completing the Prime Minister's order, He was removed through Marand to Máh-kú, the 'Open Mountain', the home town of Vazír Áqásí near the western border with Turkey. The great empty fortress lay above the town, a stronghold nesting under the monstrous lip of a mountain hollow which faced westward into Ottoman Turkey five miles away; many miles beyond reared the 16,800-foot Mount Ararat on which the legendary Noah purportedly had grounded his ark upon the ebbing of the Flood. Fifty miles north of the bald mountain, beyond the Aras* River, lay the border of Russian Azerbaijan, west of which was Armenia. In and from the fortress prison the Báb was able to teach His Cause with great effect to the bold Kurds and Azeri Turks of the district. Nine months of increasingly fruitful activity were permitted by the soon-sympathetic and later worshipful chief jailer 'Alí Khán, a lifelong associate of Prime Minister Áqásí. During this period the Báb dictated to His secretary the fundamental and distinguishing features of His Dispensation in His Book the Bayán (the Utterance), a few copies of which were promptly circulated by couriers from the fortress to the Bábí nerve centre in Teheran and to sundry individual recipients. And during late March of 1848 the Báb's first disciple Mullá Ḥusayn arrived with his companion Qanbar 'Alí, having walked more than one thousand miles from Mashhad, near Persia's northeastern borders. He stayed nine days

* The river known in ancient times as the Araxes.

before the Báb, with the command: '*Proceed toward the land of Khá!*', sent him on the long walk back to Khurásán to raise the Black Standards* of religious fulfillment and revolt.

A peremptory order from Prime Minister Aqásí interrupted this creative period of the Báb and brought His transfer into mountainous Persian Kurdistan, beyond Khuy and Salmás (now Shápúr) to the even more inaccessible prison fortress of Chihríq, situated on the slopes of '*the Grievous Mountain*', as He termed that spot. Here too He won His jailers' hearts and excited a great response from the inhabitants of that turbulent border area adjoining Turkish Kurdistan. And from Chihríq the Words of the new Revelation continued to flow out to the eager Bábís.

During this period the lady Fáṭimih, known to her devotees as Qurratu'l-'Ayn (Solace of the Eyes, see Note 8) because of her great beauty, was recalled to her home by her father Ḥájí Mullá Ṣáliḥ and regretfully left Iraq for her riven home in crossroads Qazvín. In Karbilá and Kaẓimayn she had been a brave dissenter from Shi'ite orthodoxy, openly giving allegiance to the Báb as the One expected. Moreover, she taught of God's continuing Revelation throughout the centuries, and opposed sharí'a law as being outdated and to be discarded. Much vilified by the clergy for her religious radicalism and for her stand on the rights of women, she was yet given high praise by the Mufti of Baghdad, Ibn Alúsí.† En route from Karbilá, in Baghdad, Karand and Ṣaḥna she won many adherents for the new Faith through her inspired teaching. In Kirmánsháh she engaged in ardent preaching to which there was violent response from the traditionalists. And in Hamadán her bold challenge to the local divines brought her precipitate departure for Qazvín.

Home in Qazvín, she produced a predictable tumult through her open and articulate espousal of the Báb's Message. Then, coincidental with the Báb's transfer to Chihríq, circa 15–20 August 1847,

* See fn, Chapter 6, p. 100, for a Qur'anic quotation on the meaning of the Black Standards.

† The Mufti of Baghdad, Ibn Alusí, confined the outspoken Qurratu'l-'Ayn in his own home, and there had abundant opportunity for discussions and observations. Of her he says: '. . . she stayed in my house about two months and so many discussions took place between me and her in which there was no taqiya (dissimulation) or apprehension. Verily, I saw in her such a degree of merit and accomplishment as I rarely saw in men. She was a wise and decent woman who was unique in virtue and chastity . . .' This quotation is from secondary sources, but is thought to be from an incomplete and unpublished work of Alúsí's. (See Maneck, 'Táhirih: A Religious Paradigm of Womanhood', *Journal of Bahá'í Studies* 2:2:1989, p. 48.)

Qazvín became a new crisis center. A bold young priest of the Shaykhí doctrines named Mullá 'Abdu'lláh (Ṣáliḥ) of Shíráz, furious at the crude hostility of Ḥájí Mullá Taqí, the hate-spewing chief ecclesiastical judge of Qazvín, waylaid him in his own mosque one dawntide and mortally stabbed him through his mouth. Escaping unseen from the mosque, the murderer brought tacit blame for the fatal assault upon those whom Taqí was then vilifying, the Bábí converts of Qazvín. And of those Bábís there was one luminous target, the beautiful and singularly talented poetess Fáṭimih, Taqí's own niece and former daughter-in-law, divorced only weeks before after three years of separation, her three sons seized by her fanatical former husband. Taqí and his son, Mullá Muḥammad, the vindictive ex-husband, were furious at Qurratu'l-'Ayn's challenge, both to their theological eminence and to their masculine dominance. Her authentic assumption of equality as a woman in an Islamic man's world was almost more insulting than her espousal of a new Faith. Added to this challenge of feminism, she could defeat them in open religious debate, for hers was a gifted mind and a voice of rare eloquence; she was 'a burning brand of the love of God, a lamp of His bestowal'.[4] Indeed, the rumblings in the Persian households were in the end graver than the Bábí threat. For where might the repressed female chattels of Persian men find a finer champion than this beautiful woman of extraordinary learning, flaming spirit and matchless tongue? She was thirty years old, richly gifted, mother and rebel, philosopher and poetess, and of the tissue from which epic heroines are made. Her ex-husband, his relatives and friends were unitedly bent upon a compound revenge: for Islám, for manhood, and for the soul of the benighted Taqí.

Qurratu'l-'Ayn was taken from her brother's hospitality and confined by her father Ḥájí Mullá Ṣáliḥ in the cellar of her childhood home. In that fine large abode of brick and plaster with its lancet bas-relief arches over the doors, her loving father, a scholarly priest of high rank, had tutored his unique offspring with rare awareness of her thirst for knowledge, but with a reluctant acceptance of her genius. At this juncture young Mullá 'Abdu'lláh surrendered, confessed his guilt in the presence of Ḥájí Mullá Ṣáliḥ, was identified by the dying Taqí, and exonerated the Bábís of any complicity whatsoever.

Nevertheless a number of Bábís were seized and with the assassin were hurried to Teheran to be held in the home of a ward chief, Khusraw Khán. Simultaneously the vengeful relatives sought some legal excuse to kill them all, whether guilty or innocent, and probed for a way to justify the execution of the indomitable Fátimih.

Mírzá Ḥusayn-'Alí in Teheran was informed of their plight. Since he was acquainted with the official in whose home they were confined, he decided to intervene on their behalf after first discussing such intervention with Sh̲afi' Kh̲án, the Prime Minister's chamberlain. He then rode to the house of the ward chief accompanied by police. There Kh̲usraw Kh̲án, avaricious and deceitful, and fully aware of the well-known generosity of Mírzá Ḥusayn-'Alí, greatly exaggerated the misfortune of the unhappy captives, hoping to gain thereby. Said he:

'They are destitute of the barest necessities of life. They hunger for food and their clothing is wretchedly scanty.'[5]

Mírzá Ḥusayn-'Alí immediately extended financial assistance for their relief, and urged the ward chief to ameliorate the severity of their unjust confinement. A few were relieved of the weight of their chains, and for the rest their hardships were reduced, for it was a cold autumn. Informing his superiors that Mírzá Ḥusayn-'Alí was supplying food and funds for those in house custody, and hopeful of personal reward, Kh̲usraw conspired with these officials to derive every possible advantage from the liberality of the young nobleman.

The house in Qazvín in which Qurratu'l-'Ayn had been tutored by her father Ḥájí Mullá Ṣáliḥ and, during the vicious reactions following the killing of her uncle Ḥájí Mullá Taqí, the high priest, was confined in its cellar, only to make a dramatic escape with the aid of Mírzá Ḥusayn-'Alí.

At that moment the murderer Mullá 'Abdu'lláh escaped from custody and fled with one companion, Riḍá Khán,* Bábí son of the Sháh's Master of Horse. The relatives of Qurratu'l-'Ayn in Qazvín, their passions accentuated, then accused Mírzá Ḥusayn-'Alí of complicity in the murder. Called to a hearing, the young man sharply denied any involvement, saying;

'The kad-khudá pleaded their cause . . . and enlarged upon their sufferings and needs. He himself bore witness to their innocence and appealed to me for help. In return for the aid which in response I was impelled to extend to his invitation, you now charge me with a crime of which I am innocent.'[6]

Threatening then confirming his immediate imprisonment, the officials confined Mírzá Ḥusayn-'Alí in the ward chief's home, seeking to extort the sum of a thousand tumans† for his freedom. He remained in house custody for several days until a number of well-placed friends, including Lt. Colonel Ja'far-Qulí Khán, a fellow Núrí and brother of Mírzá Áqá Khán, intervened on his behalf, upbraiding the ward chief with blunt words, effecting his release without payment, and eliciting abject apologies from Khusraw Khán and his superiors. On this event Mírzá Ḥusayn-'Alí later stated that:

'The first confinement to which we were subjected followed the slaying of Mullá Taqí of Qazvín, and was occasioned by the assistance we were moved to extend to those upon whom a severe punishment had been undeservedly inflicted.'[7]

In Qazvín the ruthless relatives of Taqí, despite a public outcry against their evil intentions and despite disapproval voiced by the Sháh, falsely charged, then viciously murdered the mild and pious Ḥájí Asadu'lláh, and incited a mob to butcher Mullá Ṭáhir and Mullá Ibráhím, while the noble Shaykh Ṣáliḥ was killed in Teheran, the four thus becoming the first Bábí martyrs. Plainly it was a critical hour for the very life of the precious lady Qurratu'l-'Ayn, whose estranged ex-husband Mullá Muḥammad now planned to poison her. At this juncture she boldly predicted to him, now become Chief Priest of Qazvín in his father's place, that her deliverance from confinement would occur in nine days.

It was October 1847 when, in the midst of a prince's wedding in

---

* Both 'Abdu'lláh and Riḍá Khán joined Mullá Ḥusayn and his followers, fought at Fort Shaykh Ṭabarsí and were killed there in combat. (See Chapter 6.)

† A tuman a century and a half ago was worth approximately the equivalent of two American dollars of that time before the gross inflations affecting both currencies, hence the sum of 1,000 tumans, or 2,000 dollars of 1847, was a princely sum, an enormous exaction.

Teheran, Mírzá Ḥusayn-'Alí was alerted to the grave dangers facing Qurratu'l-'Ayn.* He determined immediately to demonstrate the truth of her words and to frustrate the deadly plans of her enemies. Áqá Muḥammad-Hádí Farhádí, a Bábí who had secretly escaped to Teheran from Qazvín, was entrusted with her immediate release and transfer to Mírzá Ḥusayn-'Alí's own home in Teheran. He was charged to deliver a sealed letter to his wife Khátún-Ján, deeply aggrieved at the martyrdom of her beloved father Ḥájí Asadu'lláh; her instructions were to proceed, disguised as a beggar, to the house where her dear friend was confined. There she was to deliver the letter directly into Qurratu'l-'Ayn's hands and wait unobtrusively at the house entrance for her escape. Both were then to hasten down byways to the Sháhzádih Ḥasan gate of the city to meet the waiting Muḥammad-Hádí.

'*As soon as [Qurratu'l-'Ayn] has joined you,*' thus instructed Mírzá Ḥusayn-'Alí, '*start immediately for Teheran. This very night I shall dispatch to the neighborhood of the gate of Qazvín an attendant, with three horses, that you will take with you and station at a place outside the walls. You will conduct [Qurratu'l-'Ayn] to that spot, will mount the horses, and will, by an unfrequented route, endeavor to reach at daybreak the outskirts of the capital. As soon as the gates are opened, you must enter the city and proceed immediately to my house. You should exercise the utmost caution less her identity be disclosed. The Almighty will assuredly guide your steps and will surround you with His unfailing protection.*'[8]

Fortified by Mírzá Ḥusayn-'Alí's confidence, Muḥammad-Hádí set out immediately to fulfill his instructions. All went as planned: the beggar woman delivered her note, the bold Qurratu'l-'Ayn slipped away from her prison, and together they traversed familiar streets to emerge for the rendezvous with the waiting men. Nothing untoward occurred and, as planned, the attendant and Muḥammad-Hádí, with the two anonymous shrouded ladies, rode the more than ninety hard miles from Qazvín through the villages of Kulah/Daríh and Ishtihárd through the long day and the cold October night when few were abroad. Stopping briefly at the Shrine of the Imám Zádih† near Teheran, they entered the city at the next daybreak just as the

* Some few details of the story of Ṭáhirih derive from the book by the distinguished early teacher of the Faith, the journalist Martha Root. She visited Qazvín in 1920, saw the sites of the heroine's life, and recorded her deeds as gleaned from her relatives and from Bahá'í friends. Much of her data, however, is unreliable, and generally only items which are also reported by Nabíl are included.

† There are two Imám-Zádih shrines, both located west of Teheran, hence the entry would probably have been via a western gate, not the northern Shimírán gate. See Chapter 8.

western Qazvín city gate was opened by somnolent and careless guards and, following well-known streets, proceeded to the mansion of Mírzá Ḥusayn-'Alí.*

The sudden and mysterious disappearance of the noble Qurratu'l-'Ayn, fulfilling her own prediction of release, was early discovered and filled her friends with joy, her enemies with confusion. A search of possible places of hiding in Qazvín was set afoot, but no trace of the fugitive was found. Moreover, the hour she had set for her own deliverance found her housed in an upper apartment of the mansion of Mírzá Ḥusayn-'Alí, accepting there a sacred hospitality whose import she strongly felt, for she intuitively perceived the spiritual power of her benefactor. Indeed, in 1844, while in Karbilá, she had alluded in an ode to her recognition of the Truth he was to reveal: 'The effulgence of thy face flashed forth and the rays of thy visage arose on high; / Then speak the word "Am I not your Lord?" / And "Thou art, Thou art," we will all reply.'[9]

During the period of her late autumn stay in that blessed house, Bábí friends perhaps were able to come to hear Qurratu'l-'Ayn's discourses given in the principal room of the rented mansion, its multicolored jewel windows brightening its colorful carpets, or perhaps it was too dangerous to reveal her place of shelter.[10] Yet this productive time in hiding, under the sheltering presence of Mírzá Ḥusayn-'Alí, permitted chosen ones to come in contact with the illumined Fáṭimih of Qazvín, Qurratu'l-'Ayn. However, as Mírzá Ḥusayn-'Alí recalled:

'We were unable to accommodate her indefinitely in Our home. Accordingly, We arranged for her transference from Our house to that of the Minister of War,† who, in those days, had been disgraced by his sovereign and had been deported to Káshán. We requested his sister, who still was numbered among Our friends, to act as hostess to [Qurratu'l-'Ayn].'[11]

Thus, through the winter of 1847–1848, she lived and taught the Bábí Faith in another great Núrí mansion now become a second refuge from her vindictive relatives.

During this period Mullá Ḥusayn with his companion Qanbar-'Alí

---

* It is worthy of comment that the rescue of lady Fáṭimih Qurratu'l-'Ayn from the house of her father, Ḥájí Mullá Ṣáliḥ, was carried off so efficiently and with such apparent ease by her close friend Khátún-Ján because of Khátún-Ján's intimate knowledge of the home, its setting, its routines, its personnel, and through her own inventiveness; furthermore, she was devoted to her teacher, her idol. It also speaks for Mírzá Ḥusayn-'Alí's skill in arranging the details of so risky a venture.

† Mírzá Nasru'lláh of Núr, Áqá Khán, neighbor of Buzurg and Mírzá Ḥusayn-'Alí's family in Núr district, was to become the second Prime Minster of Násiri'd-Dín Sháh in 1852.

made his long pilgrimage on foot from Mashhad to visit the Báb in Máh-kú, and then back through Teheran. Met in the capital by Mírzá Músá and three Bábís, he was also able secretly to meet Mírzá Ḥusayn-'Alí on the journey to Máh-kú, and later openly on his return, thus receiving sustenance from him for his mission and for the coming days of trials.[12]

As the spring of 1848 approached, Mírzá Ḥusayn-'Alí sent messages requesting certain principal disciples, Mírzá Muḥammad-'Alí of Bárfurúsh and Fáṭimih Qurratu'l-'Ayn of Qazvín, and many other Bábís to assemble at a gathering in Khurásán province.

To meet this summons Mírzá Ḥusayn-'Alí asked his brother Mírzá Músá to make all arrangements for lady Qurratu'l-'Ayn's safe passage to the east. First, with Mírzá Músá as escort, she and her maid-servant Qánitih, swathed as required by custom, their eyes vigilant in the slits above the veils, rode boldly through the northern gate, although they knew that the guards had been ordered to refuse women without a permit to pass through the gates. Some seven to eight miles east of the capital the three paused at an orchard in whose center was a furnished house, empty because of a dispute between tenant and owner; its elderly custodian was willing to watch over the two women for the seven days of their preparation for the arduous travel ahead. Their happy escape from Teheran and safe temporary harborage in a beautiful setting at the foot of a mountain greatly pleased Mírzá Ḥusayn-'Alí, who termed that orchard the '*Garden of Paradise*' in praise of the jewel-like woman who had found a brief asylum therein. He said to Mírzá Músá:

'*That house has been providentially prepared for your reception, that you may entertain in it the loved ones of God.*'[13]

When Mírzá Músá's careful preparations were completed and all necessary supplies assembled, Qurratu'l-'Ayn set out on the northern road toward Khurásán accompanied by her maid-servant, by Áqá Muḥammad-Hádí, her rescuer, and several others. During this period Mírzá Músá was making similar preparations for Mírzá Ḥusayn-'Alí who, having entrusted the safety and well-being of his family in Teheran to his loyal and able brother, departed several days later with another company of Bábís and with the miscellaneous supplies and equipment needed for the housing and conduct of the conference. Both parties were traveling the main east-west highway of the north, with its many camel, mule, donkey and horse trains, to the town of Sháh-rúd which lay about four hundred kilometers northeast of Teheran at the half-way point to Mashhad in Khurásán Province. The already dusty highway traversed the treeless rolling country along the foothills of the southernmost range of the Alborz mountains. It was the upper edge of the great Persian desert, with the salt sink of Kavír to the south, lofty Mount Damávand in sight to the north. The slow journey of perhaps fifteen to twenty miles per day by horse or muleback howdah was as uncomfortable as ever for the patient women, but more endurable for the horsemen accustomed to long rides in the saddle. Mírzá Ḥusayn-'Alí pressed his companions to reach the chosen site in good time to procure provisions and establish a proper setting for the conference. It was late June 1848.

First reaching Sháh-rúd, the hamlet of Badasht not far southeast, Mírzá Ḥusayn-'Alí rented three fallow gardens with a mountain stream flowing through them for the assemblage of the friends. A featureless rural village lying at the eastern edge of the Alborz ranges was Badasht, of no significance and wholly inconspicuous. By contrast, nearby Sháh-rúd* was a large key town occupying an angle of the rugged mountains on the routes northward to the east Caspian coast and eastward to Mashhad. It was the place of assembly of caravans which combined their joint defenses against possible Turkoman raids during the long four hundred kilometers of semi-desert to Mashhad.

It was the turn into summer, and the fruit trees were in full leaf. With the mountain ridges a blue-purple backdrop, the fresh verdure of growing things was joyously heartening, a setting of beauty pleasing the eyes and calming the ardor of the zealous men and women gathered there. The season well befitted the high spirits of this group being reborn through the Words of the new Messenger of God. Moreover, the key participants were accounted for with the summons to Mírzá Muḥammad-'Alí of Bárfurúsh, the eighteenth Letter of the Living who with Mullá Ḥusayn had been proclaiming the Bábí Faith in Mashhad. Thus were called to Mírzá Ḥusayn-'Alí's side Fáṭimih Qurratu'l-'Ayn of Qazvín and Muḥammad-'Alí of Bárfurúsh, the two most gifted ones of the Báb's disciples, they who would 'revolve around that Day-Star of Truth, seek his advice, reinforce his efforts and prepare the way for His coming Revelation'.[14]

Three tents in three gardens were the focal point of the encampment, each with its mats and carpet floor. One garden was assigned to Qurratu'l-'Ayn, with Qánitih as her attendant, and Mírzá Muḥammad-Ḥádí as her doorkeeper. A second garden was given to Mírzá Muḥammad-'Alí of Bárfurúsh, his occupancy held secret until

* Now renamed Imámshahr.

Mírzá Ḥusayn-'Alí brought him from Sháh-rúd after his long ride from Mashhad. A third was that of the host, the nobleman of Núr. Occupying the cluster of lesser tents surrounding those of the three protagonists were a number of Letters of the Living and many others. Notable for their absence from among the major Bábí disciples were four: the fiery Mullá Ḥusayn, held in police custody by Prince Hamzih at Mashhad, the fearless Mullá 'Alí of Basṭám already in prison in Iraq, the illustrious Siyyid Yaḥyá of Dáráb, and the irrepressible Mullá Muḥammad-'Alí of Zanján, then under house arrest in Teheran. Nonetheless, the three principals were the best possible selections for the impending grand drama.

The eighty-one companions who had gathered in Badasht were content with momentary obscurity, for the high tensions of the anticipated meeting, with its unknown agenda, temporarily muted their zeal. It was to be a time of counsel together and of deeper understanding of the Báb's Mission, for as yet the Bayán* was known only to a limited number of disciples following its composition in Máh-kú. It would be a time of clarification of Bábí relationships with Islám and also of possible plans for freeing the Báb from prison. And all, for the time of their arrival to the day of dispersal, were to be the guests of Mírzá Ḥusayn-'Alí, the quiet master of events.

On every day of the twenty-two days of that sojourn he revealed a Tablet which Sulaymán of Núr chanted in the presence of the believers. Upon each one of the Bábís he bestowed a new name as his Bábí title. Henceforth each would normally be addressed by his fellows only by that distinctive title of honor. He designated himself as Bahá, the Glorious One, nor apparently was this title taken amiss by critical Bábís, a tribute to his palpable excellence. Upon the last Letter of the Living, Muḥammad-'Alí of Bárfurúsh, he conferred the appellation of Quddús, the Most Holy One. And upon Fáṭimih of Qazvín he bestowed the new title of Ṭáhirih, the Pure One. However, the identity of him who had conferred the new names upon them was not made, although each surely conjectured according to his degree of perception. For each companion a special Tablet was later revealed by the Báb, each addressed by the new name of great symbolic and personal meaning.

---

* The Bayán is of two parts, one in Persian, one in Arabic. The Persian Bayán, the Utterances or Exposition, is of nine Váhids (units) of nineteen chapters each. The Arabic Bayán is shorter and more concise. Both were composed in Máh-kú in 1847–1848.

On every day of that memorable gathering a law or a tradition of Islám was abrogated, followed by lively discussion among these able and articulate men and the few women, each with a unique background and ideas. The veils guarding the sanctity of the laws and ordinances of Islám were rent asunder for the Bábís, to be replaced by the Báb's new Words of Revelation.[15] No one knew the origin of these innovations, nor was anyone apprised of the hand which steered their course. Yet surely not a few surmised that Mírzá Ḥusayn-'Alí, Jináb-i-Bahá, was the spirit, the mind, the source.

One day Jináb-i-Bahá* was confined to his bed by an illness. Quddús hastened to his host's tent and, when ushered into his presence, seated himself at his right hand. Other solicitous companions were gradually admitted to the tent and stood in close array around the sickbed. No sooner had they assembled than Muḥammad-Ḥasan of Qazvín suddenly entered and conveyed to Quddús an insistent invitation to visit Ṭáhirih in her own garden.

'I have severed myself entirely from her,' Quddús replied. 'I refuse to meet her.'

The messenger immediately retired, soon returning to reiterate the same urgent invitation to heed her call.

'She insists on your visit,' were his words. 'If you persist in your refusal, she herself will come to you.'

Perceiving Quddús' unyielding attitude, the messenger unsheathed his sword and laid it at the feet of Quddús, saying 'I refuse to go without you. Either choose to accompany me to the presence of Ṭáhirih, or cut off my head with this sword.'

'I have already declared my intention not to visit Ṭáhirih,' was Quddús' angry retort. 'I am willing to comply with the alternative which you have chosen to put before me.'[16]

Muḥammad-Ḥasan seated himself at the feet of Quddús and extended his neck for the sword stroke when suddenly Ṭáhirih, adorned but unveiled, appeared in the mouth of the tent before the astonished Bábís.

All stood aghast before this unexpected vision. Disciplined by harsh Islamic custom which stringently limited women's garb and behavior, that these men might see the comely face of Ṭáhirih unveiled was inconceivable. Such men felt it to be highly improper even to gaze at the shadow of her whom they regarded as the incarnation of Fáṭimih, the holiest woman of Islám, who was their

* Jináb-i-Bahá (the Honorable Glorious One), the title of Mírzá Ḥusayn-'Alí used from that day onward.

very emblem of chastity.* Some may 'have recalled with throbbing hearts the Islamic tradition foreshadowing the appearance of Fáṭimih herself unveiled while crossing the Bridge (Ṣiráṭ) on the promised Day of Judgment'.[17] Mírzá Áqá Ján, later Jináb-i-Bahá's secretary, commented on this dramatic event, saying, 'The face of Fáṭimih must needs be revealed on the Day of Judgment and appear unveiled before the eyes of men. At that moment the voice of the Unseen shall be heard, saying, "Turn your eyes away from that which ye have seen." '[18]

Silently Ṭáhirih stepped forward and seated herself at Quddús' right hand. Her serenity contrasted with the startled countenances of those who were gazing upon her face, mixed anger and bewilderment curdling their Islám-conditioned souls. 'Abdu'l-Kháliq of Iṣfahán, excited, disturbed, slashed his throat† and bloody, shrieking, fled from the tent. A number were frozen, speechless, confounded. Some discovered their legs and ran forth. But during this dramatic entrance the enraged Quddús remained seated, the unsheathed sword in his hand, poised as though awaiting the proper moment to kill Ṭáhirih, violator of tradition.

His threatening attitude produced no effect. Her radiant countenance was one of dignity and confidence but also, shining from within, were triumph and joy. She rose from her seat and, undeterred by the tumult raised in the hearts of the Bábís, addressed the assemblage in language strikingly similar to that of the Qur'án, appealing with fervor to her fellow disciples to understand and meet the challenges of the new day of God, and ending with a verse of the Qur'án:

'Verily, amid gardens and rivers shall the pious dwell in the seat of truth, in the presence of the potent king.'[19]

And so saying, she glanced toward both Jináb-i-Bahá and Quddús, yet those watching were unable to determine to which one she was alluding. Without pause she declared:

'I am the Word which the Qá'im is to utter, the Word which shall put to flight the chiefs and nobles of the earth!'[20]

---

* Fáṭimih, the wife of the Imám 'Alí, was the daughter of Muḥammad, and a powerful symbol of ideal womanhood in Islám. Among her other attributes she was the symbol of chastity.

† Self-inflicted cuts of the throat are typically shallow, one-sided and bloody, for the intending suicide usually reacts to the first pain and shock of the wound by failing to press home the blade, particularly if his intentions are weak ones; thus usually only the superficial veins are severed, often producing spectacular bleeding. (A physician's note.) 'Abdu'l-Kháliq survived his act of would-be suicide, to serve and die at Fort Shaykh Ṭabarsí.

Turning then to Quddús, she rebuked him for having failed to perform in Khurásán those things which she deemed to be essential to the welfare of the Faith.

Quddús reacted sharply to this criticism, retorting: 'I am free to follow the promptings of my own conscience. I am not subject to the will and pleasure of my fellow-disciples.'

Ignoring him then and turning to the gathered men, Ṭáhirih invited those present to befittingly celebrate this memorable occasion, and concluded:

'This day is the day of festivity and universal rejoicing, the day on which the fetters of the past are burst asunder. Let those who have shared in this great achievement arise and embrace each other.'[21]

Before there could be other reactions to Ṭáhirih's momentous act, Jináb-i-Bahá took command, calling for a recitation of the Qur'ánic Súrih of the Resurrection, whose inner meaning was that mankind was about to pass through the Day of Judgment into a new cosmic cycle, for which new laws and customs were indispensable. Thus the reader began:

'When the inevitable day of judgment shall suddenly come, no soul shall charge the prediction of its coming with falsehood: it will abase some, and exalt others. When the earth shall be shaken with a violent shock, and the mountains shall be dashed in pieces, and shall become as dust scattered abroad . . .'* and so to the end of this overpowering passage, which concludes:

'Therein they shall hear no idle talk, no cause of sin, only the saying "Peace, Peace".'[22]

So ended the central act of that memorable gathering, on a day of enlightenment when the master hand of Mírzá Ḥusayn-'Alí, Jináb-i-Bahá, had created and staged a dramatic and crucial severance from the Islamic past, to make clear that a new religion had come into being, and to set the Bábí 'dawn-breakers' free to become the first among a new race of men and women fit to lead the way into the Day of God.

'*How great was the consternation that seized the companions on that day!*' recalled Jináb-i-Bahá years later. '*Fear and bewilderment filled their hearts. A few, unable to tolerate that which was to them so revolting a departure from the established custom of Islám, fled in horror from before her face. Dismayed, they sought refuge in a deserted castle in that neighborhood.*

---

* The Súrih [Chapter] of the Resurrection is Súrih LXXV entitled 'The Inevitable' by translator Sale, but given different titles by translator Arberry: 'The Event' or 'The Terror'.

Among those who were scandalized by her behavior and severed from her entirely were [Siyyid Muḥammad-'Alíy-i-Nahrí] and his brother Mírzá Hádí, to both of whom we sent word that it was unnecessary to desert their companions and seek refuge in a castle.'*[23]

The days which followed witnessed radical changes in the life and habits of the Bábís. Discarded were the customs and ceremonies of Shí'ite Islám by which these devout believers had been shaped in the past. Understandably, a great confusion prevailed even among these ardent reformers of Islám. A few condemned the new ideas and actions as heresy. Some now saw the radical Ṭáhirih as the arbiter of change, while others held to the apparently conservative Quddús. Still others saw the days as a time of separation of 'the true from the false, the faithful from the disloyal'. And some considered the conference a failure, this great drama as the collapse of fruitful consultation, particularly since a plan for the rescue of the Báb did not materialize.

Ṭáhirih repudiated the authority of Quddús, declaring: 'I deem him a pupil whom the Báb has sent me to edify and instruct.'[24]

For his part Quddús denounced Ṭáhirih as the author of heresy and categorized her followers as the victims of error. Others of rigid and cautious temper of mind accused her of casting out time-honored traditions, their complaints coming to the ear of the Báb, who later vindicated her with His powerful confirmation:

'*What am I to say regarding her whom the Tongue of Power and Glory* [Bahá] *has named Ṭáhirih?*'[25]

Tension between the two was finally openly resolved by Jináb-i-Bahá, who felt it timely to reconcile them before the eyes of their fellows. He saw, too, that the purposes of the conference had been won, the Old Order cast out and the New Order begun. The Báb was now free to carry further the demolition of centuries of Islamic religious detritus through His new Voice from God. No longer were the Bábís to consider themselves as belonging to a reform offshoot of Islám. Now they knew that while their roots were set in the Qu'rán and also in preceding Holy Books, their Bábí roots of faith had put forth a new trunk, branches and leaf cover under the ever-shining

* The brothers Siyyid Muḥammad-'Alíy-i-Nahrí and his brother Mírzá Hádí were respectively the father and uncle of Fáṭimih of Iṣfáhán who long years later was to become the bride of 'Abdu'l-Bahá. When she came to 'Akká she was named Munírih, the Illumined One, by Bahá'u'lláh. After Badasht Mírzá Hádí, the husband of Ṭáhirih's devoted and ardent Bábí friend Shams-i-Ḍuḥá, was 'attacked, tormented, stoned and subjected to such ordeals that finally, in a ruined caravanserai, he died. His brother buried him there by the roadside.' (See *Memorials of the Faithful*, p. 180.)

Sun of Revelation. It was the ending of the season of frost, the thawing of the frozen soil of Islám. The first plants of the divine Springtime were visible.

Most probably the conference at insignificant Badasht was called for the very purpose of making clear the Báb's claim of distinct Prophethood, but particularly to abrogate outworn or invented Islamic laws. Clearly Ṭáhirih had led the way in open renunciation of the sharí'a code of Muslim canon law, for high among these laws was the unhappy and demeaning tradition which required the veiling of women before the eyes of authoritarian men who saw them as physical property and as temptresses to sinful behavior. Jináb-i-Bahá had been in constant contact with the Báb via extensive correspondence; and indeed they might well have jointly planned the principal elements of this decisive meeting of the eighty-one Bábís. Further, as the Bábí Cause had expanded, it was plain that action should everywhere be encouraged. The newly converted Bábís, many of whom were trained to be Muslim teachers of theology and preachers, required stern re-education. In the main they were resolute and courageous individuals, usually Muslim liberals, many of them former followers of Shaykh Aḥmad and Siyyid Káẓim, and most were daring men and women quite willing to jump into the unknown despite its ultimate perils. Certainly the Báb had been educating His followers from prison, by word of mouth through His stream of visitors, and through a prodigious outflow of letters. Spiritually most telling, at the critical moment of Badasht, at His trial in far-off Tabríz the Báb had challenged His interrogators with the declaration that He was the promised Qá'im expected by the faithful of Shi'ite Islám.

The twenty-two days at Badasht constituted a profoundly revolutionary religious classroom. Mírzá Ḥusayn-'Alí, Jináb-i-Bahá, was palpably the *deus ex machina*. Through him Ṭáhirih was saved to be escorted from Teheran to Sháh-rúd; without her sheer bravery and spiritual eminence, where was the high drama to strike to the hearts and souls? Through him the valiant Quddús became co-actor and the proper foil for Ṭáhirih's heroism, blunting by his well-acted stance the enormity of her deed as felt by his conservative associates. With his organizational skill and wealth, Jináb-i-Bahá chose and prepared the place, then played the complete host. His opening stroke was profound: each Bábí received a befitting new name, a title symbolic of his altered personality and destiny as a dedicated servant of the new Cause. Preparatory and foreshadowing was his naming Ṭáhirih as the Pure One, she who became the 'blast of the trumpet'. After the day-to-day elimination of Islamic laws there occurred the climactic act of point-counterpoint staged by Ṭáhirih and Quddús, who were ostensibly and perhaps in some part authentically at odds. At Badas͟ht the poetess won her high place in religious history through her unveiling which swept away outdated religious traditions. The break had been accomplished, the die cast. Hereafter not one of the faithful might doubt that a new race of women and men was in process of creation.

By mid-July the company of Bábís had gone their ways, some to join Mullá Ḥusayn as he gathered Bábís. Others with Jináb-i-Bahá, Quddús and Ṭáhirih set out northward across the mountains to avoid the dusty main road and to reach the far pleasanter roads to Núr in Mázindarán by following the green forested Caspian lowlands westward. This path avoided also the highroad through Astrabad with its possible dangers should there have been a report of the gathering and an ordering of interception by the authorities. Quddús and Ṭáhirih chose to ride in the same howdah, now as true compatriots. And each day the poetess composed an ode which she taught to the company trudging behind them. Their exuberant shouts and chants echoed through the mountains and valleys as they proceeded, the words of the odes announcing the death of old ideas and the birth of the new day.

The track led upward along the Mojen River and over a high pass into the headwaters of the Nika River's long valley to the Caspian Sea. Excited and disturbed by the events at Badas͟ht, and particularly by the unveiling of the saintly Ṭáhirih, which upset a keystone of their Muslim code of thought and behavior, some unstable members of the party were ripe for trouble. Along the mountain valley road through the village of Níyálá, these few were guilty of provocative acts towards the village women. Camping then in the vicinity of that village, the party was, in Jináb-i-Bahá's words: '. . . *at the hour of dawn . . . suddenly awakened by the stones which the people of the neighborhood were hurling upon us from the top of the mountain. The fierceness of their attack induced our companions to flee in terror and consternation. I clothed Quddús in my own garments and despatched him to a place of safety, where I intended to join him. When I arrived, I found that he had gone. None of our companions had remained in Níyálá except Ṭáhirih and a young man from S͟híráz, Mírzá 'Abdu'lláh. The violence with which we were assailed had brought desolation into our camp. I found no one into whose custody I could deliver Ṭáhirih except that young man, who displayed on that occasion a courage and determination that were truly surprising. Sword in hand, undaunted by the savage assault of the inhabitants of that*

*village, who had rushed to plunder our property, he sprang forward to stay
the hand of the assailants. Though himself wounded in several parts of his
body, he risked his life to protect our property. I bade him desist from his act.
When the tumult had subsided, I approached a number of the inhabitants of
the village and was able to convince them of the cruelty and shamefulness of
their behavior. I subsequently succeeded in restoring a part of our plundered
property.*'[26]

With his characteristic presence of mind, the courageous Jináb-i-
Bahá had made the most of an ugly situation, recovering some of the
goods stolen from their camp and reestablishing the confidence of the
people. Most important, he had sent the estimable Quddús in
disguise to temporary safety in Bárfurú<u>sh</u> and again rescued the
noble Ṭáhirih, symbol of all the brave women who would hereafter
espouse the new Cause. Soon, wary that the beauteous Ṭáhirih
would be recognized and apprehended, he consigned that precious
woman, with her attendant, to the protection of <u>Sh</u>ay<u>kh</u> Abú Turáb,
who was asked to escort her in safety to Núr. There she might live
quietly, writing in relative obscurity, guarded by the faithful Bábís,
and under the protection of Jináb-i-Bahá. She was now homeless,
her beloved children stolen from her under Islamic law which
mandated custody to her unworthy ex-husband. Plainly she was
marked for grave new perils. Asylum was her present need.

Proceeding to the port town of Bandar-Gaz, Jináb-i-Bahá fell sick
and was given hospitality by Bábí friends. And during the relatively
short period in Bandar-Gaz, the estimable Bábí Mírzá Masíḥ died, he
whom Jináb-i-Bahá termed '*spirit personified*', for whom he not only
held a memorial meeting but also wrote a Tablet of Visitation.

Meanwhile, in Teheran, those opposed to Mírzá Ḥusayn-‘Alí,
including the persistently hostile Prime Minister, were reawakening
the suspicions of the gravely ailing Muḥammad <u>Sh</u>áh by reporting
the Núrí nobleman to be the prime mover of the suspicious and
incendiary Bábí gathering near <u>Sh</u>áh-rúd, and creator of the distur-
bance at Níyálá. In the end they succeeded in stirring the sovereign's
latent antagonisms into evil decision.

'I have hitherto refused to countenance whatever has been said
against him. My indulgence has been actuated by my recognition of
the services rendered to my country by his father. This time,
however, I am determined to put him to death.'[27]

To carry out his deadly intention, through Prime Minister Áqásí
he commanded an officer in Teheran to instruct his son in Mázindarán to arrest Mírzá Ḥusayn-‘Alí and accompany him to the capital
for execution. The officer's son received these orders in Bandar-Gaz

on the day prior to his own planned reception for Mírzá Ḥusayn-'Alí, for whom he had a strong attachment. Sorely distressed, he was deeply reluctant either to tell the grim news or to carry out the order, although he knew he must obey his king. Mírzá Ḥusayn-'Alí, however, observed the effect of the unknown message, and relieved the young man's acute apprehensions by advising that he put his trust in God.

The next day, as Mírzá Ḥusayn-'Alí was being accompanied by the officer's son to the home of a notable, they encountered a horseman hastening from the direction of Teheran. The young man intercepted the courier to inquire of his mission and, as he rejoined Bahá, exultantly exclaimed: 'Muḥammad S͟háh is dead!'* And so saying, he flourished the imperial summons, now without force. Thus that night the planned reception was a time of joy, relief and gratitude at God's intervention, striking down the S͟háh's hand raised to carry out a baneful act in his last hours.

Jináb-i-Bahá, well and for the moment safe, thereafter made his way with his companions through '*the district of Hizárjaríb, village by village and town by town, until he entered the land of Núr*'. Said he: '*Praise be to God that from the rays of the Sun of Truth all those regions became illumined in those days . . .*'†

The coastal road to Núr led through Sárí and Bárfurús͟h where Jináb-i-Bahá appears to have sought out Quddús, perhaps to consult on affairs of the Bábí Cause. During that brief interval he has recounted that: '*Whilst in Sárí, we were again exposed to the insults of the people. Though the notables of that town were, for the most part, our friends and had on several occasions met us in Teheran, no sooner had the townspeople recognized us, as we walked with Quddús in the streets, than they began to hurl their invectives at us. The cry "Bábí, Bábí!" greeted us wherever we went. We were unable to escape their bitter denunciations*'[28]

And so the Honorable Bahá came home to Dárkalá, Tákur and

---

* Muḥammad S͟háh died on September 4, 1848, unmourned by his people because of his tyrannical reign, which in cruel misdeeds was probably exceeded by his son Náṣiri'd-Dín S͟háh.

† Some time later Bahá'u'lláh recorded His memories of the days after Badas͟ht, of the journey home to Núr, during portions of which Quddús and Ṭáhirih accompanied Him. The Tablet *in toto* has not been found, but a fragment of it is published in Fáḍil Mázindarání's *Z̧uhúru'l-Haqq* (the Manifestation of Truth), Volume 3, p. 112, and was excerpted by Balyuzi. It is as follows: '*Those lands* (of Mázindarán) *are blessed lands, because from S͟háh-rúd this Wronged One travelled towards those territories until He entered Gaz* (now Bandar-i-Gaz), *visited its environs, then, before arriving at As͟hraf* (now Behshahr), *He travelled through the district of Hizárjaríb, village by village, and town by town, until He entered the land of Núr. Praise be to God that from the rays of the Sun of Truth all those regions became illumined in those days . . .*'

Teheran, to family, friends and the pressing affairs of the Cause, feeling the rising hostility against the new Faith. However, just as the plague in Shíráz had spared the life of the Báb, the Will of God spared the greatest disciple of the Báb, by smiting the king himself.

Most of the people of Persia are steeped in deception and idle fancy . . . People for the most part delight in superstitions. They regard a single drop of the sea of delusion as preferable to an ocean of certitude. By holding fast unto names they deprive themselves of the inner reality and by clinging to vain imaginings they are kept back from the Dayspring of heavenly signs.[29]

Bahá'u'lláh

The tomb-shrine of Shaykh Aḥmad of Ṭabarsí, place of the crude fortification defended by the heroic 313 Bábís, Mullá Ḥusayn and Quddús commanding and making possible an incredible defence against overwhelming odds. Today it is a forgotten oasis in the forest, lovingly preserved by Bahá'ís.

Sháh-rúd, above, small city at the eastern end of the Alborz Mountains, way station on the highway from Teheran to Mashhad, situated in the mouth of the Mojen River valley. A place of assembly of caravans organizing against potential Turkoman raids during the long 400 kilometers to the Holy City of the Imám Riḍá. Below: Badasht, rural hamlet in the plains southeast of Sháh-rúd; a productive farm community with well irrigated fields served by mountain runoff streams. Fallow gardens such as these were the site of the Badasht gathering, place of the Bábí rupture from Islám.

The Citadel of Tabríz, where the Báb was briefly held at the time of His trial before the Governor and priests. Below: a modern view.

6 Clash: The Bábís and Reform of Shí'ite Islám

. . . I stand, life in hand, ready; that perchance, through God's loving-kindness and grace, this revealed and manifest Letter may lay down his life as a sacrifice in the path of the Primal Point, the Most Exalted Word.[1]

Bahá'u'lláh

After the Báb had been imprisoned for three months in fortress Chihríq (see Note 9), during which time the Bábís flooded the nearby tiny Kurdish community, Prime Minister Áqásí ordered Him to Tabríz to stand trial on charges of heresy. It was July when He was conducted to the town of Urúmíyyih, the reputed birthplace of Zoroaster, on the huge salt lake of that name. It was a city slowly recovering from the wounds of the great earthquake of 1840. There He was respectfully welcomed by the Governor, Prince Malik Qásim, who accepted Him in his home as a guest, then took the opportunity to test the powers of this reputed great new Teacher of so commanding a spiritual presence. The Báb's spontaneous winning of a particularly fractious and hostile horse given Him for His ride to the public bath evoked the enthusiasm of all and the conversion of many as His fame spread like wildfire throughout the region. Here, too, the Governor's chief painter, Áqá-Bálá Big, rendered His only portrait from life.*

To avoid Khuy because it was disturbed by the ebullience of His new Bábí converts, the Báb was taken around the southern end of the lake, then northwest through Marághih and over the high passes to dour graystone Tabríz, surrounded by its toothed mountains and

* The Báb's visit to Urúmíyyih was marked by enthusiastic acceptance of Him by the authorities and populace, who felt His power and spirit through several extraordinary incidents recorded by Nabíl. The original of the Báb's portrait is now held in the International Bahá'í Archives in Haifa.

marked by its threatening massive stone and brick citadel.* The public reaction to His coming was fed by rumors of His purported supernatural powers, and such a stir was created among the populace that He was held outside the gates of the city proper lest in their zeal His presence might disturb public order.

Brought then to face a group of five chief divines of Tabríz in the mansion of the Governor, the seventeen-year-old Crown Prince Náṣiri'd-Dín soon to mount the throne, the Báb entered the grand reception hall to find it crowded with an audience keenly sensitized to the content of the interrogation, which was rumored to concern a radical heresy of greatest importance. One central seat was unoccupied, that reserved for the Prince. Calmly, confidently, with majestic gait and an emanation of great power, the Báb walked directly to the royal seat and sat down amidst deep silence.† When the Prince had arrived and was seated next to the Báb, the high priest opened the questioning by bluntly asking: 'Who do you claim to be, and what is the Message which you have brought?'

'*I am, I am, I am the Promised One!*' was the bold answer. '*I am the One whose name you have for a thousand years invoked, at whose mention you have risen, whose advent you have longed to witness, and the hour of whose Revelation you have prayed God to hasten. Verily I say, it is incumbent upon the peoples of both the East and the West to obey My Word and to pledge allegiance to My Person.*'[2]‡

Upon this shocking claim there followed what can only be described as a travesty of an interrogation purportedly designed to

* The citadel had walls one hundred and twenty feet high, and twenty-five feet thick at the base. Perilous steps led to the top, from whence faithless wives were cast to their deaths. (See Richards, *Persian Journey*, p. 216.)

† The very rare phenomenon of emanations of power by Great Spirits lends itself by its nature to infrequent reports by those considered to be objective observers, although those under the influence of religious leaders often tell of it. The bold move of the Báb to take the seat of the Crown Prince Governor, carried out without stern action by officials, suggests a radical suppression of ordinary protocol because of strong reluctance to confront Him Who might be the Mihdí, and Who acted as if He were indeed the long-awaited One. Very probably He was felt to have spiritual power by those present. Of this surcharged phenomenon of Great Souls, 'Abdu'l-Bahá told of Bahá'u'lláh's relating to Varqá that: 'At stated periods souls are sent to earth by the Mighty God with what we call "the Power of the Great Ether". And they who possess this power can do anything; they have *all* power . . .' (Blomfield, *The Chosen Highway*, p. 134.) By the power of the Great Ether possibly also is meant the power of creation, of cosmic power, of God's power.

‡ At Tabríz, the Báb unequivocally stated His role to be that of the Mihdí, the One Who is Guided, a title given to the Twelfth Imám. The expectation of the return of the hidden Imám, presumed to be in occultation, i.e. in concealment, was a strong belief of Shí'ite Islám. The expectation of the return/coming of the Qá'im, the living One, the One Who would Arise, centers about the prophecy concerning the child

assess its validity. To irrelevant criticisms of His spoken and written Arabic grammar, and to insolent and pejorative comments about His person – these insults primarily deriving from Mullá Muḥammad Mámaqání, a hostile one-eyed <u>Shaykh</u>í priest – the Báb returned deft replies, repeating firmly His claim to be the Qá'im.* He ended His testimony with the Qur'ánic verse: '*Far be the glory of thy Lord, the Lord of all greatness, from what they impute to Him, and peace be upon His Apostles!*'[3] So saying, He abruptly arose and left the assemblage.

Following further acrimonious consultation among the divines after this unsatisfactory conclusion of a gathering which had not gone at all as planned, they agreed that the Báb should receive a humiliating punishment, the bastinado, because of His asserted discourteous conduct. But when both the Prince and the police refused to inflict the penalty, He was taken to the home of Mírzá 'Alí-Aṣ<u>gh</u>ar, the high priest, who himself inflicted eleven strokes of the rod upon the tender soles of His feet. Twice He was brought for examination to the Irish physician, Dr. William Cormick,† first for a judgment of His sanity in relation to a possible death sentence, and later for medical treatment of His injured feet. The doctor recorded his observations in a singular vignette, one passage of which is notable for its description of the Báb:

'. . . He was a very mild and delicate-looking man, rather small in stature and very fair for a Persian, with a melodious soft voice . . . his whole look and deportment went far to dispose one in his favor . . .' And the doctor's report was of a nature to spare His life.[4]

Imám Muḥammad, who disappeared in 260 AH (873 AD); he was but five years old when he entered a crypt near Samarra, never to emerge according to the tradition, thus making the town a holy place. These Shi'ite traditions are presented *in extenso* in Balyuzi, *Muḥammad and the Course of Islam*, and in Momen, *Shi'i Islám*.

* In a letter of Náṣiri'd-Dín <u>Sh</u>áh written probably in the 1870s in connection with the questioning of Bábís arrested in Teheran, the <u>Sh</u>áh recalls that in Tabríz when he was Crown Prince the Báb affirmed clearly and repeatedly His claim to be the Qá'im. Moreover, in that letter of critical evidence for the Báb's Declaration, the hostile <u>Sh</u>áh reveals that he is nevertheless keenly interested in the Báb's precise Message, doubtless having lingering questions despite the tone of His message. (Balyuzi, *The Báb*, p. 145.)

† Dr. William Cormick, Irish physician of Prince Náṣiri'd-Dín <u>Sh</u>áh when he was the Governor of Tabríz, was the only western person known to have met the Báb. Summoned to examine the Báb before His bastinado principally to determine His sanity, and later to examine His swollen and damaged feet, he wrote an account of these visits to Reverend Benjamin Labaree of the American Mission in Urúmíyyih. A full account is given in Momen, *Bábí and Bahá'í Religions*, pp. 74–75. Apparently insanity was no consideration as a factor, either in Cormick's report, or in the effect upon the trial; Cormick's comments, not known, may well have been based upon his observations of the Báb's personality and character, even though he could not converse with Him.

The Báb was returned to Chihríq in early August and promptly wrote a denunciatory letter to Prime Minister Áqásí. This searing letter, known as the Sermon of Wrath, was sent to Mullá Muḥammad-'Alí of Zanján, titled Ḥujjat (the Proof) by the Báb, who in those days was confined in Teheran, instructing him to deliver it in person to the Prime Minister. Gaining permission to visit the Vazír, that bold spirit dared to confront Áqásí, sharply quoting the message to him. During that September the Minister's patron, Muḥammad Sháh, had just died at Tajrish in the Shimírán district near Teheran, and so he heard the condemnatory message without the power of reprisal, and with the specter of early ignominy and death facing him as a just reward for his evils. Years later Jináb-i-Bahá, then Bahá'u'lláh, recalled that, in his home in Teheran:

'I was in the company of Mírzá Masíḥ [of Núr] and a number of other believers when [Ḥujjat] arrived. He recounted the circumstances attending the delivery of the Tablet, and recited before us the entire text, which was about three pages in length, and which he had committed to memory.'[5]

Ḥujjat's bold act and his fiery spirit of dedication could not but bring renewed confirmation to his embattled co-religionists.

In Mashhad on 21 July 1848, just after Badasht and the trial in Tabríz, Mullá Ḥusayn, at the Báb's behest, raised the Black Standards* referred to in a well-known Islamic tradition from the Prophet as the symbol of the coming of the Mihdí, the One Who is guided. With this first troop of Bábís mustered in Mashhad he departed westward for Mázindarán province, calling for all the faithful to join him, saying: 'This is the way to our Karbilá,' the path to a heroic end even as the Imám Ḥusayn won his death in battle.[6] By the end of September his band of armed followers† had greatly increased through Bábí arrivals and through conversions as they

* When Mullá Ḥusayn raised the Black Standards at Mashhad in July of 1848, and proceeded with his small band to Shaykh Tabarsí, he was fulfilling a cryptic saying ot the Prophet Muḥammad that: 'Should your eyes behold the Black Standards proceeding from Khurásán, hasten ye towards them, even though you should have to crawl over the snow, inasmuch as they proclaim the advent of the promised Mihdí, the Viceregent of God.' It is small wonder that the Bábís, knowing this saying, converged upon his company, and that many new adherents joined Mullá Ḥusayn en route to the great siege. (See Nabíl, *The Dawn-Breakers*, p. 351.)

† Among the Bábís there was a retention of Muslim military action, which in Islám was permitted for self-defense. In addition, the Bábís were Persians, a society in which training in the use of weapons was commonly given or permitted to the boys and young men, hence the men of the Black Standards possibly saw themselves as troops gathering for defense of the new Faith which was sure to provoke further violent confrontations with those Muslims incited by the priests, or perhaps they saw themselves as defenders of a new law and a new justice.

proceeded westward through Nishápúr* of the poet Omar Khayyam, then through Sabzevar and Míyámay. Along the southern edge of the Alborz mountains the party passed through Sháh-rúd, then proceeding through Mihmán-Dúst to Chishmih-'Alí to Urim where hostility greeted them, and so over the mountains to Bárfurúsh, home town of Quddús, arriving in September 1848.[7] There the chief priest incited the local population to attack the Bábí company, in which melée and repulse of the attackers Mullá Ḥusayn performed prodigies of valor. Retreating from Barfurúsh after a nine-day standoff, and accompanied by local tribal brigands under one Khusraw of Qáḍí-Kalá, the little Bábí troop was treacherously attacked by Khusraw's hundred horsemen acting under secret orders of the chief priest, but many of the hundred attackers, including the commander himself, died at the hands of the aroused Bábís. Perceiving no way westward, and harassed by villagers, on October 12 Mullá Ḥusayn brought his party through the swamps, forests, rice fields and open meadows of this sparsely occupied area to the tomb-shrine of a local saint, one Shaykh Aḥmad of Ṭabars, situated some thirteen miles southwest of Bárfurúsh. It was a place of thickets and groves, of higher open land and swampy lowlands, much of which had been converted to rice paddies, with the Talar river passing through. The population was scant and impoverished, the area generally inhospitable.†

Around this insignificant shrine building set in the brushland and fields, with muddy paths leading to it, the Bábís began to throw up earthworks strengthened by vertical tree trunks, and fortified with small towers, to establish a base capable of resolute defense during the anticipated oncoming siege, with each segment of the wall defended by men coming from the same home areas.[8] In Teheran, the new Prime Minister Taqí Khán heard alarming reports of these events, viewed them as an armed rebellion and, wishing to show strength as a determined defender of the young Sháh Náṣiri'd-Dín's

---

* The poet and scientist Omar Khayyam of Nishápúr, city of emeralds and gateway to Persia from Central Asia, lived in the second half of the eleventh century. He composed the poem entitled 'The Rubaiyat' made famous in the western world through its translation into English in the 19th century by the poet Edward Fitzgerald.

† Dr. Edward G. Browne visited Fort Shaykh Ṭabarsí in 1888, and his description of the site provides an early eyewitness view of that section of the well-watered Caspian plain not far from the mountains. One can understand that the army found it difficult to operate in such forbidding terrain. (See Momen, *Bábí and Bahá'í Religions*, pp. 97–99.) In 1973 the spot was still forested, uncouth, inhospitable, the small Shrine preserved by Bahá'í surveillance and maintenance at the time of the author's visit.

power, immediately ordered troops to quell the purported insurrection.

While the fortifications around the half-ruined small shrine were rising and its moat deepening, but before the arrival of imperial forces, Jináb-i-Bahá appeared with companions from Núr. This first meeting with Mullá Ḥusayn was an exciting one, a fusion of great spirits, in which Jináb-i-Bahá promptly put his finger upon the key requirement for the defense: an even greater depth of spiritual leadership. Inspecting the fort with sharp eyes and expressing his satisfaction at the work accomplished, he conveyed to Mullá Ḥusayn many details which he perceived to be vital to the morale and welfare of the Bábís, and suggested:

'*The one thing this fort and company require is the presence of Quddús. His association with this company would render it complete and perfect.*'[9] But Quddús was known to be in confinement in Sárí, a number of miles farther west, and had been held there for three months since his arrival from Badasht.

Jináb-i-Bahá thereupon instructed Mullá Ḥusayn to dispatch to Sárí the courageous Mullá Mihdí of Khuy with six horsemen to demand the immediate release of Quddús from the chief priest Muḥammad-Taqí. And he gave the bold seven a confidence in their obviously rash ride into the lion's mouth of hostile Sárí by predicting the outcome of their confrontation with the high priest, saying:

'*The fear of God and the dread of His punishment will prompt him to surrender unhesitatingly his captive.*'[10]

Upon his departure from Shaykh Ṭabarsí, Jináb-i-Bahá enjoined upon the brave hundreds the necessary patience and resignation to the will of the Almighty and expressed the hope that:

'*If it be His will, we shall once again visit you at this same spot and shall lend you our assistance. You have been chosen of God to be the vanguard of His host and the establishers of His Faith. His host verily will conquer. Whatever may befall, victory is yours, a victory which is complete and certain.*'[11] And with this stirring prediction, one to be realized only in future centuries unimaginable to the defenders, he departed for Núr, and so to Teheran.

Acting to free Quddús, the seven armed horsemen leading a riderless steed boldly entered the town of Sárí and halted outside the house of the chief priest. Mullá Mihdí peremptorily issued a demand for the release of Quddús, to which Muḥammad-Taqí immediately succumbed. Freed, the indomitable Quddús returned with them to the fort, there to infuse with new power the Black Standards flying above the soon-beleaguered Bábí island in the forests. With the liberation of Quddús from his ninety-five-day house confinement, his flaming spirit and utter sincerity of purpose vastly strengthened the exemplary leadership of Mullá Ḥusayn. Thus, when Quddús rode into the Shrine compound and dismounted, he faced the three hundred thirteen valorous ones and uttered a momentous, if veiled, declaration concerning the Qayyúm, He Who would arise, saying:

'The Remnant of God (Baqíyyatu'lláh) will be best for you if ye are of those who believe!*

Immediately he asked for news of Jináb-i-Bahá from Mullá Ḥusayn, to whom he later entrusted his homilies on the Báb, on Bahá and on Ṭáhirih to be read to the Bábís for their confirmation. By his coming a potent charge was injected into the small band of defenders, now ready to withstand whatever might portend. Soon arrived the Sháh's troops, increased in numbers by local levies of soldiery to a total of some twelve thousand men. With command headquarters at the village of Vás-kas, the army began its siege with infantry, cavalry and artillery drawing a tight noose around the unprepossessing small fort. Yet the great odds were sharply reduced by the low morale of the superstitious and largely ignorant soldiery who doubtless felt uneasy at being sent to destroy the followers of one rumored to be the promised Qá'im. Some surely were even receptive to the Faith of those they faced. Moreover, the Báb's spiritual leadership was said to be superhuman, that He was acting as the very arm of God.

There ensued a series of attacks and counter-attacks, week after grim week, wherein the astonishing bravery of the essentially untrained Bábís was displayed again and again to such effect that the government soldiers were badly beaten several times. Once they were put to flight with their commander, the Governor of Mázindarán, Prince Mihdí-Qulí, fleeing his camp when it was overrun in the middle of the night. During the months of siege and growing hardship for the Bábí defenders, the inspired Quddús compiled his eulogy on 'He Who Shall be Made Manifest', a commentary begun during his imprisonment in Sárí which anticipates the Supreme Messenger of God shortly to reveal Himself to the world.

In fulfillment of his promise, Jináb-i-Bahá left Teheran for Núr at

* This quotation by Quddús was a cryptic saying, a prophecy of Muḥammad Himself concerning the Qá'im, and would have been immediately understood by the companions, who were thorough Qur'ánic scholars, although here Quddús plainly meant Jináb-i-Bahá, Bahá'u'lláh. It would have brought forth a powerful response from the Bábís as being a further confirmation of the truth of their new Faith.

the beginning of December, bringing provisions and supplies for the besieged Bábís, even though he told Ḥájí Mírzá Jání of Ká<u>sh</u>án, the self-chosen historian of the Bábí Cause, that '*If we go* (to <u>Sh</u>ay<u>kh</u> Ṭabarsí), *they will not suffer us to reach the fort, for this is unattainable, and the matter is otherwise predestined.*' Nevertheless, he proceeded toward <u>Sh</u>ay<u>kh</u> Ṭabarsí with eleven Bábí friends, all determined to share the fate of those beleaguered ones. This momentous journey he later recalled.

'*We had intended to send 'Abdu'l-Vahháb, one of our companions, in advance of us, and to request him to announce our approach to the besieged. Though encompassed by the forces of the enemy, we had decided to throw in our lot with those steadfast companions, and to risk the dangers with which they were confronted. This, however, was not to be. The Hand of Omnipotence spared us from their fate and preserved us for the work we were destined to accomplish. In pursuance of God's inscrutable wisdom, the intention we had formed was, before our arrival at the fort, communicated by certain inhabitants of Núr* to Mírzá Taqí, the Governor of Ámul, who sent his men to intercept us.*' The party reached an abandoned village not far from Ámul and settled there for the night, and were planning to try to force their way into the fort on the morrow, but . . . '*While We were resting and taking Our tea, We found ourselves suddenly surrounded by a number of horsemen, who seized Our belongings and captured Our steeds. We were given, in exchange for Our own horse, a poorly saddled animal which We found extremely uncomfortable to ride. The rest of Our companions were conducted, handcuffed, to Ámul.*'[12]

When the little party was arrested by the Governor's men, the leader Jináb-i-Bahá immediately put his captors on their mettle, for both the officers and the largely peasant soldiery of that feudal state knew well the mortal hazards of unwise handling of a powerful and well-placed noble. Hence, alone of the Bábís he remained without fetters on the ride into Ámul. En route he instructed his party to dispose of any documents which would identify them as adherents of the Báb. Although surely all were presumed to be Bábís, Jináb-i-Bahá anticipated an ecclesiastical trial in the presence of a violent Persian mob, where judicial insecurity induced by lack of specific

* Apart from those Núrís who were hostile to what they considered new heresy, the seething complexity of feudal Persian families of that time could have readily produced radical differences of opinion, feelings and purposes among the many relatives of Mírzá Ḥusayn-'Alí, notable among whom was his uncle 'Azíz. Jealousy of his superior position in the family groupings, combined with hidden intrigues perhaps, would induce some to feel themselves willing to conspire to eliminate him from their intimate social competition.

evidence might well spare their lives. Crossing a stream, most of the party discarded their precious Writings, wetting the spoilable inks of the handwritten pages. But one man decided otherwise, upon whose disobedience hinged a significant element of the later trial.

Taken to the Deputy Governor's house in Ámul, Jináb-i-Bahá was quick to feel the fundamental goodwill of Mírzá Muḥammad-Taqí, who also was uneasy in his dealing with a personage from a great family, a man of obviously formidable intellect, courage and presence. In the morning a hearing was held in the mosque, and '*such was the turmoil which the people had raised that above four thousand persons had congregated in the masjid and had crowded onto the roofs of their houses.*'[13] In the mosque, before the local divines, Mírzá Muḥammad-Taqí reprimanded Jináb-i-Bahá for his action in coming to support the embattled Bábís, this in hope of allaying the excitation of the hostile gathering. To his words Bahá gave a sharp rejoinder:

'*We are innocent*', he declared, '*of the guilt they impute to us. Our blamelessness will eventually be established in your eyes. I would advise you to act in a manner that will cause you eventually no regret.*'[14]

When the acting Governor asked the priests to question Jináb-i-Bahá as they wished, to their queries he returned explicit and convincing replies. The chief priest then '*questioned Us regarding the Mission of the Báb. We informed him that, although We had never met Him face to face, yet We cherished . . . a great affection for Him. We expressed Our profound conviction that He had, under no circumstances, acted contrary to the Faith of Islám.*'[15]

The mullá refused to believe this explanation, saying that it was a perversion of the truth. At this moment, those who were searching Bahá's companions discovered in the pocket of Ḥájí Mírzá Jání a manuscript recognized as possibly one of the Báb's Writings. When this was handed to the chief priest he scanned it, then put it aside, crying out to the audience:

'These people, who advance such extravagant claims, have in this very sentence which I have read, betrayed their ignorance of the most rudimentary rules of orthography!'

To which Bahá replied: '*Esteemed and learned divine, these words which you criticize are not the words of the Báb. They have been uttered by no less a personage than the Imám 'Alí, the Commander of the Faithful, in his reply to Kumayl, [son of] Zíyád, whom he had chosen as his companion.*'[16]

To this unassailable fact there could be no satisfactory rejoinder by the chief priest. But a siyyid among the divines vehemently urged death for the followers of the Báb, and other siyyids of Ámul insisted that the Deputy Governor comply with their demands. Much embarrassed, Mírzá Muḥammad-Taqí realized that any indulgence on his part would be fraught with personal danger. By inflicting a befitting punishment upon the captives, he sought to check the mob passions and therefore ordered the bastinado.[17]

Taken to the prayer-house of the chief priest, the first to be bound in order to receive the bastinado was Mullá Báqir of Tabríz. Said he, 'I am only a groom of Mírzá Ḥusayn-'Alí . . .' Whereupon Jináb-i-Bahá intervened and succeeded in inducing his captors to release him. So too he interceded for Ḥájí Mírzá Jání, the merchant of Káshán who, he said, was a mere tradesman and whom he regarded as his guest, so that he himself was responsible for any charges brought against him. Mírzá Yaḥyá, his half-brother and ward, was also set free as soon as Jináb-i-Bahá had declared him to be his attendant.

'*None of these men*', he told the acting Governor, '*are guilty of any crime. If you insist on inflicting your punishment, I offer myself as a willing victim of your chastisement.*'[18] And so, reluctantly, the acting Governor gave orders that Bahá alone should suffer the indignity which he had intended only for his companions. When he had been bound in the humiliating bastinado position, his legs in the air, bare feet exposed and lashed to a bar held by assistants, Mullá Zaynu'l-'Ábidín, Jináb-i-Bahá's paternal uncle and one of the company, threw himself in front of Jináb-i-Bahá's feet, was thrashed, and fainted from the pain. Bahá was beaten then with rods until his feet bled, and removed with his companions to one of the rooms of the mosque, to be held there against the return of the Governor from his visit to Fort Shaykh Ṭabarsí.

The acting Governor was resolved, however, to protect his prisoners from what could too easily be a murderous surprise attack fomented by the divines, and he saw that the mosque was all too vulnerable. Thus he instructed his servants to cut through the bricks of the mosque wall into the captives' room and he engineered an escape in the small hours of the morning, leading the prisoners to his home for their protection. En route they encountered one of the siyyids, who threatened Jináb-i-Bahá with a club. The alarm raised, a crowd of ruffians gathered to shout and hurl stones and rubbish. With cool heads and determination the armed attendants of Mírzá Muḥammad-Taqí escorted the captives to the strongly walled home of their master. Thereafter, for the days of Jináb-i-Bahá's sojourn there, that fortified house lived under veritable siege, with armed men on guard against attack. He recounts that:

The Mosque of Ámul where Mírzá Ḥusayn-'Alí and his eleven companions, captured en route to join the defenders of Shaykh Ṭabarsí, were subjected to a hostile hearing, whereupon Jináb-i-Bahá took upon himself the punishment of all: the bastinado. Below, a typical bastinado scene. (Photograph from Persia, The Awakening East, *by W.D. Cresson)*

'No prisoner has ever been accorded the treatment which I received at the hands of the acting governor of Ámul. He treated me with the utmost consideration and esteem . . . My host was afraid lest the governor (a relative of one of the commanders of forces at the siege) might return from the fort of Ṭabarsí and inflict injury upon me.' To dispel his apprehensions, Bahá assured him that: '*The same Omnipotence Who has delivered us from the hands of the mischief-makers of Ámul, and has enabled us to be received with such hospitality by you in this house, is able to change the heart of the governor and cause him to treat us with no less consideration and love.*'[19]

Suddenly awakened one night by the clamor of people gathered outside the gate-house and anticipating a fresh attack upon them, the Bábís were startled to hear the returned Prince-Governor rebuking the crowd, saying:

'For what reason have these miserable wretches chosen to treat so disrespectfully a guest . . . who has not been given the chance to defend himself? What is their justification for having demanded that he be immediately put to death? . . . If they be sincere in their claims to be devotedly attached to Islám . . . let them betake themselves to the fort of Shaykh Ṭabarsí and there demonstrate their capacity to defend the Faith of which they profess to be the champions.'[20]

Amazing was such a reaction from the Governor. But what he had seen of the heroism of the defenders of the fort had quite changed his heart and mind, filling him with admiration for a Cause formerly despised and whose progress he had strenuously resisted.[21] Humbly and respectfully he apologized to Jináb-i-Bahá for the insolence of the inhabitants of this town which he had been chosen to govern. He paid a glowing tribute to Mullá Ḥusayn, expatiating upon his resourcefulness, his intrepidity, his skill, his nobleness of soul. A few days later he arranged for the safe departure of Jináb-i-Bahá and his companions for Núr and Teheran.*

The Ámul incident well reveals the resourcefulness, hardihood and selflessness of the thirty-one-year old nobleman of Núr, now so

* In another reference to the Ámul incident, Bahá'u'lláh states: '*While confined in the prison of the Land of Mím (Mázindarán) We were one day delivered into the hands of the divines. Thou canst well imagine what befell Us.*' (Bahá'u'lláh, *Epistle to the Son of the Wolf*, p. 77.) With regard to the entire Ámul incident involving Bahá'u'lláh and His party, Balyuzi relates a story which is considerably different from this narrative which draws heavily upon Bahá's own words. Balyuzi adds material from the story as told by 'Abdu'l-Bahá in August 1919, while Nabíl's account apparently draws solely upon the event as recalled by Bahá'u'lláh Himself. (See Nabíl, *The Dawn-Breakers*, pp. 368–376 and 582–584; Balyuzi, *Bahá'u'lláh, The King of Glory*, pp. 56–60.)

deeply engaged in the hazardous venture of a new Faith. It is not surprising, moreover, that informants in Núr might apprise the authorities of the intention of a small party of well-identified Bábís to join the defenders of besieged Ṭabarsí, particularly since there had been a summons to the Bábí faithful that they should hasten to enlist under the Black Standards in Mázindarán. Many had answered, slipping into the fort to reinforce the Bábís. It was to the interest of the imperial forces to cut off any further additions of men and supplies which would shore up the losses of the Ṭabarsí defenders. The roads around the fort were therefore watched by the populace and its militia, aroused and eager to destroy the Bábí heretics.

The defense of Shaykh Ṭabarsí was a lost cause from the outset, its defenders aware of, and even eager for, their martyrs' fates. The spirit of their dying for a great Cause in the Path of God was later expressed very powerfully by Bahá'u'lláh in *The Hidden Words*. '*O Son of Being! Seek a martyr's death in My path, content with My pleasure and thankful for that which I ordain, that thou mayest repose with Me beneath the Canopy of majesty behind the tabernacle of glory*'.[22] '*O Son of Man! By My Beauty! To tinge thy hair with thy blood is greater in My sight than the creation of the universe and the light of both worlds. Strive then to attain this, O servant!*'[23] In this spirit of self-sacrifice the brave defenders went to their deaths:

First the dauntless Mullá Ḥusayn was slain in battle and buried inside the Shrine close to the tomb of the saint Shaykh Ṭabarsí, thus to hallow that spot for future centuries of pilgrimage. After an agonizing seven months of siege, lasting from October 1848 to May 1849, with progressive attrition of deaths, and with consumption of the scant supplies and water, the starving survivors under command of a wounded Quddús laid down their arms following an offer of honorable surrender, sworn upon the Qur'án by the Sháh's commander. Ruthlessly betrayed, the Bábís died under the swords of the vengeful soldiers whom they had humbled in many fierce engagements.*

Quddús was taken alive, only to perish gloriously on 15 May 1849 in the streets of his home town of Bárfurúsh, chanting the praises of God, his body then torn to bits by the mob. And yet the blood of the

* The many western accounts of the Shaykh Ṭabarsí siege are covered in the excellent chapter of Momen's *Bábí and Bahá'í Religions*, pp. 91–99. Dr. Momen's own descriptive commentary adds a proper view of the facts as opposed to the often highly imaginative and unfounded elements of the reports made by sundry members of the diplomatic corps, and by those who had access to private or other sources of biased and usually very inaccurate information.

Bábís, including no less than half the first disciples, the Letters of the Living, was far from wasted in this total defeat ordained from the outset. Rather it provided the most profound of stimuli for intensive teaching of the new Cause by the few survivors and by the Bábís far and wide.

In September 1848 Ṭáhirih was reported to have been in Bárfurúsh, a main trade center of that time. Then for about a year she was in hiding in Vaz village, south of Ámul; there she was betrayed, her host killed, and was taken to Teheran in about January 1850. She was interviewed by Áqá Khán and her arrest was communicated to the Sháh, who knew that she was a distinguished poet, famous too for her inspired oratory and extraordinary theological knowledge which made her a match for the most learned of priests. Further, she was reported to be of great beauty and of the highest intellect, a womanly prodigy (see Note 10).

While confined to the house of the kalantar, and in response, it seems, to an offer of marriage from the Sháh if she would but recant her faith, the poetess composed an ode in couplet form, the last four lines of which express what appear to have been her feelings: 'For thee, take Alexander's pomp and throne, / For me, the ways and habit of the nun. / If that is good, welcome art thou to it, / If this is bad, then good is it for me.'[24]

On 26 November 1849, the Báb dispatched from Chihríq the priest Ádí-Guzal of Maraghih, entitled 'Alíy-i-Sayyáḥ, the traveler, to make a pilgrimage on His behalf to the now holy spot of Shaykh Ṭabarsí, where the blood of His devoted ones had sanctified the ground. Sayyáḥ was instructed to offer tribute to the martyrs and to bring back earth from the graves of Quddús and Mullá Ḥusayn. These he did on 23 January 1850. Returning through Teheran from his mission, his heart now afire, he came to visit Jináb-i-Bahá. The faithful brother Mírzá Músá has recounted how . . .

'Despite the cold and snow of a rigorous winter, he appeared attired in the garb of a dervish, poorly clad, barefoot and dishevelled. And no sooner had Siyyid Yaḥyá of Dáráb, Vaḥíd, coming from Yazd that winter and then a guest in the home of Bahá, had been informed of the return of Sayyáh from the fort of Ṭabarsí, than he, oblivious of the pomp and circumstances to which a man of his position had been accustomed, rushed forward and flung himself at the feet of the pilgrim. Embracing his legs, which were covered with mud to the knees, he kissed them devoutly.'

Said Mírzá Músá of that moment: 'I was amazed that day at the many evidences of loving solicitude which [Bahá] evinced toward

Vaḥíd. He showed him such favors as I had never seen him extend to anyone. The manner of his conversation left no doubt in me that this same Vaḥíd would ere long distinguish himself by deeds no less remarkable than those which had immortalized the defenders of the fort of Ṭabarsí.'[25]

While the wondrously learnèd Vaḥíd was yet a guest in the home of Mírzá Ḥusayn-'Alí, an extraordinary discussion occurred between himself and Ṭáhirih, two singularly endowed fellow Bábís. Upon Vaḥíd's arrival, the poetess had come from the house of the mayor for a permitted visit,* and sat in the parlor of lady Ásíyih's room listening to him from behind a door curtain as he discoursed with fervid eloquence on the signs and verses that pointed to the advent of the new Manifestation. The five-year old 'Abbás, son of the host, was sitting in her lap as she followed the remarkable testimonies flowing ceaselessly from the lips of that matchlessly erudite man.† Suddenly interrupting him and raising her voice, she vehemently declared:

'O Yaḥyá! Let deeds, not words, testify to thy faith, if thou art a man of true learning. Cease idly repeating the traditions of the past, for the day of service, of steadfast action, is come. Now is the time to show forth the true signs of God, to rend asunder the veils of idle fancy, to promote the Word of God, and to sacrifice ourselves in His path. Let deeds, not words, be our adorning!'[26] Challenged by these ringing words which she applied to them both, Vaḥíd was further galvanized to meet his great destiny.

Of these days Ḥájí Mírzá Jání wrote: 'I observed in [Vaḥíd's] august countenance the signs of a glory and power which I had not noticed during my first journey with him to the capital, nor on other occasions of meeting . . .'[27] Indeed, the great scholar was being surcharged with spirit in that mansion of Jináb-i-Bahá as he prepared to return to Yazd and thereafter to his home town of Nayríz in the far south.

---

* Although Ṭáhirih had been held in house confinement since her arrival in Teheran in early 1850, Balyuzi expresses the conviction (*Bahá'u'lláh, The King of Glory*, pp. 63–64) that it would have been easy for someone of the status of Jináb-i-Bahá to arrange for a brief release to his hands, under guarantee of her return. Perhaps it was known, too, that she had won a certain favor from the Sh͟áh, and this made such an action more permissible.

† The story of Ṭáhirih and Siyyid Yaḥyá, Vaḥíd, was a memory of 'Abdu'l-Bahá, told years later, but which He recalled very distinctly despite His then being five and one-half years of age, so powerful an experience was it. (See Blomfield, *The Chosen Highway*, p. 22; Balyuzi, *Bahá'u'lláh, The King of Glory*, pp. 63–64, and 'Abdu'l-Bahá, *Memorials of the Faithful*, p.200).

Before the departure of Sayyáḥ for Chihríq, Jináb-i-Bahá entrusted him with an epistle, the text of which he had dictated to half-brother Mírzá Yaḥyá, sending it in the youth's name to the Báb. In due time a reply in the Báb's own handwriting was received, in which he committed Mírzá Yaḥyá to the care of Bahá and urged that attention be paid to his education and training.

However, apart from such open exchanges of correspondence via Bábí couriers such as Sayyah, there is evidence of a more crucial communication of confidential letters between the Báb in Chihríq prison and His greatest fellow and equal, Jináb-i-Bahá in his Teheran mansion. Their shared foresights anticipated severe trials for the Bábís which would threaten the very survival of the young Faith. The Bábís had to be sustained and directed, their enthusiasm constantly renewed, their Islamic conditioning steadily converted to new patterns of behavior. To undertake these spiritual and intellectual tasks of education Jináb-i-Bahá clearly had the necessary sagacity and intuitive bonding with the gentle Báb.

During this period began Bahá's intensified tutelage of his young Bábí half-brother and ward Yaḥyá whom, during later dissensions, he admonished to '*remember how we nurtured thee by day and night for service to the Cause*'.[28] Meanwhile, the Báb knew that His Mission was soon to end, and many were His allusions to the Great One Who would soon come. Many too were His promises to sundry disciples that they would see and know the Qayyúm, the Most Great One Who would arise.

In those days when Jináb-i-Bahá had returned to Teheran from the Ámul incident to again make his home the center of Bábí activity, an eighteen-year-old shepherd and theology student, Yár-Muḥammad of Zarand,* arrived to learn fully of the Faith at this hour when the Bayán, the great primary Book of the Báb's Revelation, was being disseminated. At Jináb-i-Bahá's mansion he met his esteemed hostess Ásíyih Khánum, who healed his sore eyes.† Also meeting Mírzá Yaḥyá in that household, he was startled at his features and his conversation which scarcely matched the rumors of a high destiny. But he became enamored of the beautiful boy 'Abbás, whom he was

* The youth Yár-Muḥammad (Yár means 'intimate friend') of Zarand earned the title Nabíl-i-A'ẓam, the noble or excellent one, through his zeal, loyalty, and assiduous collection of eyewitness stories of the events of the Bábí-Bahá'í religious emergence. His *The Dawn-Breakers* qualifies as the definitive early history of the Faith; much of it was read or heard by Bahá'u'lláh Himself.

† Trachoma and other forms of chronic eye infections were dangerously common in nineteenth-century Iran.

able to serve on a number of occasions. And as the troublous year of 1850 began in the capital city, his and many other appraising eyes saw clearly that Jináb-i-Bahá was the axis of this evolving Faith.

In Teheran in early February 1850, fourteen Bábís had been arrested for their Faith. Held in the house of the mayor, Maḥmúd Khán (where Ṭáhirih was held in an upper room), the men were subjected to dire pressures. Under threat of death seven recanted their Faith and were released. The other seven, representing many classes of Persian society, were sentenced to execution by Prime Minister Taqí Khán, who was determined to extirpate the emergent Faith which threatened to become a powerful force in the land, particularly since it had demonstrated its attraction for men and women of diverse origins and ranks, cogently persuading them of its truth. Thus on February 19 or 20 he sent the seven to the public headsman in the Sabzih-Maydán, that great square close to the palace around which lived the foreign ambassadors. Each of the seven sold his life with such spirit and selflessness, with such phenomenal bravery and fortitude in proclaiming his newfound Faith to the very moment of decapitation that many onlookers, however hardened to the crudities of Persian injustice, were compelled to admiration and even homage. For three days the corpses and heads of the Seven Martyrs of Teheran were left in the square to be reviled and desecrated, and were then cast into a common grave, a pit outside the Gate of Sháh 'Abdu'l-'Aẓím.

The illumined Siyyid Yaḥyá Vaḥíd, after wonderfully fruitful days of teaching during 1849, had set forth in the autumn for Qazvín, Qum and Káshán, and on to Iṣfahán, Ardistán and Ardikán. Wherever he went he fearlessly taught the Faith from the pulpits of the mosques, winning many new Bábís. In mid-winter he briefly returned from Yazd to Teheran, there to encounter Sayyáḥ on his return from Shaykh Ṭabarsí and to be challenged by Ṭáhirih. Rejoining his wife, daughter and three sons in Yazd for the Persian New Year in March 1850, he vigorously and dramatically expounded the Cause of the Báb, exciting a great response and many converts, but also inducing active opposition instigated by those fearful of his influence. Not wishing to sponsor an insurrection, Vaḥíd departed on May 10 with two sons and two disciples for Nayríz, not far from Shíráz, where he met the warmest of welcomes from the people and announced to them, 'O people! I have come unto you with a life-giving Tablet from 'Alí (the Báb), the Sovereign Lord.'[29] Attacked by the forces of the local Governor, Vaḥíd took refuge in the nearby ruined fort of Khájih with some of his followers, and with them was able, through sheer inspired valor, to disperse a thousand-man force besieging them. When the Governor of Shíráz sent additional forces, the out-manned Bábís still confounded the soldiery, until by treachery the army captured Vaḥíd and massacred the entire population of Bábís of the area, Vaḥíd's heroic death occurring on 29 June 1850. The valedictory from Jináb-i-Bahá is an ultimately befitting one: '*Great is thy blessedness, O Yaḥyá* [Vaḥíd], *inasmuch as thou didst fulfil thy pledge in the Day when the heavens and the earth were created, didst receive the Book of God with such resolve as is born of thy faith, and through the vitalizing breezes of His days thou hast been attracted to the sanctuary of His beauty.*'[30] '*Therefore God hath caused his name to be inscribed by the Pen of Glory upon the Scrolls of immortality. Manifold were the woes and sufferings that befell him, yet patiently did he bear all his tribulations and he was always thankful and long-suffering under dire circumstances.*'[31] And of the brave Bábís who died with Vaḥíd he uttered an ultimate accolade: '*Know ye of a certainty that God hath inscribed your names upon His sacred Scrolls and ordained for you a glorious station in the all-highest Paradise.*'[32]

The succession of tragic events produced Bábí sufferings beyond measure, and not only saw the elimination of a high proportion of the Báb's most effective supporters, but also of several thousands of believers; together and singly the tragedies evoked deep sorrow in the blessed Báb. From Máh-kú and Chihríq fortresses His flow of letters reflected an ultimate sadness of heart; for how many were the precious humans sacrificed, fulfilling God's purpose with their spilled lifeblood! And His sadness deepened as the shadows darkened about Him.

With Bábí bonfires flaring here and there – and who could know where next? – Prime Minister Taqí Khán determined to eliminate the prime source of the dissent, the Báb Himself, saying: 'Nothing short of the remedy I advocate can uproot this evil and bring us the peace for which we long.'[33] In addition, he saw himself as protector of the young and inexperienced Sháh, the disturbances as a test of his authority and competence. Indeed, his successive steps of suppression and planned elimination of the Bábís were described by them as a catastrophe.

The Báb had, however, anticipated the mortal threat many months before the actual event and began to close out His affairs. Already He was busy instructing His disciples in their special missions, was writing letters of instruction, and was quietly delivering the spiritual leadership and organizational responsibilities to Jináb-i-Bahá. In early June He placed His documents, Tablets, pen-case, seals and agate rings in a specially prepared coffer, then entrusted the box to Mullá Báqir, one of the Letters of the Living. In a letter to Mírzá Aḥmad, His secretary, He enclosed the key to the coffer. Thereupon Mullá Báqir hastened to Qum, seat of fanatical Shi'ite Islám in Persia, to find Mírzá Aḥmad for delivery of the priceless articles.

When Mírzá Aḥmad opened the coffer, he found a scroll of pale blue paper, of the most delicate texture, on which the Báb, in His exquisite shikastih* script and in the form of a pentacle, had penned about five hundred verses containing some three hundred and sixty derivatives of the word Bahá. The scroll was in a state of perfect preservation, and at first sight gave the impression of being a printed rather than a written page. So fine and intricate was the penmanship that, viewed from a distance, the writing appeared as a single wash of ink on the paper. Replacing the scroll in the coffer, Mírzá Aḥmad proceeded to nearby Teheran on the very day he received the charge from the Báb, divulging only that the trust was to be delivered into the hands of Jináb-i-Bahá.[34] Thus clearly, if obliquely, the nobleman of Núr, given the highest trust by the Báb, became the center of the Bábí Cause.

The hour of the Báb's sacrifice was close. In early June, despite attempted interventions by Mírzá Ḥusayn-'Alí and Ḥájí Sulaymán Khán,† the Prime Minister ordered Prince Ḥamzih, the just and kindly Governor of Azerbaijan, to transfer the Báb from castle Chihríq to Tabríz. On the heels of the first order came a second: to execute his Prisoner on the day of His arrival in Tabríz. But Prince Ḥamzih refused to carry out so despicable a task, and Mírzá Ḥasan Khán, brother of the Prime Minister, was ordered to fulfill the edict.

With the Báb, four other companions were taken for martyrdom. Three were spared. The impassioned youth Muḥammad-'Alí of Zunúz, entitled Anís (the Companion) alone was allowed to share with the Báb the honor of facing the Bahádurán Christian regiment of Urúmiyyih, commanded by colonel Sám Khán, erstwhile admirer of Mullá Ḥusayn.[35] It was that fateful noon of 9 July, 1850, in the barracks square of Tabríz, close to the Árg (citadel), an immense crowd on the rooftops round about. When Sám Khán expressed to the Báb his deep displeasure at being called upon to execute so noble

* The shikastih script is a beautifully graphic form of the Arabic or Persian writing. Its occurrence in correspondence or writings of that time immediately stamped its author as being from among the highest religious or secular classes.

† Ḥájí Sulaymán Khán was the son of Yaḥyá Khán, once army chief and head of the royal stewards of Prince 'Abbás Mírzá in Azerbaijan.

a person, he was told by the Báb to do his duty. Thereupon the regiment fired its volley at the two suspended by ropes from a spike fixed in a pillar, only to discover, when the black powder gunsmoke had lifted, that the youth Anís stood before them unscathed. The Báb had disappeared, having returned to His nearby cell to complete certain unfinished affairs. Ordering his men from the barracks and refusing any further duty, Sám Khán marched his men away from their personal miracle.

A Muslim regiment under Colonel Áqá Ján Khamsih was ordered to replace the Christians, and this time their volley found its mark, the gentle Báb and his faithful follower, their bodies hammered into one fused tissue by the musket balls of the soldiery, their heads remaining essentially unscathed. The great Forerunner had fulfilled His Ministry and hallowed with His blood the coming of that Great One soon to reveal Himself.[36] One supernal life had gloriously ended. It was the moment before the rising of the Sun.

Say: verily the king of Persia hath put the Beloved of the world to death in order to quench the resplendent light that God hath ignited amidst His creatures and to keep back the people from the waters of everlasting life that have streamed forth in the days of God, the Mighty, the Most Generous.

Bahá'u'lláh

The barracks square in Tabríz, where at noon on July 9, 1850, the Báb with Anís, His companion, was executed by a regimental firing squad. The 'X' on the fourth pillar from the left marks the spot of the spike from which the two young men were suspended to face the lethal volley.

7 Banishment and First Recognition

Ye slew Him, however, in such circumstances as no man hath ever witnessed. The heavens wept sore over Him, and the souls of them who are nigh unto God cried out for His affliction . . .[1]

Bahá'u'lláh

The shattered bodies of the Báb and Anís were exposed to the sun, winds and dust, and to the carrion birds and beasts at the edge of the moat near the city gate. And on the day after the execution the Russian consul Anitchkov sent an aide with an artist to record the tragic results.* Thereafter Ḥájí Sulaymán Khán, abetted by his close friend the Ṣúfí mayor of Tabríz, teamed with one Ḥájí Alláh-Yár to remove the holy remains from the moat, acting in the black night before the second morning. The sentinels, well-bribed and sleeping, did not interfere.[2]† Sulaymán Khán then secretly shrouded the shattered bodies in white silk, placed them in a chest, and conveyed

---

* This drawing has been long sought by Bahá'ís, but never found in the Russian records of that time and place. It was a 'faithful portrait' of the Báb, as recorded by one Ḥájí 'Alí-'Askar in Nabíl, *The Dawn-Breakers*, p. 518.

† Before His death, the Báb is reported to have sent a sealed letter to Ḥájí Sulaymán Khán of Tabríz. His orders were to open it only upon His martyrdom, and therein were given the following instructions: 'Six months from the time of writing this, on such-and-such a day, I shall suffer martyrdom in Tabríz along with one named Mírzá Muḥammad-'Alí. Be it incumbent on thee [to observe an attitude of] patience and self-restraint, neither must thou contend with anyone. Two nights after my martyrdom thou must go, and, by some means or other, buy my body and the body of Mírzá Muḥammad-'Alí from the sentinels for four hundred tumáns, and keep them in thine house for six months. Afterwards lay Áká Muḥammad-'Alí with his face upon my face, place [the two bodies] in a strong chest, and send it with a letter to Jenáb-i-Bahá.' (Browne, *New History*, p. 310.) Unfortunately, for much of the introduction of the Bábí-Bahá'í Faith to the West, Dr. Browne was thoroughly duped by the followers of Azal and by Azal himself, often accepting whole-cloth versions of events gravely slanted to favor their point of view. (See Balyuzi, *Edward Granville Browne and the Bahá'í Faith*.) Nevertheless, certain portions of *The New History* provide useful details of events reported, where no need existed to corrupt the facts, as seems to be true of this purported letter.

them surreptitiously to a silk factory owned by Mírzá Ḥusayn, a Bábí of nearby Mílán. Deeply grieved that his ardent hope to rescue the Báb by ruse or by force had not been realized, for he had arrived home in Tabríz too late, Sulaymán Khán nevertheless had been able to contrive the first preservation of the priceless remains.[3]*

He promptly sent a rider at all speed down the long, rocky and mountainous road to report to Jináb-i-Bahá hundreds of miles and many days away in Teheran. Forthwith Bahá instructed his brother Músá to dispatch a chosen messenger who would secretly convey the remains from Tabríz to the capital. This decision was prompted by the wish of the Báb Himself, as expressed in a Tablet revealed on the exile journey to Máh-kú when He was not far from the Shrine of 'Abdu'l-'Aẓím close to old Rayy,† the ancient and once-populous capital of the kingdom of Medea whose ruins lay south of Teheran.

'Well is it with you,' the Báb addressed the buried saint, 'to have found your resting place in Rayy, under the shadow of My Beloved. Would that I might be entombed within the precincts of that holy ground.'[4]

Sulaymán Khán, his guidance made clear by the courier, was alerted to carry out the early transfer of the bodies from Mílán to Teheran when it was safe to do so. Clandestinely, in nightly forced hard rides, the remains were transported to the capital and hidden first in the Shrine of 'Abdu'l-'Aẓím and later in that of the Imám-Zádih Ḥasan. Later, the hallowed chest was removed to Sulaymán Khán's Teheran house in the Sar-Chishmih Quarter, thence to a hiding place in the Shrine of the Imám-Zádih Ma'ṣúm.

Mírzá Naṣru'lláh of Núr, Áqá Khán, was the first official in Teheran to hear of the extraordinary drama surrounding the martyrdom of the Báb. Earlier, when he had been the Sháh's Minister of War, he had been bastinadoed and banished in disgrace to Káshán at the very time when the Báb was passing through that city in 1847. Also, during that autumn and winter one of his unoccupied homes in Teheran had sheltered Ṭáhirih, his sister acting as her hostess. He had been taught the precepts of the new Faith by Ḥájí Mírzá Jání of

* There are a number of stories of the rescue of the Báb's remains from the moat, and this account seeks what seems to be the most logical and consistent among the details of that feat.

† The Shrine, located south of Teheran, near old Rayy, houses three tombs: those of the saint Abu'l-Qásím 'Abdu'l-'Aẓím (d. 861 AD), of a holy lady whose death dates to before the time of Islám, and of the Báb's beloved Imám-Zádih Ḥasan, son of the seventh Imám, Músá Káẓim.

Ká<u>sh</u>án, and had promised Jání that, if the love he bore the new Revelation would cause him to regain his lost position, he would exert his utmost endeavor to secure the well-being and safety of the persecuted community. Jání reported the promise to the Báb, whereupon His reply conveyed assurances to the humbled minister that ere long he would be summoned to Teheran to be invested by the sovereign with a position second only to the <u>Sh</u>áh himself. He warned Mírzá Áqá <u>Kh</u>án not to forget his promise, but to strive to realize it. Delighted with the happy prediction, Mírzá Áqá <u>Kh</u>án repeated his pledge of future aid to the Bábís.[5]

When news of the martyrdom reached him, he had already regained kingly favor, had been named a Trustee of the Government, and hoped for appointment as Prime Minister. Quick to inform Mírzá Ḥusayn-'Alí, his neighbor and distant relative of Núr and Teheran and his frequent guest at Af<u>ch</u>ih, and confident that the new Cause would not long survive the death of its Author, he strongly expressed the hope that the fires of Bábí religious dissension would now be extinguished.

'*Not so,*' was Mírzá Ḥusayn-'Alí's sharp rejoinder, '*if this be true, you can be certain that the flame that has been kindled will, by this very act, blaze forth more fiercely than ever, and will set up a conflagration such as the combined forces of the statesmen of this realm will be powerless to quench.*'[6]

Mírzá Áqá <u>Kh</u>án was older than Mírzá Ḥusayn-'Alí by several decades. With his pouchy hooded and prominent eyes, a dense and unruly beard crowding his lips and cheeks, he already showed the wear and tear of the highly dangerous and stressful roles he had played. Deeply indebted to his young neighbor, for he had been cured by him of an assertedly incurable illness and several times had been given Mírzá Ḥusayn-'Alí's financial aid, he partook of the general respect accorded the brilliant youth whose aspirations were so different from his own. A son, then a Director of Public Order, on one occasion asked him whether he did not think that Mírzá Ḥusayn-'Alí, who of all the sons of the late Vazír Buzurg had shown himself the most capable, had failed to live up to the traditions of his father, disappointing the hopes reposed in him. To this his father replied:

'My son, do you really believe him to be an unworthy son of his father? All that either of us can hope to achieve is but a fleeting and precarious allegiance which will vanish as soon as our days are ended . . . Not so . . . with [Ḥusayn-'Alí]. Unlike the great ones of the earth, whatever be their race or rank, he is the object of a love and devotion such as time cannot dim nor enemy destroy.'[7]

Such a tribute from a worldly court politician of long acquaintance was justly earned. As a neighbor, family friend, distant relative, and former associate of Mírzá Buzurg, Áqá Khán had actually observed the young man, both at home in Núr and in the capital city. He was therefore willing to predict so great a destiny, prophetic as it was, and mixed as may have been his own feelings about the extraordinary young man.

There were others of the court who wished to fathom the depths of knowledge shown by the young noble, to seek his surprising insights. Thus, one day in Teheran the Prime Minister Taqí Khán of Faráhán, who had been responsible for the Bábí persecution, summoned him to an interview. The Minister knew Mírzá Ḥusayn-'Alí well, hence his interrogation was a friendly one on the surface, although its true purposes might be something other. His bold direct gaze upon the mild young Núrí, his shaggy beard emphasizing that roughness of character which tended to negate his excellent reformist purposes, Taqí asked whether there was any reference to himself in the Qu'rán. Mírzá Ḥusayn-'Alí responded surprisingly:

'*Yes, where it states, "I take refuge in the God of Mercy from thee! if thou art Taqí, [pious]*" '[8]

Repressing his anger, the Prime Minister asked again: 'And what of my father?'

Again Mírzá Ḥusayn-'Alí responded, '*In the verse which states: "God has made a covenant with us, that we believe not any Messenger until He brings us a qurbán [a sacrifice] which fire shall devour.*" '[9]

Harmless as were the citations, yet dangerously clever in revealing the young man's Qur'ánic knowledge, Mírzá Taqí Khán was quick to see the infuriating implications of both. Particularly the second, for his father Qurbán had been a cook in the service of the Qá'im-Maqám, a former Prime Minister. And surely he envied those of noble birth, and seethed when his humble origins were suggested.*

The martyrdom of the Báb had created a ferment of confusion, indignation and righteous anger among the Bábís, who now felt themselves to be bereft of sure guidance. It was scarcely surprising, then, that disorders began in the turbulent town of Zanján in Khamsih, a district of Gílán province, the dissension centering about the fiery Mullá Muḥammad-'Alí, entitled Ḥujjat (the Proof) by the Báb. Accounted by many as the most learnèd and effective of the

---

* Chapter 14 of Balyuzi, *Bahá'u'lláh, The King of Glory*, pp. 69–73, relates the career of Mírzá Taqí Khán in some detail, and presents a balanced picture of this able and brave, if ruthless man.

Mírzá Taqí Khán, the first Grand Vizier of the young Náṣiri'd-Dín Sháh. Ruthless, resolute, resourceful, determined to stamp out the Bábí hazard to stability of the realm, but also a reformer bent upon steps of modernization in backward Persia.

The minor Shrine of the Imám-Zádih Ḥasan, noted for the beauty of its dome, a tomb near to and west of Teheran which served as the second place of concealment of the precious remains of the Báb and Anís.

Báb's disciples and exponents, he had triumphed in theological debate over the priests of both Zanján and Teheran. It was he whose resolute followers had not been allowed by the Báb to rescue Him from His guards on the journey to Máh-kú after He had passed through their humble town. When polarization of the Zanjání populace brought open conflict and a summoning of troops, the Bábís fortified a portion of the town, fought bravely against great odds for several months until, on 8 January 1851, Ḥujjat died of battle wounds, and soon thereafter his followers were betrayed and butchered. But again the deaths were so nobly endured that the Faith won prestige and new followers, even as the heroic martyrdom of the Báb was stiffening Bábí determination to believe and to resist.

In the confused and turbulent days following the Báb's martyrdom there were a number of Bábís who had the temerity to see themselves as leaders of the community, and who displayed various levels of spiritual and intellectual capacity which in their own minds logically gave them the position of the Báb's successor. No less than twenty-five Bábís ultimately asserted their pretensions to leadership. Among them the most prominent and demanding were the blind Siyyid Baṣír of India, and Mullá Shaykh 'Alí of Turshíz who had been entitled 'Aẓím (the Great One) by the Báb. At the calm center of the Bábí vortex at this time of interregnum was the family of Mírzá Ḥusayn-'Alí in Teheran and Núr.[10] Here lived a person considered by the Bábís to be the nominee for the dangerous post of successor: the eighteen-year-old Yaḥyá, whose supporters began to use the high-flown if vague title of Ṣubḥ-i-Azal (the Morn of Eternity) taken from a passage in the Báb's Writings. Addressed to the recessive and unassuming Yaḥyá there was the simple signed letter of the Báb wherein, in an almost offhand manner, He had stated: '. . . *verily thou art a mighty way of truth*'. The Báb Himself had effaced from the Bayán the question of succession by saying: '*There will be no mention of a successor in this Dispensation,*'* nor indeed was it within His role or power to do so. His other Writings made reference only to 'letters' and 'mirrors' among His outstanding disciples; one 'mirror' was Yaḥyá.[11] In any event, the primary thrust of the Báb's Writing was to tell of the imminent coming of 'Him Whom God will make Manifest'. (See Note 11.)

From Badasht onward Jináb-i-Bahá had quietly assumed both organizational and spiritual leadership of the Bábís, his high destiny apparently fully known to the Báb during the years of their

* Section 6, Chapter 14, of the Persian Bayán.

correspondence. Some others could perceive the truth and were convinced that Bahá was the *deus ex machina* of the ardent Bábís. For example, one Siyyid 'Abdu'r-Raḥím, a close student of the Báb's extant Writings, had collected many verses which he felt pointed to the young nobleman of Núr as the Qayyúm, the Most Great One Who was to be made manifest. He had been strengthened in his conviction through observing the great respect shown to Jináb-i-Bahá by Quddús and Ṭáhirih at that turning-point gathering of Badasht, and came to Teheran to confirm his opinion, considering Yaḥyá to be a person and name without substance. Thus, meeting Jináb-i-Bahá in the bazaar, 'Abdu'r-Raḥím was startled to be invited to his home. There Bahá called for tea, and Yaḥyá brought the samovar and served the tea, the while standing silently in the presence of his elder brother, who expatiated with great eloquence upon meaningful subjects. When the tea was finished, Jináb-i-Bahá stood up, turned to Yaḥyá, and said simply: '*He has come to see you!*' and withdrew. 'Abdu'r-Raḥím bowed low to express his respect, but Yaḥyá said nothing, nothing at all.[12]

In early June of 1851 the Grand Vazír Taqí Khán, who was now the Sháh's brother-in-law, expressed the wish to have a visit with Mírzá Ḥusayn-'Alí. At the meeting in his office the Minister was superficially cordial, yet great tension must have been tangible in that elegant chamber of the second most powerful person of the land. The Vazír's pearl-studded kingly robe contrasted with the severity of his tall black hat, emphasizing the hostility felt from the broad-faced, ruthless man behind the rough beard. Quickly, sharply, with his close-set icy eyes he impaled the calm, unafraid, luminous young man, revealing his purpose for the polite summons by saying in gently insinuating fashion:

'I am well aware of the nature and influence of your activities, and am firmly convinced that were it not for the support and assistance which you have extended to Mullá Ḥusayn and his companions, neither he nor his band of inexperienced students would have been capable of resisting for seven months the forces of the imperial government. The ability and skill with which you have managed to direct and encourage those efforts could not fail to excite my admiration, but I have been unable to obtain any evidence whereby I could establish your complicity in this affair. I feel it a pity that so resourceful a person should not be given an opportunity to serve his country and sovereign. The thought has come to me to suggest that you visit Karbilá in these days when the Sháh is contemplating a visit to Iṣfahán.* It is my intention to be enabled, upon your return, to confer upon you the position of Amír-Díván (Head of the Court) a function you could admirably discharge.'

Mírzá Ḥusayn-'Alí protested vehemently at these accusations and refused to accept the position offered as a bribe. But he well knew how close to the heart of Bábí viability the Prime Minister was stabbing when on circumstantial evidence he so blandly accused the young Núrí of sedition, and then almost casually banished him from the capital and the country. Reflecting upon this near-strike by Taqí Khán, Mírzá Ḥusayn-'Alí commented that:

'*Had the [Prime Minister] been aware of my true position, he would certainly have laid hold on me. He exerted the utmost effort to discover the real situation, but was unsuccessful. God wished him to be ignorant of it.*'[13]

Indeed, Prime Ministers are chosen in recognition of their shrewd judgments of men and for their complex reach of mind, since key national officers are invariably besieged by contending personalities and must confront highly complicated issues. This able first Prime Minister of the youthful Sháh was a bold reformer, upright within his code of behavior, innovative and industrious. An outstanding contribution was his sponsorship in 1852 of the first Persian institution of higher learning, the College of Arts and Technologies located inside the palace compound,† with the Austrian engineer Major August Krziz as his technical adviser. But he was also a man thoroughly fitted for and adapted to his hideously corrupt world, strong-willed, imperious, determined to survive in often deadly power games. He was intensely sensitive to the Bábí movement, whose dynamics could so easily come to be a destabilizing force within the Islamic church-state which he administered. Perhaps despite himself he even felt something of the spirit of the new Faith which so energized its believers. His politician's gambits with the thirty-four year old Mírzá Ḥusayn-'Alí were classic: remove the dangerous young man temporarily from friends and resources, and simultaneously seek to buy him as a promising lieutenant if he proved corruptible, perhaps as a move against his rivel Áqá Khán.

---

* A recollection of this event was this: '*At the time when His Majesty the Sháh . . . was planning a journey to Iṣfahán, this Wronged One . . . visited the holy and luminous resting-places of the Imáms, may the blessings of God be upon them!*' (Bahá'u'lláh, *Epistle to the Son of the Wolf*, p. 20.)

† Bahá'u'lláh saw clearly the great educational needs of Persia saying: '*. . . most of the people in Persia continue to be deprived of the benefits of profitable counsels and remain sorely lacking in useful sciences and arts.*' *Tablets of Bahá'u'lláh*, p. 91.)

But behind the suggestion and the offer was the threat. Karbilá and Najaf were swarming with expatriate Persian pilgrims willing to supply surveillance for a price. And of course the suggestion was a firm order of banishment.

The immediacy of departure had not been specified at that momentous interview. But a few short days of preparation and of farewells to wives and children, relatives and friends were necessary before Mírzá Ḥusayn-'Alí could depart, accompanied only by kinsmen Shukru'lláh of Núr and Muḥammad of Mázindarán, a survivor of Fort Shaykh Ṭabarsí. Left behind was a grieving and worried family, keenly aware of the official nature of his exile but unsure of the true plans of the dangerous Taqí Khán, who might easily be plotting his death in Iraq, far from his loyal relatives and friends.

The dusty road led westward to Kirmánsháh across the four-thousand-foot Iranian plateau ribbed with its mountain spines; there he spent the month of Ramaḍán, the Islamic period of fasting. And there he was sought out by Mullá Muḥammad of Zarand, Nabíl, come to visit his mentor Mírzá Aḥmad who had been actively teaching the Bábí precepts to Íldirum Mírzá, the Prince Governor of Khurram-Ábád. Coming to meet their esteemed visitor Jináb-i-Bahá, Mullá Muḥammad and Mírzá Aḥmad found him engaged in reading the Qur'án aloud to guests, then citing and commenting upon selected verses. To him Muḥammad presented Prince Íldirum's written message to Mírzá Aḥmad in which he assured him of his devotion to the Cause of the Báb. After perusing the letter, Bahá spoke candidly:

'*The faith which a member of the Qájár dynasty professes cannot be depended upon. His declarations are insincere. Expecting that the Bábís will one day assassinate the sovereign, he harbors in his heart the hope of being acclaimed by them the successor. The love he professes for the Báb is actuated by that motive.*'[14]

Within a few months the Bábís knew the truth of that judgment, for Prince Íldirum ordered the cruel killing of blind Siyyid Basír of India, he who had claimed so high a station after the Báb's death and who had become well known to Jináb-i-Bahá during the four months he had once spent in Núr.

During those same days of July and August in 1851, soon after the departure of Jináb-i-Bahá from the capital but in pursuance of his instructions, it was propitious to move the remains of the Báb and His disciple to another hiding place. Brother Músá with Mírzá Aḥmad took the sacred dust from the Shrine of Imám-Zádih Ma'ṣúm to a place of utmost secrecy, telling no one of the spot, for at all costs they must contrive to preserve the priceless remains for posterity's sake.

Crossing the western ranges into Iraq in late August, Jináb-i-Bahá tarried a few days in sweltering midsummer Baghdad and its environs, for there was no haste. Arriving on or about 28 August in Karbilá of the Imám Ḥusayn, his spiritual forebear, Jináb-i-Bahá sought out the Bábís, but also those of receptive heart and spirit. In a group gravely misled by one Siyyid-i-'Uluvv he found hearts ready but confused by the Siyyid's claims to be the incarnation of the Holy Spirit. Through wise counsel and loving kindness Jináb-i-Bahá won over 'Uluvv's chief student, Shaykh Sulṭán, an Arab who had been converted to the Bábí doctrines by Ṭáhirih when she was in Karbilá; his returning to the Cause of the Báb strongly influenced his associates to abandon their teacher. And through the words and example of Bahá a singularly zealous group of new seekers after truth came into the fold. Among those who also felt the power of Jináb-i-Bahá's persuasion and the light of his presence were Shaykh 'Alí-Mírzá, Shaykh Salmán and young 'Abdu'l-Vahháb, all of Shíráz, and also Muḥammad 'Aliy-i-Ṭabíb of Zanján, four of the most ardent souls yet to enroll in the new community. All were destined for distinction in the propagation of the Faith and in their sacrifices for it. The youth 'Abdu'l-Vahháb had first met Jináb-i-Bahá in Káẓimayn and there became singularly attached to his mentor, pledging undying devotion to him.[15] Shaykh 'Alí-Mírzá was the young nephew of Shaykh Abú-Turab, the priest who in Shíráz had cleverly protected the Báb at the time of His public statement of mission in the Vakíl Mosque. Another who received marked favors and attention from Bahá was the worthy Ḥájí Siyyid Javád of Karbilá.[16]

But in Karbilá a special person awaited Jináb-i-Bahá, an elderly Bábí named Shaykh Ḥasan of Zúnúz, quietly going about his life as a scribe and quite unknown to the community of Bábís. He had been an early disciple of Siyyid Káẓim and one who during his days among the Shaykhís in Karbilá had fleetingly encountered the youth 'Alí-Muḥammad of Shíráz, not yet known to be the One awaited, visiting Him with Siyyid Káẓim when first he had arrived from Shíráz (see p. 15). During his first months of conversion as a Bábí he had journeyed to Kurdish Chihríq to join the Báb in that distant prison, there to act as transcriber of His works. It was then 1848 and Shaykh Ḥasan was moved to join the valiant defenders of Fort Shaykh Ṭabarsí, for the mustering summons had gone forth to the faithful. He expressed his wish to the Báb, only to be startled by His countermanding the intention.

'Participation in that struggle is not enjoined upon you. You should proceed to Karbilá and should abide in that holy city, inasmuch as you are destined to behold, with your own eyes, the beauteous countenance of the promised Ḥusayn. As you gaze upon that radiant face, do also remember Me. Convey to Him the expression of My loving devotion!' And then He added, *'Verily I say, I have entrusted you with a great mission! Beware lest your heart grow faint, lest you forget the glory with which I have invested you.'*[17]

Soon thereafter Shaykh Ḥasan departed from the fortress-prison of Chihríq, journeyed to Karbilá in Iraq as instructed and settled into life in that city. Fearing that a prolonged stay in that center of pilgrimage might arouse suspicion, he decided to marry and to earn his livelihood as a scribe. He lived thus for two years until he heard of the martyrdom of his Master in Tabríz, and then waited through another year of anticipation.

On the day of 'Arafih in the year 1267 AH,* Shaykh Ḥasan passed by the gate of the inner courtyard of the Shrine of the Imám Ḥusayn, and there for the first time he saw Mírzá Ḥusayn-'Alí of Núr, Jináb-i-Bahá. Later recalling that highest point in his life, he exulted: 'What shall I recount regarding the countenance which I beheld! The beauty of that face, those exquisite features which no pen or brush dare describe, his penetrating glance, his kindly face, the majesty of his bearing, the sweetness of his smile, the luxuriance of his jet-black flowing locks, left an indelible impression upon my soul . . . How lovingly he advanced towards me! He took me by the hand and, in a tone which at once betrayed power and beauty, addressed me in these words: "*This day I have purposed to make you known as a Bábí throughout Karbilá.*" Still holding my hand in his, he continued to converse with me. He walked with me all along the market-street, and in the end he said: "*Praise be to God that you have remained in Karbilá, and have beheld with your own eyes the countenance of the promised Ḥusayn.*" I recalled instantly the promise which had been given me by the Báb. His words, which I had regarded as referring to a remote future, I had not shared with anyone. These words of [Jináb-i-Bahá] moved me to the depths of my being. I felt impelled to proclaim to a heedless people, at that very moment and with all my soul and power, the advent of the promised Ḥusayn. He bade me, however, to repress my feelings and conceal my emotions. "*Not yet,*" he breathed into my ears. "*the appointed Hour is approaching. It*

* 5 October 1851.

has not yet struck. Rest assured and be patient." From that moment all my sorrows vanished. My soul was flooded with joy. In those days I was so poor that most of the time I hungered for food. I felt so rich, however, that all the treasures of the earth melted away into nothingness when compared with that which I already possessed. "Such is the grace of God; to whom He will, He giveth it: He, verily, is of immense bounty." '[18]

Shaykh Ḥasan's predestined encounter momentarily opened the door into the coming day of light, revealing the key Spirit of the future in a first flash of brilliance, a luminous moment of self-identification. Moreover, it showed Jináb-i-Bahá's own inner realization of his high mission, thus fulfilling the millennial circadian rhythm of Divine Revelation whereby at about one-thousand-year intervals a great Teacher appears by God's own timing to meet the needs of an evolving society. He was also fulfilling the Shi'ite expectation of the return of the Imám Ḥusayn, grandson of the Prophet Muḥammad, killed on Muḥarram 61 AH.* How fitting that Taqí Khán should send the mature Mírzá Ḥusayn-'Alí to Karbilá, the place of his spiritual predecessor, there to be discovered in the very month of the battle death of the Imám, this through the Báb's prescience in dispatching a disciple to Karbilá for the unique mission of first recognition of the Great One! And from that moment Shaykh Ḥasan had the bounty of discovering his new Bábí brothers in the holy cities of Iraq.

No prohibitions had been made in the terms of his banishment, hence Jináb-i-Bahá felt free to undertake constructive activity on behalf of the Báb's Cause. With great energy he cast himself into the task of finding receptive persons among the horde of pilgrims who had come to the city of the Imám Ḥusayn, Prince of Martyrs. Thus he passed the nine months of his exile in direct teaching, and during this period discovered and activated many ready souls, some of great capacity. He visited Káẓimayn and Baghdad and doubtless nearby Najaf, discovering responsive new individuals, and assiduously fortifying the spirits and knowledge of the leaderless community of fugitive Bábís. Also the sands of time were running, for the Báb's prophetic lunar 'year nine', dated from His 1844 Declaration, was fast approaching. It was time to return to Iran to seize the charged strands of Bábí life and leadership. And so Jináb-i-Bahá informed friends and close associates of his imminent departure. 'Abdu'l-Vahháb, out of his deep attachment, pleaded to accompany him to

* October 680 AD.

Teheran, but Bahá advised him to remain, giving him a small sum of money to improve his business in Karbilá, saying:

'*Since you are an only son, you must stay with your father, and this will be deemed as being the same as being with me on my journey.**

In the spring of 1852, during Jináb-i-Bahá's latter days in Karbilá, events in Persia had taken a decisive turn. The vindictive and intemperate young Sh̲áh ordered the murder of his able Prime Minister, Mírzá Taqí K̲h̲án of Farahán, allegedly because of having obtained protection from the Russian Government through its minister Prince D.F. Dolgorukov.† By his forceful character, his progressiveness in matters of education and his drive for secular reform of the many corruptions of the kingdom, Taqí K̲h̲án had become known as the Amír-Kabír, the Great Emir. Indeed, after only three years of intense service he had settled the twenty-year-old Sh̲áh firmly on his throne. Banishing his great administrator to Kás̲h̲án, the Sh̲áh sent his Chief Prosecutor Ḥájí 'Alí K̲h̲án there to assassinate him, a heinous deed carried out by opening his veins in the public bath at nearby Fín. Thus was gravely stained the early years of that Sh̲áh who during his long reign well earned the title of 'The Tyrant of Iran'. Yet the deed only replicated the fates of a number of Prime Ministers of his Qájár predecessors, for Fatḥ-'Alí Sh̲áh murdered one Grand Vazír by boiling him in oil, and Muḥammad Sh̲áh had one of his Chief Ministers strangled. Energetic and able though he was, Taqí K̲h̲án's ruthlessness was revealed in the death of the Báb and his savage persecution of the Bábís; indeed, his brief time of power was disastrous to the young Faith upon whose eradication he had set his heart.[19]

Thereupon, as predicted by the Báb, the Sh̲áh appointed as his new Prime Minister the ambitious Mírzá Áqá K̲h̲án of Núr, Taqí's long-time rival, who assumed the honorific Ṣadr-i-A'ẓam (the Greatest One), a title taken from the time of the Ottoman sultans. Recalling then his promise to the Bábís, Áqá K̲h̲án took steps to effect a reconciliation between the yet-threatening small group of Bábís and the Government of which he was now the administrative head. Since he considered Mírzá Ḥusayn-'Alí to be by far the most capable of the Báb's followers, he promptly dispatched to his friend a warm letter of invitation to leave Karbilá, expressing his eagerness to

* An excellent brief biography of the youth 'Abdu'l-Vaḥháb entitled 'The Story of a S̲h̲írází Youth' is contained in Balyuzi, *Bahá'u'lláh, The King of Glory*, Chapter 18, pp. 94–98.

† See Kazemzadeh, *Russia and Britain in Persia*, p. 123.

see him. Thus he officially extended a pardon and simultaneously an order for his return to Teheran.

> You ask, was the path that these followed uncertain or easy
> and plain?
> It is easy to find by the milestones built white with the bones
> of the slain.[20]
>
> **Anon**

Mírzá Naṣru'lláh of Núr, Áqá Khán, Ṣadr-i-A'ẓam, second Grand Vizier of Náṣiri'd-Dín Sháh. Neighbor of Mírzá Buzurg and his family, treacherous friend, and ultimately he who exiled Jináb-i-Bahá forever from homeland Persia.

Kirmánsháh, major city of the western mountains, where Jináb-i-Bahá, banished from the capital by the Prime Minister Taqí Khán, spent Ramadan 1851 en route to Baghdad and Karbilá in Iraq. (Seyhoun)

Chahabád in Shimírán district, north of Teheran, where the Alborz Mountains begin their reach into the skies, range upon range. A place of the well-to-do of the city, place of water and developed beauty spots. (Seyhoun)

The summer palace of the Sháh at Niyávárán in Shimírán district.

Estate of the Russian Consul, Prince Dimitri Dolgorukov, at the village of Zárkandih in Shimírán, near to a home of the Prime Minister. Here Jínab'i'Bahá gained a brief asylum with the Prince, whose secretary was Mírzá Ḥusayn-'Alí's brother-in-law.

8 The Torrent and the Maiden

God is My witness, O people! I was asleep on my couch, when lo, the Breeze of God wafting over Me roused Me from My slumber, His quickening Spirit revived Me, and My tongue was unloosed to voice His Call.[1]

Bahá'u'lláh

Each hoof-fall of the returning exiles' horses was light and lilting, for it was April and another springtime, and they were homeward bound after nine months of separation from families and friends. The small company of riders, climbing sharply into the Zagros mountains from the flatlands of the Tigris, exulted in the spring floral display of crocuses, cyclamen and narcissi, in the meltwater gurgling down the rocky gullies, in the herbs and grasses bursting from the raw hillsides and the almond blossoms shining pale pink, in the sharp air of this the best of seasons in Persia. A festival spirit suffused them through the long days on horseback through the barrier ranges which protect Persia at its western border. As they passed through the abject, deprived hamlets, ragged mountaineer peasants and grubby townsmen alike quietly snarled at the clattering passage of the nobleman and his escort, grumbling at their wretched lot in these hard-scrabble valleys, wishing ill to all who were landed and titled and rightly blamed for the deep ills of Persian life. Even with the sunlight glancing from spring seeps or crystalline rocks in the high screes, even with the joyous song of returned migrant birds, the men of soil and flock and craft remembered too well the physical hungers of winter in their den-like hovels of stone and mud, of blanket doorways and crude box windows, the symbols of their serfdom. Little wonder that they muttered helpless hatred for those who were the living evil of their once-great land. Every Persian in his way felt the apathy and despair of a famine of the spirit, a winter of the heart. And every Persian was well entitled to venomous feelings against those who had ruined Iran for their power and pleasure. Insulated by hate and calloused by toil, how could they feel the latent power and profound good will of the young man who passed by so errantly?

Reunion with loved wives and children filled each traveler's thoughts, for soon again each must pick up the skeins of his life affairs. Even in slow-paced Persia a nine-month hiatus had brought for Jináb-i-Bahá many endings, mendings and beginnings. Foremost was the Bábí ferment of mind and motive which energized each traveler as he rededicated himself to the propagation of the new reformation, whatever the dangers to life and possessions; how much more intense the thoughts of him who was the heart of the Bábí Cause! It was the month of Rajab, early May of 1852, as the party crossed the uplands of Persia, passing through hospitable Karand so receptive to the Bábís, then through Kirmánshah and Hamadán en route to the capital.

Arriving in the outskirts of Teheran in the middle of May, Mírzá Ḥusayn-'Alí was met by a fellow Núrí, Lt.Col. Ja'far-Qulí Khán,* brother of the Prime Minister Áqá Khán, who had been directed to receive him, doubtless to monitor his actions and screen his associates. Not knowing the time of his return, Lady Asíyih and the children had repaired to Yálrúd and Tákur, as was their wont for the blazing summer months; indeed, from Kirmánsháh Jináb-i-Bahá had sent a loving gift of sweets to them through Mírzá Músá. For a full month he was the honored guest of the Prime Minister in his home in Teheran, where the notables and dignitaries who flocked to see him were so many that he found it difficult to attend to family and personal affairs.[2] By means of this political hospitality the Minister possibly wished to keep this powerful spirit, whom he knew so long and well, away from his home base and under observation, thus not easily or quickly to re-establish active relationships with his benighted Bábí companions. Also, he may have hoped for a lasting reconciliation with the followers of the Báb, and such marked favor

* When the Zanján incident involving Ḥujjat and his devoted followers was in full cry in late 1850, the Governor of Zanján, Aṣlán Khán, appealed to the Government for military aid, presenting to Prime Minister Taqí Khán a highly colored and misleading account of the events preceding and during the organized resistance by the Bábís. Wishing to send to Zanján as a commander of infantry and cavalry Lt.Col. Ja'far-Qulí Khán, Mírzá Taqí Khán was amazed to have him excuse himself, saying: 'I am not an Ibn Ziyád, to go and make war on a band of siyyids and men of learning of whose tenets I know nothing, though I should be ready enough to fight with Russians, Jews or other infidels.' Certain others, notably the 'Alíyu'lláhís (of Karand and elsewhere), also refused service against the Bábís perhaps because they felt that the Lord of the Age might well have appeared. (Browne, *New History*, fn. p. 139.) Ibn Ziyád was a notoriously cruel persecutor of the Imám Ḥusayn and his followers, hence was execrated by all Shí'as. It would have been surprising indeed if, in their hours together as neighbors, Ja'far-Qulí Khán had not heard expositions of the Bábí tenets from Jináb-i-Bahá.

shown to Mírzá Ḥusayn-'Alí might be persuasive. After that month Jináb-i-Bahá was free to leave the city for Shimírán, to renew ties of family and Faith. Then, because of the 'excessive heat prevailing in the capital' he sought the familiar mansion of the Vazir in Afchih, forty miles northeast in Lavásán, from which began the mountain crossing to Yálrúd and Tákur to the north.

Sometime during this homecoming period Mullá Shaykh 'Alí of Turshíz, entitled 'Aẓím, approached Jináb-i-Bahá to enlist his support and gain his advice for a plan of Bábí revenge against the young Sháh and his new Prime Minister who were deemed to be the source of the continuing persecutions. Supported by his group of Bábí conspirators, 'Aẓím also aspired to be the successor of the Báb, for the Báb had promised that '*we have granted you a mighty station on our part*'. Besides, the Sháh's death might be a propitious time for the advancement of the Bábí Cause. But Jináb-i-Bahá condemned his designs, advised him in most emphatic terms to abandon the plan he had conceived, and disassociated himself entirely from the intended rash act, warning him that fresh disasters of unprecedented magnitude would thus be precipitated.[3]

Notwithstanding this strong dissent expressed to 'Azím by the sagacious Jináb-i-Bahá, independent plotting by such hot-tempered reckless men could easily go forward without hindrance within the scattered and disorganized Bábí community. Thus, on Sunday 15 August, when the Sháh had left his summer palace in the Shimírán district for a hunting camp nearby, three Bábís – Ṣádiq of Tabríz, Fatḥu'lláh of Qum, and Qásim of Nayríz – waited outside the camp for the king's morning ride to the hunting site. As he emerged from the palace grounds, preceded by equerries and a vanguard of armed nomad riders, the three waited quietly near the garden of Mírzá Muḥammad Ḥasan, Director of the Treasury, until the king came abreast. Dressed as gardeners, two on one side of the road, one on the other, they bowed low as the unsuspecting Sháh came opposite them, and cried out together in the traditional formula of appeal:

'We are your sacrifice! We make a request!'

But instead of waiting for whatever kingly response might be his whim, they rushed upon him, shouting, 'We make a request!'

Surprised and alarmed, the king cried out: 'Rascals, what do you want?'

Ṣádiq, on his right, seized the bridle of the king's horse while firing his pistol. The two on his left fired at the same time, but the pellets of shot only inflicted minor injuries. Fatḥu'lláh and Qásim dragged the Sháh from his saddle to dispatch him with knives, but his own defense and a careening horse prevented their quick success, giving time for the startled retinue to leap to the protection of their master. The grand equerry and one of the nomad riders cut down Ṣádiq with their swords. Other lords flung themselves upon the remaining two, disarmed and bound them. Spared momentarily by the angry retainers, the two captives declared that they were Bábís, and that the assassination attempt had been made to avenge their Master's blood spilled in Tabríz and that of their brethren shed at Fort Ṭabarsí, Zanján, Nayríz and Teheran. Silent through intensive interrogation by the Sháh's police, Fatḥu'lláh had molten lead poured down his throat, while Qásim was publicly tortured, then killed. Ṣádiq's body was halved, then suspended from two city gates as a summary warning.[4]*

Despite the confessions of the would-be assassins, there was the usual and predictable suspicion that some rival claimant to the throne had instigated the act in order to seize power. Indeed, rumors circulated in the capital that the attempt had been successful, and this heightened the tensions in that intrigue-ridden city. The furore aroused nobility, policy and populace to sharp action against the Bábís of Teheran, identified by the attackers as the source of the conspiracy. Swooping down upon all known Bábís, the police were aided by the sorry betrayal of many believers by one 'Abbás, a Bábí page of the spirited courtier-martyr Ḥájí Sulaymán Khán in whose home, a center of Bábí activity, a dozen prominent believers were surprised and arrested. Through methodological searches the authorities ultimately netted eighty-one believers of the city, thirty-eight of whom were active teachers of the new Faith.

At the time of the attempted assassination, the Prime Minister's brother Col. Ja'far-Qulí Khán was also in Shimírán. Immediately he dispatched a message informing Mírzá Ḥusayn-'Alí of the crisis, for he had '*proceeded to Lavásán on account of the excessive heat prevailing in the capital*',[5] to the home of Áqá Khán in familiar Afchih, forty miles distant.

'The Sháh's mother', he wrote, 'is inflamed with anger. She is denouncing you openly before the court and people as the would-be

---

* There are a number of highly inconsistent official and unofficial recorded versions of the attempt upon the Sháh written by Gobineau, Lady Sheil, Muslim historians, Browne (per Ṣubḥ-i-Azal and others) and Nabíl-i-A'ẓam. The version here used comes principally from Nabíl, Gobineau and Balyuzi. This brief sequence seeks a reasonable consensus of details of those conflicting versions. Jináb-i-Bahá in his own words focuses upon Ṣádiq as the most determined of the would-be assassins. (See Chapter 9, p. 160.)

murderer of her son.' She was also seeking to involve the Prime Minister, accusing him of being an accomplice. Ja'far-Qulí Khán was by no means on the best of terms with his brother, yet he knew how false were the accusations of Jahán Khánum, the Queen Mother, with respect to his brother and Mírzá Ḥusayn-'Alí, fellow Núrís. He was also intensely aware how inflammatory the incident could become when the emotions of the oppressed and resentful Persian people were aroused; their shallow loyalties could be readily directed to widespread violence visited upon scapegoats of any kind. He was also Mírzá Ḥusayn-'Alí's official guardian and host since the return from Karbilá; a certain culpability might be ascribed to him should his guest be found guilty of complicity in the plot. Feeling sure of Bahá's innocence and protecting himself, he urged his friend to seek concealment in the neighborhood of Afchih until tempers had cooled and confusion dissipated; and the messenger was a trusted old retainer ordered to be at his service.[6]

Refusing to go into hiding despite the consideration shown him by his host, and ignoring the messenger, the next morning Mírzá Ḥusayn-'Alí rode out with calm confidence westward toward the headquarters of the imperial army, then camped near the summer palace of Níyávarán, north of Teheran.[7] Arriving at the village of Zarkandih, about three miles from Níyávarán, he was met by Mírzá Majíd-i-Áhí, husband of his younger sister Nisá* and secretary of the Russian Consul, Prince Dimitri F. Dolgorukov. His brother-in-law promptly invited him to seek asylum in his home within the grounds of the Russian legation. However, attendants of Ḥájí 'Alí Khán, the Chief Prosecutor of the Government and recent murderer of the former Prime Minister Taqí Khán, recognized Mírzá Ḥusayn-'Alí and informed their master, who quickly relayed the information to the Sháh to secure his order of arrest. The news was also quickly transmitted to the officers of the nearby army.[8]

The Sháh and officers alike were surprised at the bold step of voluntary return to Teheran by the man accused of being the chief instigator of the assassination plot. The Sháh sent an officer to the Russian legation, demanding that the accused be delivered into his hand, but Dolgorukov refused. Instead, he requested Mírzá Ḥusayn-'Alí to repair to the nearby home of Mírzá Áqá Khán, the Prime Minister, a place which he considered the most appropriate

* Nísá, the younger (Malik-Khusraví says the elder) full sister of Jináb-i-Bahá, was a believer and supporter of her brother. Sadly, she died in childbirth; her body was sent by Jináb-i-Bahá to Baghdad for burial.

under the complex circumstances of the hour. He then formally communicated to the Grand Vazír his wish that this man, the trust of the Russian Government now delivered into the Vazír's hands, should be assured safety and protection, while warning the Minister that he would hold him responsible should he disregard his wishes. In reply the Prime Minister gave the fullest assurances required and received his old friend into his home with every mark of respect. But the Vazír was fearful of his position and felt that he dared not risk displeasing the Sháh and the Queen Mother at this tense moment, hence promptly handed over his guest to the authorities.

As Mírzá Ḥusayn-'Alí was leaving the village of Zarkandih under arrest, the Russian Minister's daughter, esteeming their noble friend and distressed at the acute dangers which surrounded him, broke into tears and upbraided her father, saying:

'Of what use is the authority with which you have been invested, if you are powerless to extend your protection to a guest whom you have received in your house?'

The Prince, moved by her tears and angered by the Prime Minister's betrayal of trust, affectionately sought to comfort his daughter by reassuring her that he would do all in his power to avert the dangers confronting Mírzá Ḥusayn-'Alí.[9]

In a society where justice was utterly haphazard and based upon the powers of the king, his nobility and his appointees but with absolute authority in the hands of the Sháh, where the value of life was small and the innocent were freely seized and sacrificed with the guilty, in a populace where most lives were wasted, who cared about a few murdered innocents? Of this critical moment Jináb-i-Bahá relates that '*they arrested Us and brought Us to the prison in Teheran, from Níyávarán, which was then the seat of the royal residence; on foot, in chains, and with bare head and feet, for a brutal fellow who was accompanying Us on horseback. snatched the hat from Our head, and many executioners and farráshes hurried us along with great speed and put Us for four months in a place the like of which has not been seen.*'[10]*

The road from Shimírán was long, up and down, rough and dusty, the August sun blazing, the few poplars at the roadside

* In a recollection of His later years, Bahá'u'lláh tells of this occasion: '*Upon Our return, We proceeded to Lavásán on account of the excessive heat prevailing in the capital. Following Our departure, there occurred the attempt upon the life of his Majesty . . . Those days were troublous days, and the fires of hatred burned high. Many were arrested, among them this Wronged One . . . We were in no wise connected with that evil deed, and Our innocence was indisputably established by the tribunals. Nevertheless, they apprehended Us . . .*' (*Epistle to the Son of the Wolf*, p. 20.)

offering little shade. It was a 'via dolorosa', a road into the shadow of death, nor was the stony Teheran landscape too unlike the bleak hills around Jerusalem remembered by Christians over long centuries. All along the route he was stoned and pelted with whatever came to bystanders' hands, and he was vilified by the crowds flocking to the scene on hearing that the prime enemy of the sovereign had been captured and was being taken to some condign retribution. The people owed no love to the monarch, and perhaps some even had benefitted from the generosity of Mírzá Ḥusayn-'Alí, but they were glad to cease their drudgeries and vent their resentments upon another hapless victim of that pitiless time. Throughout the some three hard miles to the Shimírán Gate of the northern city wall each step on the blistering, rocky, rutted roadway was torture, each slow minute perspiring in the sun without his hat a torment and a sunstroke peril to the Bábí nobleman. Then over the moat bridge and past the leering sentries at their posts inside the double-arched northern gate and so into the city, Mírzá Ḥusayn-'Alí plodding the

The road south from Shimírán to the city of Teheran, once stony, pitted, rocky, a track for wagons and four-footed beasts, the scant shade from the broken trees reminiscent of Jináb-i-Bahá's midsummer walk to the city and the Síyáh-Chál.

tortuous streets to the dread dungeon. As the company proceeded, a decrepit old woman emerged from the mob with a stone held high to cast into the face of the captive. Running to overtake the moving company, she cried out:

'By the Imám Ḥusayn I abjure you, give me a chance to fling my stone in his face!'

To his guards, Mírzá Ḥusayn-'Alí gave warning not to interfere with her, saying:

'*Suffer not this woman to be disappointed. Deny her not what she regards as a meritorious act in the sight of God.*'[11]

Wearily slogging through dusty, oven-hot Teheran with his guards, Jináb-i-Bahá was destined for the worst prison of the land, the Síyáh-Chál, the Black Pit, situated just inside the southern edge of the palace compound, '*a place foul beyond comparison*'.[12] Once it had been an underground reservoir for a public bath, and had then been emptied and converted into an intolerable prison. The Pit already held some two score Bábí victims arrested in the searches. Recalling his arrival, Jináb-i-Bahá relates that:

'*We were consigned for four months to a place foul beyond comparison . . . Upon our arrival we were first conducted along a pitch-black corridor, from whence we descended three steep flights of stairs to the place of confinement . . . The dungeon was wrapped in thick darkness, and our fellow-prisoners numbered nearly a hundred and fifty souls: thieves, assassins and highwaymen . . . There was no other outlet than the passage by which we entered. No pen can depict that place, nor any tongue describe its loathsome smell. Most of these men had neither clothes nor bedding to lie upon. God alone knoweth what befell us in that most foul-smelling and gloomy place.*'[13]

At his side, chained with him, were five other Bábís, including his nephew Maḥmúd* and Ḥájí Mírzá Jání, the merchant of Káshán who had become the historian of the Cause; their fetters were locked together with heavy bolts and screws, the chains fastened to the floor. His clothing was in shreds, and from this appalling state there was no prospect of relief. In recollection, Bahá'u'lláh says:

'*Shouldst thou at some time . . . visit the dungeon of His Majesty the Sháh, ask the director and chief jailer to show thee those two chains, one of which is known as Qará-Guhar, and the other as Salásil. I swear by the Day-Star of Justice that for four months this wronged one was tormented and*

---

* Maḥmúd, son of half-brother Mírzá Muḥammad-'Alí, was chained with Bahá'u'l-láh in the Síyáh-Chál, but on his release became an Azalí, a follower of half-brother Mírzá Yaḥyá, entitled Ṣubḥ-i-Azal (per Malik-Khusraví 1958.)

chained by one or the other of them. "My grief exceedeth all the woes to which Jacob gave vent, and all the afflictions of Job are but a part of my sorrows!" '[14]*

A barrel roof, vertical sides and a flat brick floor enclosed a dungeon space perhaps twenty meters long, lightless even when the jailers opened the single door above the last short, steep, seven steps from the access hallway to the floor of the pitch-black dungeon. To Jináb-i-Bahá who loved light, the blackness itself was a torture. At the angle of wall and floor of the two long sides of the chamber sat the prisoners side by side, the central space between their feet functioning as an aisle for the jailers. There was no drainage and no removal of wastes. Odors of foulest kinds were intermixed with offensive acrid aromatics from the ferments, molds and putrefaction. The prisoners' torments were made additionally intolerable by vermin, doubtless bedbugs, fleas and lice, possibly also with aggressive rats competing for food scraps. The chained prisoners could scarcely move in their floor-fastened shackles, and then only in concert. And they could not escape the mind-curdling din of their fellow prisoners, a confused manic chorus of despair.† For the first three days and nights, Jináb-i-Bahá was given no food or drink, and the human cacophony prevented sleep.

The family first heard of the crisis when suddenly a servant came running to lady Ásíyih at the rented mansion in Teheran, crying out that the Master had been arrested and had walked many miles, that his clothes were torn, his feet bare and bleeding, and that he had been mistreated. Quickly the storm broke about their heads as the outcries against the Bábís began and were propagated so that, alarmed, all the

---

* The Qará-Guhar fetters (lit. big and heavy), heavier than the intermediate weight of the Salásil chains (lit. iron chains) weighed about fifty-one kilograms or one hundred and ten pounds; a special wooden fork was supplied to the prisoner to help carry its weight. See Taherzadeh, *Revelation of Bahá'u'lláh*, Vol. I, p. 9, and Bahá'u'lláh, *Epistle to the Son of the Wolf*, p. 77.

† Prisoners under maximum security imprisonment experience an ultimate loneliness in the midst of fellow-sufferers, each person facing himself as a thief, murderer, arsonist, or perhaps bystander. The din of prisons in all ages is one of the predictable effects of such a human herd, confined and talking to itself, trying to maintain sanity by reviewing life, by learning and memorizing aloud, by shouting and screaming to decompress overwhelming interior tensions, declaring aloud: 'I am still alive, at least; I, about to die; I, victim of a mistake; I, vengeful, eager to settle scores however and if ever; I, soldier; I, artist; I, farmer; I, human being . . .' Then there is pain: pain from the shackles and sores which create dishonorable scars never to be lost; pain from the kicks and blows of the guards; pain of position, aches and stiffness from limitations of movement. But time dominates all: time of endless hours with nothing to do and prevention of all meaningful doing. Time: every brick of floor and roof is composed of careless time baked into their very substance. Time: endless ticks of eternity. (Note from a former prison physician.)

Núrí relatives fled their houses in Teheran and were followed by their servants, save only faithful black Isfandíyár and a single black servant-woman. The houses of Jináb-i-Bahá and his kindred were looted and stripped by plundering mobs, so that in a single day the family was reduced from wealth to poverty.

During the first day of alarms, hiding from the Bábí-hunters, the family, with younger half-brother Muḥammad-Qulí' took refuge in the house of Lady Ásíyih's aunt, whose husband was a Government official, 'Uncle Ismá'íl' to the small 'Abbás. Finding that their presence endangered the host family, lady Ásíyih returned briefly to the looted house, in which they lived in destitution. Lady Ásíyih had been able to preserve only some few items from her marriage dowry, including gold buttons from her wedding garments, to sell for what they might bring for food or other needs. From that house eight-year-old 'Abbás, venturing into the streets to obtain money from a relative, was accosted by street boys who crowded about him, jeering 'Bábí. Bábí!' Feeling that boldness was the only counter to the aggressiveness of the small hoodlums, 'Abbás rushed at them with such resoluteness that they fled precipitately, calling out that 'the little Bábí will slay us all!' in echo of the rumors of Bábí reactive violence. As he turned toward his home refuge the boy heard a man shout after him:

'Well done, you brave and fearless child! No one of your age would ever have been able, unaided, to withstand their attack!' And indeed he was never afterward molested by the street urchins.[15]

With the aid of Bahá's brother, Mírzá Músá, he himself keeping out of sight, Ásíyih Khánum and her three children fled again into hiding. Lady Ásíyih daily visited her aunt for news of her priceless husband, often remaining the entire days in anxious waiting, fearful that news of his execution would come; often she took the boy 'Abbás with her on these vigils. And soon they found two small rooms in the Sangilaj Quarter in the western maze of streets, not far from the dread prison. She was aided by the kindly Mírzá Yúsif, husband of her great-aunt and a friend of Prince Dolgorukov. At considerable risk to himself, despite his being a Russian subject, Yúsif arranged for food to be passed into the Black Pit for her precious husband, thus preventing the usual starvation planned for prisoners; he also attended the courts to keep abreast of what was occurring. Yúsif's wife was the sole visitor to those bleak small rooms and the only comforter of the anxious young wife Ásíyih.[16] For the fugitive family, hardship increased until 'there came a day when', as 'Abdu'l-Bahá recalled it, 'my mother took a little flour and shook it into my hand instead of bread, and I ate it like that'.[17] So too was little Bahíyyih offered only flour to sustain her at this time of deprivation.[18]

One morning the insistent eight-year-old 'Abbás, accompanied by a servant, visited the dungeon grounds after pleading to see his beloved father. When the door into the Pit opened, the man took the boy onto his shoulders and walked to the steps where, peering into the tunnel of darkness, they could see nothing. But a blessed voice called out, ordering the guards, '*Do not bring him!*'[19]

Upon hearing the call, the boy strained his eyes to see his father, but could not, and was then taken into the courtyard and seated, being told that it was customary to bring out the prisoners at midday for their hour of meals and limited exercise. At about noon the jailers ushered forth the sad, dirty, even naked prisoners, among them many Bábís. Jináb-i-Bahá emerged, chained to his nephew Maḥmúd, his body bent, his neck abraded with the weight and edges of the shackles, his hair and beard unkempt, his clothing tattered; visibly under great hardship, his health could readily be seen to be failing. First they took him to a pool to allow him to wash his face, and thereafter he struggled back to the dungeon. So ominous was the sight of the prisoners and particularly of his dearly loved father that little 'Abbás was overcome and fainted, his father ordering the servant to '*Take the child home!*'[20]

Those terrible days for the Bábís were described by Jináb-i-Bahá himself: '*All those who were struck down by the storm that raged during that memorable year in Teheran were Our fellow-prisoners in the Síyáh-Chál . . . We were all huddled together in one cell, our feet in stocks, and around our necks fastened the most galling of chains. The air we breathed was laden with the foulest impurities, while the floor on which we sat was covered with filth and infested with vermin. No ray of light was allowed to penetrate that pestilential dungeon or to warm its icy coldness. We were placed in two rows, each facing the other. We had taught them to repeat certain verses which, every night, they chanted with extreme fervor.*

"God is sufficient unto me; He verily is the All-Sufficing!" one row would intone, while the other would reply, "In Him let the trusting trust . . ."

One day, there was brought to our prison a tray of roasted meat which they informed us the Sháh had ordered to be distributed among the prisoners. "The Sháh," we were told, "faithful to a vow he made, has chosen this day to offer to you all this lamb in fulfillment of his pledge." A deep silence fell upon our companions, who expected [me] to make answer on their behalf.

"We return this gift to you," We replied; "we can well dispense with this offer."

The answer we made would have greatly irritated the guards had they not been eager to devour the food we had refused to touch. Despite the hunger with which our companions were afflicted, only one among them, a certain Mírzá Ḥusayn [of Qum], showed any desire to eat of the food the sovereign had chosen to spread before us. With a fortitude that was truly heroic, Our fellow-prisoners submitted, without a murmur, to endure the piteous plight to which they were reduced. Praise of God, instead of complaint of the treatment meted out to them by the Sháh, fell unceasingly from their lips – praise with which they sought to beguile the hardships of a cruel captivity.

Every day our jailers, entering our cell, would call the name of one of our companions, bidding him arise and follow them to the foot of the gallows. With what eagerness would the owner of that name respond to that solemn call! Relieved of his chains, he would spring to his feet and, in a state of uncontrollable delight, would approach and embrace Us. We would seek to comfort him with the assurance of an everlasting life in the world beyond, and, filling his heart with hope and joy, would send him forth to win the crown of glory. He would embrace, in turn, the rest of his fellow-prisoners and then proceed to die as dauntlessly as he had lived. Soon after the martyrdom of each of these companions, we would be informed by the executioner, who had grown to be friendly to us, of the circumstances of the death of his victim, and of the joy with which he had endured his sufferings to the very end.

We were awakened one night, ere break of day, by Mírzá 'Abdu'l-Vahháb [of Shíráz], who was bound with Us to the same chains. He had left Kázimayn and followed Us to Teheran, where he was arrested and thrown into prison. He asked Us whether We were awake, and proceeded to relate to Us his dream.

"I have this night," he said, "been soaring into a space of infinite vastness and beauty. I seemed to be uplifted on wings that carried me wherever I desired to go. A feeling of rapturous delight filled my soul. I flew in the midst of that immensity with a swiftness and ease that I cannot describe."

"Today," We replied, "it will be your turn to sacrifice yourself for this Cause. May you remain firm and steadfast to the end. You will then find yourself soaring in that same limitless space of which you dreamed, traversing with the same ease and swiftness the realm of immortal sovereignty, and gazing with that same rapture upon the Infinite Horizon."

That morning saw the jailer again enter our cell and call out the name of 'Abdu'l-Vahháb. Throwing off his chains, he sprang to his feet, embraced each of his fellow-prisoners, and taking Us into his arms, pressed Us lovingly to his heart. At that moment I discovered that he had no shoes to wear, We gave him Our own, and, speaking a last word of encouragement and cheer, sent him forth to the scene of his martyrdom . . .'[21]

He was slain by a brother and sons of the treacherous Prime Minister, who thus began a hellish day of planned murder,[22] one typical of the Persian character so 'fertile in device and indifferent to suffering,' as Lord Curzon expressed it.[23]

There followed the unspeakable horrors of 15 September 1852, when the Prime Minister's unholy plan for mass murder of the surviving Bábís came to pass. The execution of victims was to be divided among the classes of nobles down to those occupying different departments of the state administration, the Sháh only exempted. By this device were distributed the guilt of the martyrdoms and any risks of vengeance from relatives of the slain. The ensuing blood bath was of a calculated fiendishness befitting the worst annals of Persia's bloody pages. Twenty-seven Bábís met heroic death in horrid ways, each at the hands of a selected class of murderers: the mullás, the princes, the nobles, the soldiers, and others. Most inspired of all was the valiant Ḥájí Sulaymán Khán, who, with nine candles burning in stab wounds, went to his terrible death so passionately and poetically that his sacrifice transcended the butchery by achieving that defeat of all violence: heartfelt admiration for the victims by the killers. So bravely and well did these few spirited men give up their lives in the squares and streets of Teheran that the Cause of the Báb was indeed given that promised fiercer blaze.[24]* In a tradition of Islám, the Ḥadíth-i-Jábir from the Káfí, as authenticated in *The Kitáb-i-Íqán* (The Book of Certitude) of Bahá'u'lláh, the signs of the appearance of the Qá'im, He Who will Arise, are given: 'His saints shall be abased in His time, and their heads shall be exchanged as presents; . . . they shall be slain and

* The heroism of the Bábí martyrs has received eloquent notice, among others from Rénan, Gobineau, Nicolas and Lord Curzon. The summation by Lady Sheil (Nabíl, *The Dawn-Breakers*, fn.2, pp. 612–613) shows the fiendish conception of the massacre. The words of Lord Curzon have a particular cogency: 'If one conclusion more than another has been forced upon our notice by the retrospect in which I have indulged, it is that a sublime and unmurmuring devotion has been inculcated by this new faith, whatever it is. There is, I believe, but one instance of a Babi having recanted under pressure or menace of suffering, and he reverted to the faith and was executed within two years. Tales of magnificent heroism illumine the blood-stained pages of Babi history. Ignorant and unlettered as many of its votaries are, and have been, they are yet prepared to die for their religion, and the fires of Smithfield did not kindle a nobler courage than has met and defied the more refined torture-mongers of Teheran. Of no small account, then, must be the tenets of a creed that can awaken in its followers so rare and beautiful a spirit of self-sacrifice . . .' (Hon. George N. Curzon, *Persia and the Persian Question*, Vol. I, p. 501, quoted in *The Dawn-Breakers*, fn.1, p. 621.)

burned, and shall be afraid, fearful and dismayed; the earth shall be dyed with their blood, and lamentation and wailing shall prevail amongst their women; these are My saints indeed.'[25]

Jináb-i-Bahá's own reaction to these and other atrocities visited upon the Bábís reflects all too well the satanic spirit infecting feudal Iran: '*Gracious God!*' he wrote, '*the great and the noble in Persia glory in acts of such savagery that one is lost in amazement at the tales thereof.*'[26] '*How strange that the people of Persia, who were unrivalled in sciences and arts, should have sunk to the lowest level of degradation among the kindreds of the earth.*'[27]

Some who before were skeptical, even scornful of the new belief, now felt moved to discover whence came this strength not merely to withstand but to surmount any extreme of pain or suffering. As Bahá proclaimed:

'*Behold how . . . the worthless and foolish have fondly imagined that by such instruments as massacre, plunder and banishment they can extinguish the Lamp which the Hand of Divine Power hath lit . . . How utterly unaware they seem to be of the truth that such adversity is the oil that feedeth the flame of this Lamp!*'[28]

Alarmed at the anticipated dangers of the plot to assassinate the Sháh, Jináb-i-Bahá's half-brother Mírzá Yaḥyá had hastened home to Tákur to rally the many Bábís of the district in preparation for a possible uprising, should the murder be consummated. When the plot was a failure and news of the violence visited upon the Bábís of Teheran reached Tákur, Yaḥyá in the guise of a dervish fled westward with his uncle Mírzá Zaynu'l-'Ábidín and another companion, first hiding in the forests of Gílán province for long months until, informed of his great brother's banishment, he surreptitiously set forth for Kirmánsháh and Baghdad, alms-bowl in hand.[29]

One of Mírzá Ḥusayn-'Alí's uncles Shaykh 'Azíz, hostile to his nephew from well before the time of the attempted assassination, had sent alarming reports to the Sháh which suggested that a rebellion was imminent. Whereupon the Sháh-Savan regiment of cavalry under the command of the rash young Abú-Ṭálib Khán, nephew of the Prime Minister, was dispatched to pacify the district. Far beyond pacification, without provocation he attacked, leveled and burned Tákur village and brought widespread terror to the people of the countryside, most of whose men had run to the mountains. Despite the intervention of Jináb-i-Bahá's half-brother Mírzá Ḥasan, the evil commander of troops '*slew, moreover, some of our kindred, and plundered our property, and made our family captives in the hands of the oppressors*',[30] Jináb-i-Bahá has recorded, saying further:

'In Mázindarán a vast number of the servants of God were exterminated.'[31]*

The fine mansion of the dead Vazír Mírzá Buzurg, rebuilt after the great flash flood, and maintained by his son Mírzá Ḥusayn-'Alí, was emptied of its precious valuables, was burned in part, gravely damaged, and left in ruins. The luxurious house in Teheran was plundered. From the looting the opportunistic Prime Minister Áqá Khán acquired a priceless leather tablet of a prayer of Kumayl in the handwriting of the Imám 'Alí as rendered in Kufic calligraphy, and also a book of the poems of Ḥáfiẓ in the handwriting of Mir 'Imád, famous scholar and calligraphist, prizes which he had long coveted. Moreover, he took advantage of the débacle to transfer certain of Mírzá Ḥusayn-'Alí's properties to himself.[32]†

The Bábí-hunting spread far and wide into remote corners of Persia, but notably to Yazd and Nayríz, where many Bábís were seized and inhumanly dealt with. At Nayríz the survivors of the blood bath of the time of Vaḥíd suffered terribly, as did the believers of nearby Shíráz. Those alive after the local violence had subsided were marched the killing six hundred miles through Ábádih, where the heads of two hundred martyrs were buried, to Iṣfahán. In Teheran grim miles later those who had survived the death march were immediately executed or imprisoned. And many months were to pass before the incited hostility to the Bábís was to die down and tolerance be reestablished.[33]

During this period of savagery the malevolent Bábí-hunters turned to that unique woman who thus far had escaped their bloody hands. Long confined by order of the Prime Minister to the house of the Mayor of Teheran, the poetess Ṭáhirih had early won the heart and homage of the Mayor's wife. Through her hostess she had attracted throngs of women admirers who eagerly entered her presence to drink deeply of her knowledge, but more importantly to

---

* In a Tablet of Bahá'u'lláh we read: '*Among them* (kings of the earth) *is the King of Persia, who suspended Him Who is the Temple of the Cause* (the Báb) *in the air, and put Him to death with such cruelty that all created things, and the inmates of Paradise, and the Concourse on high wept for Him. He slew, moreover, some of Our kindred, and plundered Our property, and made Our family captives in the hands of the oppressors.*' (Shoghi Effendi, *The Promised Day is Come*, p. 70.)

† In Prime Minister Áqá Khán could be seen what Lord Curzon well described as the character of the Persian official: '. . . there is no sense of duty or pride of honor, no mutual trust and cooperation (except in ill-doing), no disgrace in exposure, no credit in virtue, no national spirit or patriotism.' (Nabíl, *The Dawn-Breakers*, p. xxix.) Taherzadeh asserts, however, that the Prime Minister sought to protect Jináb-i-Bahá's relatives in Núr, but failed. (*The Revelation of Bahá'u'lláh*, Vol. I, pp. 10–11.)

Bábul, once Bárfurúsh, a thriving town in northern Iran, birthplace of the noble Quddús and place of his heroic martyrdom after betrayal at Fort Shaykh Ṭabarsí. (Seyhoun) Below, the ruined Fort of Khajih outside Nayríz. Here the illustrious Siyyid Yáḥyá, Vaḥíd, with his valiant followers held off overwhelming Government troops until betrayal and martyrdom along with all Bábís of the area.

The House of Maḥmúd Khán, the Mayor of Teheran, in which Ṭáhirih was held for many months of house confinement before her brutal strangling in the Ílkhání Garden outside the northern city wall. Below, among the more shocking inventions of executioners is to blow a convicted man apart with a cannon blast. Here the killing group tethers a victim to the mouth of a field gun.

be strengthened by her powerful spirit which signaled that coming deliverance from bondage for which they scarcely dared hope. Ṭáhirih was a splendid, nay incomparable, teacher and an example to all Persian women; yet she was one who permitted social reforms to take their own pace as God might wish. And now she was totally vulnerable.

During the period of house arrest she had had seven inquisitions by two learnèd priests,* when she engaged them in vehement controversy, sharply criticizing their ignorance and backwardness. Not surprisingly, after a final interrogation, they secretly condemned the unrepentant poetess to death as a heretic.

One night in late August or early September 1852, the wife of the Mayor was called to the lamp-lit upper room of Ṭáhirih to find her dressed in a bridal gown of white silk, her room redolent with perfume. To her surprised hostess, she said:

'I am preparing to meet my Beloved, and wish to free you from the cares and anxieties of my imprisonment. Weep not, the time of your lamentation is not yet come. I wish to share with you my last wishes, for the hour when I shall be arrested and condemned to suffer martyrdom is fast approaching.' She requested that the Mayor's son accompany her to be sure that she would not be stripped of her gown, and that her body would be thrown into a pit and covered with stones.

Alone, praying and fasting through the night and the following day, at four hours after sunset came a harsh rapping on the door: the men of 'Azíz Khán, the Sardár, the Minister of War, demanded the prisoner. Veiled and ready, Ṭáhirih was pacing the floor in the lamplight and chanting a litany when the Mayor's wife came, trembling, to summon and escort her by lamplight down the dark stairs to the doorway and into the hands of the armed escort. Outside the house she mounted the steed sent by the Sardár and, accompanied by the Mayor's son and farrashes who walked on either side, the company clattered northward along the gloomy erratic streets. Those awakened by the hoof-falls, when only police were publicly abroad in that primitive city, shivered with knowledge of evil rampant. As she passed through the Shimírán Gate, the sentinels ogled the woman's swathed form and with their lanterns sardonically acknowledged their brothers escorting a new victim. And thus the cavalcade traversed the jumble of walled private properties to the

* Mullá 'Alí Kaní and Mullá Muḥammad Andírmání, ulamás, high level priests.

Ílkhhání Garden not far outside the city ramparts. On passing through the garden gates she called the youth to her side as they confronted a scene of debauchery, the Sardár, his adjutant, lieutenants and others noisily carousing in the malignant glare of smoky lamps. She handed a kerchief to the youth, saying:

'They apparently wish to strangle me. I set aside, long ago, a silken kerchief which I hoped would be used for this purpose.'[34]

Brought before the drunken and insulting Sardár who had ordered her death ride, she sharply declared, 'You can kill me as soon as you like, but you cannot stop the emancipation of women.'[35] Under the sorrowful and angry vigilance of the mayor's son, all occurred as she had anticipated. Upon the order of the brutal Sardár to 'Let that miserable wretch be strangled and her body be thrown into a pit!' it was done with casual viciousness, an anonymous dry well and insensate stones forever concealing a greatness ignobly snuffed out. And so fled the soul of that noblest of Bábí women, she who was the Seventeenth of the Báb's Letters of the Living,[36] she who at Badasht became the symbol of the abrogation of the out-dated religious law and a standard-bearer of the emancipation of women.*

In Teheran, the few survivors of the holocaust, both those of the original arrests and of the later ordeals in Núr, Nayríz and Shíráz, were in relative respite from the blood orgy, but remained in prison pending some unpredictable and perhaps whimsical decision of the court, even though their complicities were clearly disproven. But the implacable Queen Mother was not easily to be thwarted. When 'Abbás, the Bábí page boy of the martyr Ḥájí Sulaymán Khán, on his further rounds of forced betrayals and false identifications, was brought several times to the prison to confront Jináb-i-Bahá in chains, he refused to acknowledge that he knew this disciple of the Báb at all, holding to this denial despite threats to his life. Each time when taken into Bahá's presence, he would rub his eyes and stand for some moments gazing into the face of Bahá; but God's guidance stiffened his weak will and he would emphatically deny any knowledge of him, even though the queen had promised him a robe

* There is the account of Dr. Jacob Polak, the Austrian surgeon and ophthalmologist of the group brought by the Sháh to aid Persia, who reported that: 'I was an eye-witness of the execution of Qurratu'l-'Ayn (Ṭáhirih). The Minister of War ('Azíz Khán) and his adjutant performed it. That beautiful lady suffered her slow death with superhuman fortitude.' Dr. Polak was in Teheran in 1852, a teacher of medicine and surgery at Prime Minister Taqí Khán's Dárul-funún, the college of arts and technology. From 1855 until 1861 he was the Sháh's personal physician upon the passing away of the Frenchman Dr. Cloquet. (See Momen, *The Bábí and Bahá'í Religions*, p. 144, from *Persien*, Vol. I, p. 353.)

of honor and a position for positive identification. Frustrated in this effort to inculpate the nobleman of Núr, but in the hope of gaining favor with the Queen Mother, the jailers poisoned Jináb-i-Bahá's food, intercepting it en route from his home. With the first mouthful he had noted an altered taste and refused to eat the deadly meal; the poison only sickened the noble prisoner, for years impairing his then fragile health.*

Of this period, Jináb-i-Bahá comforted the Bábís, saying:

'*Be patient in the path of God and be not grieved by reason of that which befalleth you in the days of Him Who is the Spirit of God, for ere long ye shall, within His celestial Garden of holiness and sublimity, behold the recompense of them that endure patiently.*'[37]

Meanwhile 'Azím admitted his role as ringleader of the plot against the Sháh, with its implicit bid for Bábí leadership should the attempt have brought success. While the Sháh's mother continued to rage at Mírzá Ḥusayn-'Alí, whom she persistently regarded as the real author of the crime, his friends and relatives were busy seeking his delivery from prison, were mitigating the rigors of his confinement by taking food and drink to him, and were pressing his jailers with kindness. Surprisingly perhaps, several high-ranking visitors came to visit him in that grim place. Finally, at the insistence of the Russian minister Dolgorukov, 'Azím was taken to the Black Pit to confront Jináb-i-Bahá in the presence of the Russian minister's interpreter and a government representative.[38] There he stated without equivocation:

'The leader of this community is none other than the Siyyid-i-Báb, who was slain in Tabríz, and whose martyrdom induced me to arise and avenge his death. I alone conceived the plan and endeavored to execute it . . .' For his brave veracity, Jináb-i-Bahá later praised him, saying that '*In truth he was 'Azím, a great one.*' Delivered then into the hands of the priests, they killed him and desecrated his body.[39] But he was the last victim of that grim summer's martyrdoms, with only four Bábís left alive in the Pit. Those sacrificed were indeed the ransom paid for Jináb-i-Bahá's deliverance for his Mission. Years later Bahá'u'lláh wrote of 'Azím, saying:

'*And when ye took away His* [the Báb's] *life, one of His followers arose*

* At a later time, Bahá'u'lláh reflected on His own experience: '*At one time He suffered imprisonment in the land of Ṭá* (Teheran), *at another in the land of Mím* (Mázindarán), *then once again in the former land, for the sake of God, the Maker of the heavens. In His love for the Cause of God, the Almighty, the All-Bountiful, He was subjected there to chains and fetters.*' (*Tablets of Bahá'u'lláh*, p. 104.)

to avenge His death. He was unknown of men, and the design he had conceived was unnoticed by anyone. Eventually he committed what had been preordained.'[40]

The inquisitors' teeth were blunted, but they would not too easily loose their bite. Perhaps others might be found who would betray the charismatic nobleman of Núr fallen into this dangerous heresy and who, alive, might yet be a threat to the Sháh and his uneasy grip on a nation of discontented subjects. Thus the imprisonment continued.

The Black Pit was noisome, loathsome. Its unrelieved night was ugly with the din of the malefactors, crazed and hopeless, chained in their two facing rows. With the accumulating filth and the omnipresent vermin, the hazards of prison diseases were always imminent, but in God's wisdom Jináb-i-Bahá was spared, if narrowly. The malnutrition-to-starvation regularly induced in all prisoners by calloused jailers had been foiled by the family's gaining permission to bring food to Bahá after much persuasion and bribery of the guards. And then, perhaps during the third month of confinement, in the teeming black loneliness, in the midst of the detained and the condemned, his premonitions of Mission became a stream of consciousness of purpose welling up within him, his very imprisonment the way to glory: '*The Ancient Beauty hath consented to be bound with chains that mankind may be released from its bondage . . .*'[41] Of those highest moments of his inner Voice Jináb-i-Bahá related that: '*Day and night, while confined in that dungeon, We meditated upon the deeds, the condition, and the conduct of the Bábís, wondering what could have led a people so high-minded, so noble, and of such intelligence, to perpetrate such an audacious and outrageous act against the person of His Majesty. This Wronged One, thereupon, decided to arise, after His release from prison, and undertake, with the utmost vigor, the task of regenerating this people. One night, in a dream, these exalted words were heard on every side: 'Verily, We shall render Thee victorious by Thyself and by Thy Pen. Grieve Thou not for that which hath befallen Thee, neither be Thou afraid, for Thou art in safety. Erelong will God raise up the treasures of the earth – men who will aid Thee through Thyself and through Thy Name, wherewith God hath revived the hearts of such as have recognized Him.*'[42] Further describing those momentous times of illumination, he recounts: '*During the days I lay in the prison of Teheran, though the galling weight of the chains and the stench-filled air allowed Me but little sleep, still in those infrequent moments of slumber I felt as if something flowed from the crown of My head over My breast, even as a mighty torrent that precipitateth itself upon the earth from the summit of a lofty mountain. Every limb of My body would, as a result, be set afire. At such moments My tongue recited what no man could bear to hear.'*[43]

In that stygian blackness the mysterious Call of God was channeled to the Messenger chosen for a new era of man's spiritual progress: '*While engulfed in tribulations I heard a most wondrous, a most sweet voice, calling above My head. Turning My face, I beheld a Maiden* – the embodiment of the remembrance of the name of My Lord – suspended in the air before Me . . . Pointing with her finger unto My head, she addressed all who are in heaven and all who are on earth, saying: "By God! This is the Best-Beloved of the worlds, and yet ye comprehend not. This is the Beauty of God amongst you, and the power of His sovereignty within you, could ye but understand. This is the Mystery of God and His Treasure, the Cause of God and His Glory unto all who are in the kingdom of Revelation and of creation, if ye be of them that perceive."*[44]

How akin this mystical experience to Moses' summons by the Voice on Mount Sinai, to the descent of the Dove upon Jesus at His baptism by cousin John in river Jordan, to Zoroaster's seven visions, to the visitation of the angel Gabriel to Muḥammad in Ḥira Cave. Confirming his Mission, the Maiden appeared to Jináb-i-Bahá, expressing his Guidance in stirring words: '*Cry out before the gaze of the dwellers of heaven and earth: I am the Maid of Heaven, the Offspring begotten by the Spirit of Bahá* [Glory]'[45] 'And Bahá called her to him: '*Say: Step out of Thy holy chamber, O Maid of Heaven, inmate of the Exalted Paradise! Drape thyself in whatever manner pleaseth Thee in the silken Vesture of Immortality, and put on, in the name of the All Glorious, the broidered Robe of Light. Hear, then, the sweet, the wondrous accent of the Voice that cometh from the Throne of Thy Lord, the Inaccessible, the Most High.*'[46]

Remembering the Black Pit in later soliloquies, he amplified that potent vision of His Calling by God: '*I lay asleep on the bed of self when lo, Thou didst waken me with the divine accents of Thy voice, and didst unveil to me Thy beauty, and didst enable me to listen to Thine utterances, and to recognize Thy Self, and to speak forth Thy praise, and to extol Thy virtues, and to be steadfast in Thy love.*'[47]

Overwhelmed by the magnitude of his Summons and the supernal significance of his Designation as a Manifestation of God, he cried out in humility and exaltation. '*By My life! Not of Mine own volition have I revealed Myself, but God, of His own choosing, hath manifested Me . . . I was but a man like others, asleep upon My couch, when lo, the breezes of the All-Glorious were wafted over Me, and taught Me the*

* The Maiden: A symbol of the Spirit in the Bahá'í Revelation. See Note 12.

knowledge of all that hath been. This thing is not from Me, but from One Who is Almighty and All-Knowing. And He bade Me lift up My voice between earth and heaven . . . His all-compelling summons hath reached Me and caused Me to speak His praise amidst all people. I was indeed as one dead when His behest was uttered. The hand of the will of thy Lord, the Compassionate, the Merciful, transformed Me.'[48]* Again the Voice of Self-recognition: '*And whenever I chose to hold my peace and be still, lo, the voice of the Holy Ghost, standing on my right hand, aroused me, and the Supreme Spirit appeared before my face, and Gabriel overshadowed me, and the Spirit of Glory stirred within my bosom, bidding me arise and break my silence.*'[49]†

The Great Soul had been commanded to undertake His Mission. It was the beginning of the prophetic 'year nine' warned of by the Báb when '*the unrivalled Speaker . . . illumined the world with the joyful tidings of this Revelation.*'[50] At that moment also, as with a coronation garment, God enwrapped His Chosen One in that 'broidered robe of light' which would be seen and felt thereafter by every sincere soul who entered His presence.

> *I lay asleep on my couch, O my God, when lo, the gentle winds of Thy grace and Thy loving-kindness passed over me, and wakened me through the power of Thy sovereignty and Thy gifts, and bade me arise before Thy servants, and speak forth Thy praise, and glorify Thy word.*[51]
>
> **Bahá'u'lláh**

* See Note 13 on Bahá'u'lláh's recognition of His Mission.
† See Note 14.

Mírzá Riḍá-Qulí, physician half-brother of Jináb-i-Bahá and husband of the favored cousin Maryam. In the aftermath of the Síyáh-Chal he gave his ill and needy brother home and care toward that recovery necessary for the winter odyssey across the western mountains to Iraq.

A Persian caravan with howdahs for the women, pack animals with cargo, and a company of travellers including a spear-bearing guard.

9 Exile and Expatriate

In the city of justice it is the unrivalled Speaker Who, in the year nine, illumined the world with the joyful tidings of this Revelation . . .[1]

Bahá'u'lláh

Siyyid 'Alí-Muḥammad, the Báb, had reiterated the significance of the ninth lunar year after His Declaration, the year 1269 AH (1852–53)*† declaring: '*In the year nine ye will attain unto all good.*' '*In the year nine ye will attain unto the Presence of God.*'[2]

And long years later Bahá'u'lláh attested to the close time interval between the messages of the Báb and of Himself, saying:

'*That so brief an interval should have separated this most mighty and wondrous Revelation from Mine own previous Manifestation is a secret that no man can unravel, and a mystery such as no mind can fathom. Its duration had been foreordained.*'[3]

In His voluminous Writings, the Báb had repeatedly urged His followers to be ready for the new Manifestation of God, and had warned them of the hazards of failing to recognize Him in whatever way He might come into their ken. His exhortations to them were full of the challenge to see with unclouded sight, with the sure vision of the spirit, unconfused by loyalty to His own person and doctrines. In words of encouragement and also of unequivocal warning He adverted to the Most Great One Who would be manifest, the

---

* It should be pointed out, in the words of 'Abdu'l-Bahá concerning the close occurrence in time of two great Manifestations, that 'All the people of the world are awaiting two Manifestations, Who must be contemporaneous; all wait for the fulfillment of this promise.' 'The essential fact is that all are promised two Manifestations, Who will come one following on the other.' (Shoghi Effendi, *God Passes By*, p. 92.) The Báb Himself constantly referred to 'He Whom God will make manifest'. '*And, again, He* [the Báb] *saith: "Of all the tributes I have paid to Him Who is to come after Me, the greatest is this . . . that no words of Mine can adequately describe Him, nor can any reference to Him in My Book, the Bayán, do justice to His Cause."*' (Bahá'u'lláh, *Gleanings from the Writings of Bahá'u'lláh*, p. 10.)

† The critical lunar year nine extended from 15 October 1852 to 24 October 1853.

Qayyúm. He assured them of their singular privilege, of their rare opportunity to discover the Messenger and the Way, but He also made clear their danger of failure, saying:

'*Suffer not the Bayán and all that hath been revealed therein to withhold you from that Essence of Being and Lord of the visible and invisible.*'[4] Most pregnant of the Báb's predictions is this:

'*Well is it with him who fixeth his gaze upon the Order of Bahá'u'lláh, and rendered thanks unto his Lord. For He will assuredly be made manifest.*'[5]

In the evening of his life, Jináb-i-Bahá confirmed that:

'*In the year nine this Most Great Revelation arose and shone forth brightly above the horizon of the Will of God.*'[6] And in that year the '*requisite number of pure, of wholly consecrated and sanctified souls*' were '*most secretly consummated*'.[7]

As the momentous lunar year nine began, the scattered Bábís were scarcely offered a clear choice, nor was there an easy answer to their reflections on the many awesome allusions to that year in the Báb's Writings. Indeed, only a few of the Bábís were profound scholars or even familiar with the Bayán, for hand-transcribed copies were rare and hard to procure for study. And yet, as the year was beginning, God's wondrous pattern was being woven in the fetid gloom of the Black Pit, where His Summons was awakening and illuminating the consciousness of the One Appointed. Meanwhile, the seething court of the Sháh was providing design and action.

Jináb-i-Bahá later expressed the sorrows of that hour, saying: '*Those days were troublous days, and the fires of hatred burned high.*'[8] But by mid-November the blood-lust was dying down in the capital, and outside the prison powerful forces were engaged in efforts to save the nobleman of Núr who, still languishing in the Black Pit, represented an unresolved political and religious problem.

The family of Mírzá Buzurg well knew the many good deeds done by Mírzá Ḥusayn-'Alí of behalf of the Prime Minister, for twice the generous young neighbor of Núr had met the Vazír's financial obligations through payments of fines, and he had also arranged a government annuity for him. Moreover, in defrauding Buzurg's family after the Tákur raid and massacre, Vazír Áqá Khán was entitled to pangs of conscience, if indeed he was capable of them. Now the relatives of Mírzá Ḥusayn-'Alí brought gifts and a large sum of money to sway him to mercy, knowing also that on several occasions release had been near, but always it had been aborted by the ecclesiastics. Through informants the vigilant great-uncle Mírzá Yúsif was apprised of a plot by the mullás to kill this last surviving

Bábí of high leadership qualities, hence he hastened to approach Prince Dolgorukov, still angry at the betrayal of his trust by the Prime Minister four months before and greatly irritated at his own repeated failures to free his worthy friend. Prodded by a remonstrance from Mírzá Majíd, his secretary, the Prince determined to foil the plot by direct action, hence repaired to the palace.

In the Court where sentences of death were passed he awaited a propitious moment, then arose with permission and boldly addressed those present, although he was fully aware that his action was presumptuous in this foreign land where he lived under diplomatic sufferance. His very audacity and blunt words added force to this outcry against an imminent great miscarriage of justice to be visited upon a virtuous man already heavily penalized through false assertions of involvement in the assassination plot.

'Hearken to me!' he cried. 'I have words of importance to say to you. Have you not taken enough cruel revenge? Have you not already murdered a large enough number of harmless people, because of this accusation, the absurd falsity of which you are aware? . . . How is it possible that you can even pretend to think that this august prisoner planned that silly attempt to shoot the Sháh? . . . You know very well that this charge is not only untrue, but palpably ridiculous.

'There must be an end to all this. I have determined to extend the protection of Russia to this innocent nobleman; therefore beware! For if one hair of his head be hurt from this moment, rivers of blood will flow in your city as punishment. You will do well to heed my warning. My country is behind me in this matter.'[9]

While this stern ultimatum could well have contained an element of statesmanly bluff, the mighty and hungry Christian neighbor to the north was not to be trifled with, particularly after its successful wars with Persia short decades before in 1804–1814 and 1826–1828, wars very damaging to the Qájárs. Russia was clearly embarked on a continuing imperial expansion and might be looking for a pretext to quarrel again with a weak Islamic neighbor whose land, if subjugated, would become the route to a warm-water all-seasons port.* Of course the Prince gave no public hint of his complex motives, but

* Imperial Russia under several Czars of the latter nineteenth century had imperialistic designs upon Persia, weak and dispirited as it was after the two recent defeats by Russian forces. The diplomatic and military actions of Russia in the second half of the century are recorded and analyzed in the volume entitled *Russia and Britain in Persia, 1864 to 1914. A Study in Imperialism*, by Dr. Firuz Kazemzadeh, Yale University Press, 1968.

these possibilities were known and heeded. Perhaps, too, this voice was the additional weight tilting the scales towards those priests and courtiers who would not curry favor with the vengeful Queen Mother Jahán. Or perhaps the Court itself might be seeking a way to free the obviously innocent noble while avoiding suspicion of disloyalty to the throne.

With this intercession the Prime Minister could now comfortably send for his neighbor and erstwhile friend, however treacherously he had dealt with him, to be publicly questioned as a prelude to his release. Also, Mírzá Ḥusayn-'Alí's sister Sárih, daughter-in-law of Vazír Isma'íl of Yalrúd, had accompanied her personal plea for leniency with valuable gifts for Mírzá Áqá Khán. And in an earlier interrogation, Jináb-i-Bahá's own statement of the injustice of the charges had been masterful, focussing on Ṣadíq, the most resolute pistoleer:

'*The event itself indicates the truth of the affair and testifies that this is the action of a thoughtless, unreasoning, and ignorant man. For no reasonable person would charge his pistol with shot when embarking on so grave an enterprise. At least he would so arrange and plan it that the deed should be orderly and systematic. From the very nature of the event it is clear and evident as the sun that it is not the act of such as myself.*'[10]

It was mid-December when the Prime Minister was encouraged to send to the Síyáh-Chál a trusted representative, one Ḥájí 'Alí, to present to the noble prisoner the order for his discharge, for the Sháh had reluctantly agreed to his release and commanded his banishment from the realm.

Upon his arrival the sight which the worldly courtier beheld filled him with grief and surprise. The spectacle was one he had not fully anticipated, for perhaps he had never before been in the Black Pit. He wept dramatically as he found Mírzá Ḥusayn-'Alí chained to a floor infested with vermin, his neck weighted by galling chains, his face mirroring his privations, his person ungroomed, his clothing dirty and in tatters, his every inhalation contaminated by the pestilential atmosphere of that terrible dungeon.

'Accursed be Mírzá Áqá Khán,' he burst forth, as he identified Mírzá Ḥusayn-'Alí in the dim light provided by the guards. 'God knows that I had never imagined that you could have been subjected to so humiliating a captivity. I should never have thought that the Grand Vazír could have dared commit so heinous an act!' He removed the mantle from his shoulders, presenting it to Mírzá Ḥusayn-'Alí and entreating him to wear it when in the presence of the Minister and his counsellors.

But Jináb-i-Bahá reacted sharply to the mouthings of Ḥájí 'Alí. With his keen sense of justice he wished to emphasize the grim realities of the Black Pit there at the very edge of the palace walls. And also he sought to show his strong feelings at the failure of the Prime Minister earlier to defend his manifest innocence. Hence, refusing the mantle, weak and ragged, he walked the passageways of the palace compound to the chambers of the Grand Vazír, that craven and untrustworthy fellow Núrí so thoroughly corrupted by his high position.

The first words the Grand Vazír was moved to address to his recent captive were:

'Had you chosen to take my advice, and had you dissociated yourself from the faith of the Siyyid-i-Báb, you would not have suffered the pains and indignities which have been heaped upon you.'

'*Had you in your turn*', Mírzá Ḥusayn-'Alí retorted, '*followed my counsels, the affairs of the government would not have reached so critical a stage!*'

The Minister was immediately reminded of the conversation he had with his neighbor on the occasion of the Báb's martyrdom, the memorable prediction flashing into his mind that: '*The flame that has been kindled will blaze forth more fiercely than ever.*'

'The warning you uttered', he remarked, 'has already been fulfilled. What is it that you advise me to do now?'

'*Command the governors of this realm*', was the instant reply, '*to cease shedding the blood of the innocent, to cease plundering their property, to cease dishonoring their women and injuring their children. Let them cease the persecution of the Faith of the Báb. Let them abandon the idle hope of wiping out its followers.*'

On that day in the middle of December orders were given, through a circular issued to all the governors of the realm, bidding them desist from their acts of cruelty and shame. 'What you have done is enough,' wrote the Prime Minister. 'Cease arresting and punishing the people. Disturb no longer the peace and tranquillity of your countrymen.' As a gesture it was proper but, as later events proved, its effects were brief and of little consequence.[11]

The order for Mírzá Ḥusayn-'Alí's release permitted his return to his family. But he had scarcely arrived home when the formal decree of banishment for life came from the S͟háh, to be effective within a month from that date of mid-December 1852. He was commanded to leave Teheran for a place beyond the confines of Persia. The concurrent formal confiscation of all his possessions amounted to officially sanctioned theft of his lands and whatever goods remained after the looting and the vandalism. But the choice of the place of exile was his to make.

Prince Dolgorukov, informed of the edict of exile, offered to take Mírzá Ḥusayn-'Alí under the protection of the Russian Government, to afford asylum to him and his family, and to assist in his transfer to Russia. Although that land was close beyond Jináb-i-Bahá's beloved Alborz mountains and beyond the murky Caspian, his prescience pointed to western horizons. Nevertheless, deep gratitude was richly due the Prince for his resolute advocacy; whatever his complex and devious motivations as revealed in some part in his diplomatic reports, he had played a crucial and timely role in Jináb-i-Bahá's preservation for family and Mission, and for mankind. Indeed, Bahá's gratitude was lifelong, later expressed in an epistle to the Czar of Russia: '*Whilst I lay, chained and fettered, in the prison of Teheran, one of thy ministers extended me his aid. Wherefore hath God ordained for thee a station which the knowledge of none can comprehend except His knowledge. Beware lest thou barter away this sublime station.*'[12] And again, '*In the days when this wronged one was sore-afflicted in prison, the minister of the highly esteemed government* [of Russia] . . . *exerted his utmost endeavor to compass my deliverance. Several times permission for my release was granted. Some of the 'ulamás of the city, however, would prevent it. Finally, my freedom was gained through the solicitude and the endeavor of His Excellency the Minister* . . . *His Imperial Majesty, the Most Great Emperor* [of Russia] . . . *extended to me for the sake of God his protection – a protection which has excited the envy and the enmity of the foolish ones of the earth.*'[13]

Jináb-i-Bahá knew that Dolgorukov was but the instrument of God for his deliverance in an hour of mortal peril, and that the ultimate thanks must humbly be given to the Creator and Preserver, hence his moving soliloquy: '*Remember the grace of God towards thee when thou wast in prison with sundry others, and He brought thee out thence, and succoured thee with the hosts of the Invisible and the Visible* . . .'[14]

Directed then by his unfathomable wisdom and foresight, Jináb-i-Bahá chose the familiar environment of the Muslim Turkish empire to the west rather than the alien refuge of Russia to the north. He asked permission to settle in the Baghdad area, specifically in the Najaf-Karbilá zone which held the supreme shrines of Shi'ite Islám, and it was granted.

The prison experience had brought Jináb-i-Bahá to the very lip of survival itself. He was ill and emaciated, and now he must recover before the imminent midwinter odyssey. Moreover, from luxury to poverty, from great estates to empty-handedness had been the life change wrought during his four months of imprisonment. With his ancestral home at Tákur looted and burned, his mansion in Teheran stolen by Qájár princes, his rented home near the Shimírán Gate pillaged and abandoned, his close family in straitened circumstances, he himself a sick man not recovered from dire hardship, Jináb-i-Bahá could now say in intimate fellowship with the Hebrew prophet Job: 'The Lord gave and the Lord hath taken away; blessed be the Name of the Lord!'[15] His 1863 Baghdad commentary on Job echoes His feelings on what had befallen Him '*in the days of Him Who is the Spirit of God*', saying: '*O Lord! dire affliction assaileth me from every side, yet Thou art the One Whose grace pervadeth all things. Have mercy then upon me by Thy graciousness and grant favor unto me through Thy loving-kindness. Thou art in truth compassionate toward Thy servants.*'[16]

Home in Teheran had shrunk to two tiny rooms, perforce crowded, but throbbing with joy that the beloved father had returned. All, anything, could now be endured, for he had come back from the maw of death. There was deep joy for the children. But there was deep worry too. Ásíyih Khánum was in advanced pregnancy; and their father was weak, ill, dangerously debilitated, his neck and legs galled from the prison irons. But only one month was permitted to prepare for the hard journey to Iraq, with a bitter January in prospect. Fortunately the decree of the Prime Minister halting the persecution had created a time of lull when harassment of the Bábís was at a low ebb, thus enabling the loving lady Ásíyih, with loyal brothers Músá and young Muḥammad-Qulí, and with other helpers, to collect and sell what scattered possessions could be retrieved, including some few of her jewels, and gold buttons of her court garments. Prayer beads made of pearls inset with emeralds had been spared but these, earlier pawned for a small amount, could not be redeemed because of exorbitant interest. In the end they were able to accumulate a pathetic four hundred tumans* to meet the expenses of the coming journey, the Government giving nothing. A deeply gratifying aid came from loyal Isfándíyár,† that estimable servant

* A tuman was then worth one English pound sterling.

† Isfandíyár was a trusted and extremely able servant of the household of Jináb-i-Bahá. As with many similar servants within Islamic society where bond-servants or slaves were treated with great regard and protection, Isfandíyár was a member of the family, entrusted with marketing and many family business affairs. Early after the attempt on the life of the Sháh, lady Ásíyih sent Isfandíyár to Mázindarán to prevent his arrest, but he returned in the midst of the turmoil to aid his loved family. He was not betrayed by 'Abbás, the servant of Sulaymán Khán, he who had identified many of the Bábís who had met at his master's house. Following the departure of his

who used his few savings to help meet the urgent needs of his beloved family and master. Indeed, Isfándíyár was a man whom Jináb-i-Bahá considered to be the model of a luminous character. But the priceless manuscripts, artifacts and furnishings of a noble family had been stolen, and the possessions of a privileged life had vanished.

For Mírzá Ḥusayn-'Alí, virtually an invalid, there was a warm refuge in the home of his half-brother, the physician Mírzá Riḍá-Qulí, whose Bábí wife Maryam was a cousin and who had learned of the Faith through him; she was also the elder sister of Fáṭimih, Bahá's second wife. With the loving care given by Ásíyih and the devoted Maryam in that hospitable home, with good food and medications to heal his sores, Jináb-i-Bahá rebounded toward his customary dynamism. But his sojourn in the Black Pit had brought more than temporary disabilities: an inner transformation had occurred which transcended all physical limitations, bathing him with that robe of light which was to be his for a lifetime. Little Bahíyyih and the entire family perceived it.

'We saw a new radiance seeming to enfold him like a shining vesture . . . At that time we were only dimly aware of the wonder of it, without understanding, or even being told the details of the sacred event.'[17]

Moreover, the poem of nineteen couplets entitled the 'Rashh-i-Amá' (Sprinklings from a Light Cloud), was written soon after his discharge from prison. Conceived in the Síyáh-Chál, it reflected his mystical experience and his transformation in the Black Pit. In language which challenges translation and which expresses multiple meanings, he sought to release the torrent of thoughts and images which, almost cyclonic within his mind, rushed forth in words somehow descriptive of the feelings and perceptions evoked in his Call to Mission. The poem is also singularly memorable in its being the first fruit of His Revelation.

Aware of the finality of exile, Jináb-i-Bahá sought to heal rifts in his family before departure. One half-sister, Sháh-Sulṭán, who lived in another quarter of Teheran, had been estranged for some time. Therefore, '*As a token, however, of our loving-kindness, our affection and mercy, we, a few days prior to our departure, visited her and her mother*

---

beloved family for Baghdad and exile, he who had wished to accompany them was employed as the trusted head-servant of Yaḥyá Khán, Governor of Mázindarán, for the remainder of his life. Yaḥyá Khán, despite Isfandíyár's appeal to return to Jináb-i-Bahá, refused to give him up, so valuable had he become. (See Abu'l-Qásim Afnán, *Black Pearls*, Kalimat Press, 1988.)

[Kulthúm], *that haply she might quaff from the living waters of faith, and attain unto that which would draw her nigh unto God, in this day.*'[18]

Finally there came the day of departure, a day also of heavy hearts at partings for all time, a day when the sickly four-year-old Mihdí, named after his deceased paternal uncle,* had to be left behind to await health and a better travel season when he could rejoin his family. His father announced that '*he was afflicted through his separation*' from his family, but that this was destined '*according to what had been ordained for him through God's irrevocable decree*'.[19] None of the relatives dared to come to say farewell on that fateful day, save only lady Ásíyih's mother who was to care for her little grandchild Mihdí.

As Jináb-i-Bahá left Teheran forever '*in evident sorrow*', He yet had a note of hope for the decadent land from which He had been banished. In a later memorable passage He anticipates a far day of true emancipation for Persia and its Bahá'ís, saying: '*Let nothing grieve thee, O Land of Ṭá* [Teheran], *for God hath chosen thee to be the source of joy of all mankind. He shall, if it be His Will, bless thy throne with one who will rule with justice, who will gather together the flock of God which the wolves have scattered. Such a ruler will, with joy and gladness, turn his face towards, and extend his favours unto, the people of Bahá. He indeed is accounted in the sight of God as a jewel among men. Upon him rest forever the glory of God, and the glory of all that dwell in the kingdom of His revelation.*'[20]

He spoke several times of the exile, saying:

'*And when this Wronged One went forth out of His prison, We journeyed, in pursuance of the order of His Majesty, the Sháh . . . to 'Iráq, escorted by officers in the service of the esteemed and honored governments of Persia and Russia.*'[21] '*We departed out of Teheran, at the bidding of the King, and, by his leave, transferred Our residence to 'Iráq.*'[22]

It was the 12th day of January, 1853, the winter having set in with exceptional severity to promise a hard crossing of the Iranian plateau and the already snow-bound western mountains. Through the southwest gate of Teheran passed the little cavalcade which included the close family of Jináb-i-Bahá, his brothers Mírzá Músá and sixteen-year-old Muḥammad-Qulí, his ward from childhood. There was a Persian escort officer of the Imperial Guard and an official of the Russian Legation, sent perhaps to watch over the precious family lest there be some treachery en route. Riding in howdahs were the

* Mírzá Mihdí, elder full brother of Mírzá Ḥusayn-'Alí, died in 1848. Thus when a son was born to Ásíyih Khánum in 1849, he was named Mihdí in memory of the deceased brother.

adult women and the children, including Ásíyih <u>Kh</u>ánum and the
seven-year-old Bahíyyih, all enduring the rolling jolting of the mules
so like a voyage on a choppy sea. Young 'Abbás was nine and able to
ride with his uncles and those others who had elected to share the
exile.

The road first led southwest across the barren plains with their
intervening ridges, traversing impoverished and often ruinous
hamlets and villages of mud-brick and stone construction. It led
them across the Saveh Pass for long upland days which culminated in
a hazardous crossing of the icy Qara Char river, dangerous in the
winter and spring. Thence a rough climbing of the snowy ridges
before passing Bibikabad, and so toward Hamadán. As the caravan
pushed forward, light snow powdered the ground, and sharp winds
produced a passage of sheer torture. Frequent stops and outdoor
camps were necessary whenever travel became too arduous, discomfort too acute. And always the laden mules and horses plodded
stolidly along the iron-hard roadway, rocky, snowy-icy, the mud
hurtfully frozen, making perhaps fifteen to twenty miles each hard
day. Sometimes they walked abreast, often in line, bells and harness
jingling. And there were moments of beauty and appreciation too of
the stark splendor of the landscapes and of the luminous starry skies
of the high desert nights.

Harborage was thankfully relished for some days in February in
Hamadán, once ancient Ecbatana of the Medes, above which reared
6,300-foot Mount Alvand. It was a time to rest, to be warm again,
and to regain courage for the arduous travel ahead.

On the road once more, the party plodded forward with the
altitude increasing as the high plateau slanted upward across the <u>Sh</u>áh
Pass through the Nahavand Mountains, whose highest peaks rear to
more than 12,000 feet; their spines and slopes were coated with
repeated snowfalls. The temperatures fell still more and the riders,
exposed to the cutting winds, suffered acutely from exposure. The
boy 'Abbás was inadequately clad, for there had not been time nor
money to prepare for the frigid days in the saddle. He was exposed to
the boreal winds for long periods of time and suffered frostbite of his
feet and fingers, injuries creating chronic and recurrent pain and
discomfort for his lifetime. After passing through Bisitun along the
Kuh-Paro ridge, it was with great relief that the company reached
the town of Kirmán<u>sh</u>áh* on the edge of Persian Kurdistán, 350

---

* Now recently renamed Bá<u>kh</u>tarán.

miles from Teheran, a town notable for its having been the capital of the Sassanian King Bahram IV. The party sought refuge for a number of days at an inn, to rest and to prepare for the hard climbs and arduous crossing of the great breadth of the lofty Zagros Mountains round about and ahead, in places deep in snow, dangerous in their frozen beauties. The inn was of comfortable design, a hollow square of two storeys surrounding a large courtyard, with rooms and a wooden veranda on the upper level. The ground floor compartments housed the animals and their baggage. There were no beds, only mats on the floor, but the inn's offerings were far superior to saddle and howdah and roadside camps.

It had been a hard journey thus far for the gentle lady Ásíyih, already in the last months of her seventh pregnancy. En route she had been able to wash clothing in the public baths of the towns, and also to bathe herself; but working in cold water with wet garments ravaged the gentlewoman's hands, which were painfully chapped. Too, food preparation for the company of travelers was difficult, but eased by the cooperation of others of the party. Tea was available as were a few eggs, cheese and coarse bread difficult for the still-ailing Jináb-i-Bahá to stomach. Yet the admirable Ásíyih not only never complained, but sought constantly to support the others, to do kindnesses, giving sympathy to each person who was enduring these midwinter tribulations. And there were incidents to remember, such as that evening in the lightless caravanserai when lady Ásíyih had procured some flour and sugar, and with joy set out to bake a sweetcake for her beloved husband. Forced to work in the dark, instead of sugar she added salt to the mix, to her consternation producing a totally inedible cake.

During the days of readying for the further, harder travel, a furtive fugitive made his presence known. It was half-brother Yaḥyá down from Gílán after his flight from arrest or death in the raid on Núr. Timid and retiring as ever, and fearful still for his life, he was scarcely the image of the Bábí nominee for leadership which some considered him to be. In Kirmánsháh he had become a vendor of shrouds for one 'Abdu'lláh of Qazvín, remaining carefully incognito and not known to the Bábís. From his brother Jináb-i-Bahá he obtained a small sum of money sufficient to enable him to buy a few bales of cotton, thereby to play the role of a cotton merchant, in which disguise he planned to follow his brother to Baghdad. In Kirmánsháh the resident Bábís were fortified in their faith by the exiles. And, as departure approached, some few pilgrims, perhaps carrying the bodies of relatives for interment in the holy cities of

The unique and dramatic town of Karand, most picturesque community of the western Kurdish mountains, set in the mouth of a canyon at the base of great cliffs. This was the home of the 'Alíyu'lláhís, friends of the Bábís and erstwhile disciples of Ṭáhirih. Here Governor Hayát-Qulí Khán welcomed Jinab-i-Bahá to his home (above) and the townspeople welcomed the exiles to their hears. (Drawings by Seyhoun)

Iraq,* chose to join the company of Bábís for safety and fellowship in that evil winter.

Departing reluctantly from the sheltered town, plodding upward through valleys heavy with snow, they happily came to Karand, that most picturesque town of the mountains, built on terraced slopes at the mouth of a great gorge, and facing a broad and fertile intermontane valley beyond the canyon. Karand was the center of the religiously tolerant Kurdish 'People of the Truth' (Ahl-i-Ḥaqq), believers in the Imám 'Alí whom they equated with God and who therefore called themselves 'Alíyu'lláhís ('Alí as God); rebellious toward the government, their messianic traditions responded to the Bábí hope and promise. It was also the home of another small minority, the equally tolerant Daoudis.

The town was notably friendly and hospitable to Bábís, for Ṭáhirih had come through Karand in 1848 bound for Qazvín after her expulsion from Karbilá and Baghdad, but exultant from the triumphs of her memorable stay at the Shi'ite shrines of Iraq. Here among friendly mountaineers of unique receptiveness she had expounded the Teachings of the Báb, exciting the interest of all classes of the inhabitants. Here, despite a pause of only three days, some twelve hundred persons had arisen to place themselves at her command, so cogent was her message of a great new day dawning.

Welcomed by Governor Ḥayát-Qulí Khán and royally housed in his fine two-storey brick residence set against the mountain slope, Jináb-i-Bahá responded so spiritedly to the open arms of the townspeople that his potent words lighted again in their hearts the ardor and urgency of the Báb's Message, and thus for a time thereafter they even considered themselves to be Bábís. These few March days of rest and recuperation in that orchard, vineyard and garden town became a personal conquest for the great exile, a visit long remembered by its people and benefiting every Bábí who passed through Karand in later days.

In a prayer revealed at that time Jináb-i-Bahá reflected upon the

---

* The Shi'ite Holy Cities of Iraq included Najaf, Karbilá, Kaẓímayn and Samarra. Very many Shi'ite Persians wished to be buried in these Holy Cities, as witness the burial in Najaf of Mírzá Buzurg, father of Mírzá Ḥusayn-'Alí. Hence parties of persons accompanying the bodies of the deceased came over the mountains throughout the year, perhaps also accompanied by pilgrim relatives. Typically, the bodies were anointed with fragrant resins and tightly swathed in long cloth wrappings, and were bound to the sides of slogging mules or camels. Wintertime transportation was also far better for preservation of the remains against deterioration during the long passage.

months past and the sufferings of the journey from his homeland, saying: '*My God, My Master, My Desire! . . . Thou has created this atom of dust through the consummate power of Thy might, and nurtured Him with Thine hands which none can chain up . . . Thou hast destined for Him trials and tribulations which no tongue can describe, nor any of Thy Tablets adequately recount. The throat Thou didst accustom to the touch of silk Thou hast, in the end, clasped with strong chains, and the body Thou didst ease with brocades and velvets Thou hast at last subjected to the abasement of a dungeon . . . How many the nights during which the weight of chains and fetters allowed Me no rest, and how numerous the days during which peace and tranquility were denied Me . . . until, finally, Thy decree was irrevocably fixed, and Thy behest summoned this servant to depart out of Persia, accompanied by a number of frail-bodied men and children of tender age, at this time when the cold is so intense that one cannot even speak, and ice and snow so abundant that it is impossible to move.*'[23]

Sadly leaving Karand to face the hard mountain passages ahead, the party crossed over a divide to reach the headwaters of the icy Holwan River, down whose rough valley the road dropped, often sharing the gravelly bottom of the fast-flowing stream. Spring was dimly visible in the valley. March flowers were scattered timorously in sunny coves among rocks and brush, spangling the little meadows and field edges. The shrubs and trees showed tender buds greening faintly from the spring warmth errantly arising from the sunny plains beyond the mountains. The hill winds at their backs hastened the caravan through the territory of the Zangana tribe and so to a crossing of the Zahab River. Passing along the still arduous road the company came to shelter in the decrepit smoke-blackened caravanserai called the Mansion of Shírín after the beauteous heroine of a well-known romantic poem.* Not far beyond they emerged from the hills to reach the Persian border town named Khusraví after Shírín's lover, King Khusraw. Before passing through the customs post, the Persian and Russian officers bade farewell and began their cold backtrack through the Zagros, while beyond the border a contingent of Turkish soldiers joined the party as escorts.

* In the famous poem entitled 'Khusraw and Shírín', the great Persian poet Nizami dramatized the love of the Sassanian King Anúshirwan (of immortal soul) for the beautiful Shírín (the sweet one), and also the fate of his luckless rival Farhad (the patient one), required to cut through the mountain of Behistun of Achaemenian history. The poet developed a colorful tale which appears largely to be the stuff of legend rather than of recorded history, for even the identity of Shírín has been insecure among the many amours of the adventurous and warlike monarch. One source has it that Shírín was the daughter of a Byzantine king. Khusraw, exiled at that time, is said to have fallen in love with her, and his love was requited.

Mírzá Músá, that spirit of service to Jináb-i-Bahá, was sent ahead to Kh́aniqayn with instructions to rent an orchard for a camp in which they might celebrate the days of Naw-Rúz, the Persian New Year. The caravan followed to settle down in an orange grove already in bloom, sibilant date palms round about, winter wheat and barley deliciously green, the ground vegetation rich in March floral displays. It was altogether a celebratory setting for the nearly exhausted travelers so deeply relieved to be out of the snow, ice, freezing runnels and brooks, to be delivered from the cold winds of mountain springtime, and to be approaching the great warm Tigris River valley after more than five hundred grim winter miles. Of this moment Bahá gave a challenging valedictory: '*It is reported in the press that this servant hath fled from the land of Ṭá (Teheran) and gone to 'Iráq . . . Not even for a single moment hath this Wronged One ever concealed Himself. Rather hath He at all times remained steadfast and conspicuous before the eyes of all men. Never have We retreated, nor shall We ever seek flight. In truth it is the foolish people who flee from Our presence. We left Our home country accompanied by two mounted escorts, representing the two honored governments of Persia and Russia until We arrived in 'Iráq in the plenitude of glory and power.*'[24]

And reflecting upon his supernal mission of spiritual guidance, he cited criticisms that '*Certain ones among both commoners and nobles have objected that this wronged One is neither a member of the ecclesiastical order nor a descendant of the Prophet.*'[25]

Passing over the fine bridge across a Silwan River tributary, thence over the rough broken country of the Hamrin Range and so through villages of the plains to Abú-Jisra, a welcome stopover permitted Jináb-i-Bahá to teach the Bábí doctrines to the open, simple Arab villagers, a number of whom espoused the Cause. This pleasant land of the Silwan, now called the Diyala, was once densely populous and highly developed for agriculture through extensive irrigation systems dating back to Assyrian and Babylonian times; now its canals were clogged and functionless, its soils salted. But the land could well be the Biblical garden 'east of Eden' and the Diyala was probably the Biblical Gihon,* the 'river (which) went out of Eden to water the Garden.'[26] (See Note 15.)

Joyously proceeding down the banks of the Diyala, beginning to show its spring freshet level, the little party was accompanied by the new Arab believers. All crossed the river at Ba'qubah with the

* Gihon is also the name of a famous spring close to the old city of Jerusalem in Israel; its waters were brought by tunnel into that city.

minarets of Baghdad on the horizon, and passed through K͟hán Bani-Sa'ad. These converts who came to the gate of Baghdad with Jináb-i-Bahá were the first of a large company of believers who were addressed in later letters as 'those residing in the land of Qáf', a reference to Ba'qubah; the first Bahá'í center of Iraq was in one of their villages, Awás͟híq.*

On 8 April, after a night in a caravanserai, deeply fatigued and at the limit of their resources, the exile party passed through the Báb'u'l-Wastání,† the ancient eastern gate protecting the moat bridge into the city, and came to a place of relative comfort in the old city, there to remain for three days of recuperation. They had traveled more than six hundred miles on 'that terrible journey' in the dead of winter, arduously; and as the child Bahíyyih recalled: 'On the way to Bag͟hdád we sometimes encamped in wilderness places.'[27] But now it was springtime at the threshold of Eden.

The mighty Tigris River at Baghdad.

---

* For the names of the villages and towns through which Jináb-i-Bahá passed en route to Baghdad, the illustrated booklet of Mihdí Rajabzadeh has provided the sequence and the meanings of those names, checked and modified by Da'oud Aní who has actually traveled the route. For many details of that harrowing midwinter transit of the Iranian Plateau and Zagros Mountains, the scholarship of Da'oud Aní has been essential. His Iraqi upbringing and access to local information and illustrations have been priceless in providing first-hand data.
† The Báb-u'l-Wastání (the Middle Gate) was built in 1180 AD by Caliph Abu'l-'Abbás and rebuilt in 1819 by Valí Dawud Pás͟há. In 1899 Mírzá Asadu'lláh Iṣfáhání and his companion, carrying the casket containing the remains of the blessed Báb and Anís, his disciple, passed through the gate en route to 'Akká; they spent one night in the caravanserai associated with the gate. (Per Da'oud Aní.)

After their pause in Baghdad, Jináb-i-Bahá took his small company upriver to the pontoon bridge of boats at 'Azamíyyih, and crossed from Mu'ázzam to the western bank to reach nearby Káẓimayn, only three miles distant. This holy city of the seventh and ninth Imáms, both entitled Káẓim and both poisoned in early Islamic fratricidal intrigues, was a small town set among huge date palm groves, and was largely inhabited by expatriate Persians. Here the family lived in the rented house of Ḥájí 'Abdu'l-Majíd of Shíráz.

The Sháh's representative in Baghdad, the Consul Mírzá Ibrahim Khán of Shíráz, was informed of this move. Well aware of the political and religious repercussions possible with the coming of the potent and eloquent Bábí Mírzá Ḥusayn-'Alí Núrí to this incendiary spot of many Persians, he intervened to suggest that Mírzá Ḥusayn-'Alí establish his residence in old Baghdad. Jináb-i-Bahá readily assented to this proposal and on his return to Baghdad a month later, in mid-May, rented the small house of Ḥájí 'Alí Madad in the Reṣafa Quarter of the old city, on a lane near the Mosque of Da'oud Páshá.*

The journey had been unconscionably hard, but Jináb-i-Bahá's reception had everywhere been favorable. Moreover, he had turned down gifts from those in authority and had refused to allow the escort officials to levy provisions from the peasants as was their wont. However, a deep and nagging unhappiness pervaded him: Persia was now to be only a memory, a home never to be seen again. At this irreparable loss through the edict of the Sháh he reflected that '. . . *he banished me and my family from my country, whereupon we arrived in 'Iráq in evident sorrow.*'.

The greatest Persian had lost his homeland forever, although it lived on in numerous references in his writings (see Note 16.) Ennobling his unpromising home city within that mind which saw the reality of the present but also the future of Persia, he said: '*Call thou to remembrance, O Land of Ṭá* (Teheran), *the former days in which thy Lord had made thee the seat of His throne, and had enveloped thee with the effulgence of His glory . . .*[28] *It is our wish to remember the Abode of supreme blissfulness* (Teheran), *the holy and shining city – the city wherein the fragrance of the Well-Beloved hath been shed, wherein His signs have been diffused, wherein the evidences of His glory have been revealed, wherein His standards have been raised, wherein His tabernacle hath been pitched, wherein each of His wise decrees hath been unfolded.*'[29]

* Now the Mosque of Haidar-Khán.

The pontoon bridge of boats at 'Azamíyyih, upriver from Baghdad, near to the Holy City of Káẓimayn, to which Jináb-i-Bahá came with his party and his family to live briefly in the House of Ḥájí 'Abdu'l-Majíd of S͟híráz.

He had now become a citizen of the wider world, spokesman and guide and teacher for the people of planet earth yet in travail, its unification made inevitable through the many new instrumentalities of science and society just being born and destined to be infused with his Message. In this latter half of the nineteenth century, the time of his mission, began the explosion of scientific knowledge in congruence with the new age of religious enlightenment. Jináb-i-Bahá's role was to bring to the world that essential spirit of unity, that will and common purpose to become one people, 'one soul in many bodies'. All mankind would share and enrich God's unique planet earth in peaceful cooperation and mutual love.

After that fateful year nine, his arrival in the Arab-Turkish province of Iraq began an unfolding time of creativity. The Spirit of the High Prophet had been released for His Mission.

O present hour! Rejoice thou by virtue of this Hour which hath struck within thee through the power of God, and appreciate this eternal, this imperishable and celestial food which streameth down from the clouds of holiness from behind veils of light and descendeth from the heaven of glory upon Him Who beareth the Name of God.

O present day! Shed thou illumination upon all created things through the advent of this radiant, this glorious Day which hath been manifested unto all the world from the horizon of 'Iráq.[30]

Bahá'u'lláh

Notes

1 Persian Names and Titles

Persian names and the Persian system of titles require both definition and a statement of practices employed in this text of a nineteenth-century drama. Names of persons, up to Persian governmental action in very recent times when family names were required, consisted of one or two given names, without a family name. Rather, the geographical place of birth was usually added as an identifier, e.g. Káẓim of the city of Rasht, Siyyid Káẓim-i-Ras͟htí. Titles of achievement, distinction or birth, such as Siyyid, the title given to the descendants of Muḥammad; Ḥájí for one who has fulfilled his Muslim obligation to visit Mecca and Medina as a pilgrim; mullá for a Muslim religious teacher of theology, judge or preacher; Buzurg, the Great One; these and other titles were added either before or after the compound given name and place. Also, since everyone sought an honorific title, often overblown beyond the merits of the person thus designated, these are added where known. It must be stated that the names from Islamic history are excessively repetitive and often outright confusing.

Specifically in the Bábí-Bahá'í nomenclature, titles given to individuals by the High Prophets tended to replace all former names. In Bahá'í literature these latter names have tended to become the sole ones used, e.g. 'Abdu'l-Bahá (Servant of Bahá) for 'Abbás (Effendi); Áqáy-i-Kalím (Interlocutor) or simply Kalím for Mírzá Músá, et al.

In the case of titles accruing to positions such as that of Grand Vazír (Prime Minister), the S͟háh (King), etc., the English equivalents are often used after a first statement of the Persian title, wherever this makes for clarity. English approximations are also used in such cases as kalantar (mayor), Amír Díván (chief court chamberlain), etc., wherever encountered. In any event, a glossary is supplied for reference in this often confusing encounter with a non-western culture of an earlier time. No attempt is made to explain the principles of pronunciation of Persian words. The title Mírzá as a prefix of a man's name is honorific for men who are given respect through family, profession, or achievement; as a suffix Mírzá means prince. The title Khánum after a woman's name similarly is a respectful honorific used for women of rank or achievement.

2 Sources of information

The author has had access to the common sources of Bahá'í information in English, and the advantage of expert assistance from various scholarly sources. In addition, one nineteen-day visit to Iran in 1973 provided certain on-the-spot observations and an abundance of photographs of sites associated with the Founders of the Faith. The Bahá'í World Centre photographic archive has supplied much visual detail of nineteenth-century Persia for study. As a veteran physician and public health worker, the author felt free to make observations and comments from scientific reports which have analyzed that time; and his work as a prison doctor for two years has invested the Síyáh-Chál experience of Bahá'u'lláh with a deep personal reality. Twenty-five years in Israel, the Holy Land, have permitted an experience with the ambience of a Middle Eastern country similar in many ways to Iran in social reality, but particularly in the common natural history of the two lands. Recurrent observations in 'Akká and Haifa, the Twin Holy Cities of the Bahá'í Faith, have developed a relatively deep penetration of the latter years of the life of the High Prophet, as mirrored in the book *Door of Hope* (1983).

A natural tendency to reflect a feeling for Bahá'u'lláh well beyond hagiography must be moderated through such objectivity as is possible so soon after the lifetime of the Prophet. Nevertheless, the author's subjective emotional conviction has been sustained by a steadily deepening appreciation of the Great Soul.

3 The Shi'ites of Islám

The early years of Islamic history witnessed a fundamental division between the body of Muslims and the 'party of 'Alí' (Shi'at 'Alí), a faction supporting 'Alí, fourth caliph of the Muslim community. When 'Alí was killed in 661 AD, his followers asserted the primacy of the succession of 'Alí's descendants who were known as Imáms, of which 'Alí himself was the first. The majority of the faithful, however, held to the authority contained in the Islamic traditions, the sunná. 'Alí's son Ḥusayn was defeated and killed at Karbilá in Iraq in 680 AD, but his supporters gathered behind the later Imáms, most of whom were poisoned in the internecine strife among Islamic factions. A number of sects developed: Ithná-'Ashariya (Twelvers), Ismáilí, Alawí, Zaydí, etc., usually named after their founders and following their interpretations. The largest and strongest was that of the 'Twelvers', who recognized the twelve Imáms and enunciated a strong doctrine of prediction for a return of Imáms 'Alí and Ḥusayn after the advent of the Qá'im; these Shi'ites became the dominant group and force in Iran with the coming of the Safávid Dynasty in the 16th Century.

4 The 'Ascent' of Muḥammad

The Mi'ráj, the Ascent, was a dream of Muḥammad in His early Mecca days which He recorded in the Seventeenth Súrih of the Qur'án, later entitled 'The House of Israel' or 'The Night Journey'. It reads, in the Arberry translation (17:1): '*Glory be to Him, who carried His servant at night from the Holy Mosque to the Further Mosque, the precincts of which We have blessed, that We might show Him some of our signs. He is the All-hearing, the All-seeing.*'

Followers of Muḥammad, as recorded in the traditions, spun out elaborations of the story, identifying Jerusalem as the place of the 'Ascent'. In the latter centuries Islám has generally taken the visionary journey to be from Mecca to Jerusalem, and the 'ascent' to heaven on the steed al-Burak (al-Buráq) (the Lightning) to be a literal happening rather than a dream, and the 'Further Mosque' to be Al-Aqsa (the Outer) in Jerusalem, although in early years it was thought by many Islamic scholars to be Medina's 'outer mosque'. Shaykh Aḥmad and Siyyid Káẓim had vigorously and properly portrayed the event, which had been given no geographical point, as a spiritual, not a physical, experience of the Prophet. (See Balyuzi, *Muḥammad and the Course of Islám*, p. 41.)

In recent years the archeological exposure of Islamic constructions surrounding the Temple Mount in Jerusalem has revealed new aspects of the Mi'ráj tradition. The monumental eastern Golden Gate, in Muslim times called the Gates of Mercy and Repentance from its two archways, once opened onto the Temple Mount but is now closed by masonry. It was built during Omayyad times at the end of the seventh century as an adjunct to the mosques Al-Aqsa and Dome of the Rock. The Caliph Muawiyah chose to interpret the story of Muḥammad's dream journey to heaven as having occurred from David's city and Mount Moriah, hence raising Jerusalem to tertiary significance as a Muslim holy place, and thereby providing a religious justification and pilgrimage site for his empire based in Damascus. (For complete data, see Ben Dov, *The Shadow of the Temple*, pp. 278 and 286.) It should be noted that Muḥammad Himself gave tribute to Jerusalem because of the Biblical story of Abraham, Hagar and Ishmael, but late in His Ministry made Mecca the Qiblih of prayer.

5 The Qájár Dynasty of Persia

The Qájár dynasty of Turkoman-derived Persian kings from Gurgán reigned for one hundred and forty years, from 1785 to 1925. During this long period the Qájárs promoted Shi'ite separatism from dominant Sunní Islám. Their reign was marked by steadily increasing pressures from the colonial powers of Europe, but principally from Russia and Britain. Two wars with Russia, in 1804–1814 and again in 1826–1828, left a defeated Persia with heavy losses of land, men and resources but, most importantly, with a great vulnerability to European trade, sciences and social ideas. England's role was a strong one in its intense competition with Russia for commercial and political influence which, while bringing Iran into the modern world in many ways, also had adverse effects in compounding the economic crises of the nineteenth century. The Qájárs were, moreover, responsible for encouraging the entrenchment of a highly corrupt feudalism described pungently by Lord Curzon. Their horde of progeny, born of Islamic polygamous families, bled the land and tyrannized the unfortunate people so gravely handicapped by these parasitical princes and princesses. (See Kazemzadeh, *Russia and Britain in Persia: 1864–1919. A Study in Imperialism.*)

Three Qájár Sháhs feature in the Bábí-Bahá'í early history: Fatḥ-'Alí Sháh (1797–1834). Muḥammad Sháh (1834–1848), and Naṣiri'd-Dín Sháh (1848–1896). All three were distinguished for misrule, corruption, cruelty and exercise of the many sins possible for despots. Fatḥ-'Alí Sháh lost two wars and much territory to the Russians, and opened Iran to Anglo-Russian rivalry. Muḥammad Sháh sought to revive industry and agriculture in the land, but with little success; under his rule the Bábís began their explosive origins. Nasiri'd-Dín Sháh sold national concessions to the European powers, savagely oppressed the Bábí-Bahá'í movement, and saw the emergence of a popular protest campaign which became a dramatic activity under Muẓaffar Sháh, his successor. Two later ineffectual Sháhs under the impact of dynamic world changes produced an attempt to institute a constitutional government. This was followed by civil war, with the appearance of Riḍá-Khán and his establishment of the short-lived Pahleví Dynasty in 1925, which ended in 1979 with the coming of the Khomeini government.

6 The Ṣúfís of Iran

From the teachings of Islám came a crop of religious thinkers, some fanatical and narrow, others liberal and mystical. Those who came to be called Súfís did not emerge as followers of a doctrine put forth by a single teacher of Islamic mysticism, but rather in a recurrent appearance of poets and scholars who 'at first were quietists, then ecstatics', the best known of whom was Jaláli'ḍ-Dín-i-Rúmí, greatest of the mystical poets of Persia. As Sufism widely and spottily emerged over the centuries of Islamic growth and change, it was diverse in its manifestations, 'Eclectic, absorbing and transmuting', but it 'has never been an order or a sect'. (Rice.) The pre-Crusader evolution of Sufism came to its climax in the clarifications of al-Ghazzalí, who 'harmonized philosophy with religious belief' and 'cleared the Súfí path of its extravagances'.

The name Súfí derives from 'súf', a rough woolen garment which marked the early devotees, men who espoused the varied ideas of Muslim mysticism. (See Balyuzi, *Muḥammad and the Course of Islám*, pp. 275–286.)

7 Mullá 'Alí of Bastám, Valiant Disciple

The Báb gave the learned, pious, bold and eloquent Mullá 'Alí of Basṭám the highly dangerous task of confronting the Shi'ite divines in their very strongholds in Iraq, particularly in Najaf and Karbilá. First proclaiming in Najaf the coming of the Promised One, he met the expected storm of reaction from both Shaykhís and the more orthodox priests. Then, with leonine courage he proclaimed to the Shaykhís of Karbilá the appearance of the Báb and evoked such a wave of hostility that he was arrested, turned over to the government authorities and placed in the hands of the Turkish Valí Najíb Páshá, whose hands were yet bloody from suppressing the revolt of that city in 1843. The Valí (Governor) ordered a convocation of chief priests, both Sunní and Shi'ite. These hardened divines, schooled in Islamic jurisprudence, and aware that even in prison the ardent Mullá 'Alí had converted many visitors who became enamored of the new Faith, sat in judgment upon him. The Sunnís passed sentence of death upon Mullá 'Alí for blasphemy, but in the end, the Shi'ites agreed only to his removal from Iraq although they issued a joint fatwa (death sentence) with the Sunnís. The fatwa, studied intensively by Dr Moojan Momen, reveals their differences of judgment. Najíb Páshá, asked by the Persian Government to extradite Mullá 'Alí to Iran, decided instead to remove this source of religious controversy to Constantinople. Sent to the Turkish capital, he was sentenced to hard labor and was thought to have been consigned to the naval stockyards. It must be presumed that there he died, anonymously. (See Momen, *The Trial of Mullá 'Alí Bastámí: A Combined Súnni-Shi'ite Fatwa Against the Báb*, Iran XX, British Institute of Persian Studies, 1982.)

8 Fáṭimih, Qurratu'l-'Ayn, Ṭáhirih: A Womanly Phenomenon

The extraordinary woman Fáṭimih, of Baraghan and later of Qazvín, lived a singularly momentous and important life, hence her origins and relationships deserve a certain detail of record.

Three able brothers came to Qazvín in the early 1900s from Baraghan, a village east of that city. The two elder brothers, Muḥammad Taqí and Muḥammad Salíh, undertook religious studies in Qum, Iṣfáhán and Iraq, returning after some years to Qazvín as qualified mujtahids (scholar priests), Taqí to show himself as ambitious, power-hungry and greedy, Salíh to become a scholar. The third brother, 'Alí, also of religious bent, became a follower of Siyyid Káẓim of Rasht.

Mullá Salíh's daughter Fáṭimih (b. 1817) showed herself to be a prodigy of body, mind and spirit. Moreover, under her surprisingly tolerant and loving father, she pressed forward in her studies far beyond those permitted to women of her time. Married at age thirteen to her first cousin Muḥammad, son of Mullá Taqí, she accompanied him to the holy cities of Iraq; there he completed his theological studies in thirteen years, during which time two sons were born to the couple. Fáṭimih seized upon the unique Islamic educational environment to develop her great powers, and became fully as learnèd as her husband despite his resistance to her scholarship. Here too she became acquainted with Siyyid Káẓim of Ras͟ht and the S͟hayk͟hís. Returning to Qazvín, but without recognition of her theological achievements, and with her marriage in shambles despite the birth of a third son, she declared a unilateral separation and with her devoted younger sister Marzieh returned to Iraq and the S͟hayk͟hís, arriving in Karbilá just after the passing of Siyyid Káẓim. She resided with Káẓim's widow, gathering around her a number of able and enlightened women, including the sister of Mullá Ḥusayn and S͟hams-i-Ḍuḥá, who became Bábís at the time when Mullá 'Alí of Basṭám arrived in Karbilá to challenge the priests with the revolutionary doctrines of the new Faith. Her great influence upon the Bábís came about through her radical ideas of progressive revelation which excited much controversy among Bábís and S͟hayk͟hís alike. Other elements of her teachings, which called for the dismantling of many Shi'ite ideas and traditions, were shocking; indeed, it is reported that she unveiled before a gathering of her associates in Karbilá as another act demonstrating the discarding of timeworn unhappy Islámic injunctions. In response to Bábí complaints transmitted to Him, the Báb completely vindicated her behavior and teachings, calling her '*that mirror which has purified its soul in order to reflect the word . . .*' and further declaring that '*she is a righteous, learnèd, active and pure woman*'.

She challenged the chief mujtahids of Karbilá to an open debate, but none responded. Rather, to silence her she was detained in the house of one Ḥájí Mahdí Kamúna, but was released to go to Baghdad, where she again actively taught the Faith of the Báb. There she became the center of religious controversy, and for three months was confined by order of Governor Najíb Pás͟há to the house of the Mufti Ibn 'Alusí (see fn., Chapter 5, p. 77), from which she was recalled to her home in Qazvín by a special messenger sent by her father and relatives.

Nabíl describes her, saying: 'None could resist her charm; few could escape the contagion of her belief. All testified to the extraordinary traits of her character, marvelled at her amazing personality, and were convinced of the sincerity of her convictions.' (Nabíl, *The Dawn-Breakers*, p. 270.)

The names of Fáṭimih of Qazvín, eminent poetess, brilliant vanguard leader in the emancipation of women, and the Báb's Seventeenth Letter of the Living, reflect her impact upon family, teachers and Bábí colleagues. To her family and kin she was known as Zakíyyih (the Virtuous One) and Zarrin-Taj (the Crown of Gold) and to others Umm-i-Salmih (Mother of Peace). To Siyyid Káẓim she was Qurratu'l-'Ayn (Solace of the Eyes). By Jináb-i-Bahá at Badas͟ht she was named Ṭáhirih (the Pure One) the only name by which she is known to Bahá'ís today. She was a phenomenon of her hour, perhaps the greatest of the early modern exponents of the emancipation of women, and an acknowledged and distinguished poet.

How remarkable that she should have occurred at all is made eloquently clear by Marzieh Gail who reflected that she was, 'a woman in a country of silent, shadow-women, who lived their quiet cycle behind the veil: marriage and sickness and childbirth, stirring the rice and baking the flaps of bread, embroidering a leaf on a strip of velvet, dying without a name'. (Gail, *Dawn Over Mount Hira*, p. 84.)

Her dramatic last life chapter is contained in the text. Further notes on Ṭáhirih are nos. 10, 14 and Appendix 2.

9   The Báb, An Autobiographical Life Summary

While in fortress <u>Ch</u>ihríq the Báb wrote a brief and pungent summary of His life. Because it confirms the high points of His experiences up to that time, it is given here: '*Thou art aware, O My God, that since the day Thou didst call Me into being out of the water of Thy love till I reached fifteen years of age I lived in the land which witnessed My birth* [<u>Sh</u>íráz]. *Then Thou didst enable Me to go to the seaport* [Búshihr] *where for five years I was engaged in trading with the goodly gifts of Thy realm and was occupied in that with which Thou has favoured Me through the wondrous essence of Thy loving-kindness. I proceeded therefrom to the Holy Land* [Karbilá] *where I sojourned for one year. Then I returned to the place of My birth. There I experienced the revelation of Thy sublime bestowals and the evidences of Thy boundless grace. I yield Thee praise for all Thy goodly gifts and I render Thee thanksgiving for all Thy bounties. Then at the age of twenty-five I proceeded to Thy sacred House* [Mecca], *and by the time I returned to the place where I was born, a year had elapsed. There I tarried patiently in the path of Thy love and beheld the evidences of Thy manifold bounties and of Thy loving-kindness until Thou didst ordain for Me to set out in Thy direction and to migrate to Thy presence. Thus I departed therefrom by Thy leave, spending six months in the land of Sád* [Iṣfáhán] *and seven months in the First Mountain* [Máh-kú], *where Thou didst rain down upon Me that which beseemeth the glory of Thy heavenly blessings and befitteth the sublimity of Thy gracious gifts and favours. Now, in My thirtieth year, Thou beholdest Me, O My God, in this Grievous Mountain* [<u>Ch</u>ihríq] *where I have dwelt for one whole year.*' (*Selection from the Writings of the Báb*, pp. 180–181.)

10   Ṭáhirih and the <u>Sh</u>áh

Ṭáhirih was reputed to be a great beauty, and in a fragment from her own writings she described two inconsequential details: 'Small black mole at the edge of the lip – A black lock of hair by either cheek.' Scant as this is, it tells of her lack of vanity, rather than of her Persian charms. (Gail, *Dawn Over Mount Hira*, p. 81.)

A perhaps fanciful report has it that Ṭáhirih was brought for an interview with the young Sháh. One can readily imagine the encounter: the veiled prisoner facing the nineteen-year-old king with his flowing moustache and his quizzical arched eyebrows, the woman fearless, profoundly attractive in her maturity, immune to the opulence of the palace and the splendid robes of king and courtiers, and unintimidated by the arrogance of the insecure youthful ruler, although she well knew his power of life and death. Her incandescent spirit and whatever bold words she uttered plainly challenged the worldliness of everything he stood for. Whatever his interest and despite her known religious challenge to orthodox Shi'ite Islám, the Sháh is reported to have sent a message to her saying that if she would recant her heresy, he would take her in marriage. Upon her departure under guard for return to the house of the kalantar, he is reputed to have exclaimed: 'I like her looks; leave her, and let her be!' (Browne, *A Traveller's Narrative: Episode of the Báb*, note Q, p. 313.)

11 The Báb's Letter to Mírzá Yaḥyá, His Shield Role

The principal text of the letter, omitting the salutations, in English translation by E.G. Browne, is cited in Balyuzí, *Edward Granville Browne and the Bahá'í Faith*, p. 38, as follows: '. . . This is a letter from the presence of God, the Sovereign Protector, the Self-Subsistent; to God, the Sovereign Protector, the Self-Subsistent. Say: "All return unto God." This is a letter from 'Alí before Nabíl, the Remembrance of God unto the worlds; unto him whose name is equivalent to the name of the Sole One, the Remembrance of God unto the worlds. Say: "Verily all originate from the Point of the Bayán. O Name of the Sole One, preserve what hath been revealed in the Bayán, and what hath been commanded; for verily thou art a Great Way of Truth." ' (See also *New History*, translated by E.G. Browne, Appendix IV, No. 11, pp. 426–427.)

Mírzá Yaḥyá, Ṣubḥ-i-Azal's role is fully explained in the following passage of 'Abdu'l-Bahá's *A Traveller's Narrative*, pp. 37–38: 'Now since a great celebrity had been attained for Bahá'u'lláh in Ṭihrán, and the hearts of men were disposed towards Him, He, together with Mullá 'Abdu'l-Karím, considered it as expedient that, in face of the agitation amongst the doctors, the aggressiveness of the greater part of (the people of) Persia, and the irresistible power of the Amír-Nizám, whereby both the Báb and Bahá'u-'lláh were in great danger and liable to incur severe punishment, some measure should be adopted to direct the thoughts of men towards some absent person, by which means Bahá'u'lláh would remain protected from the interference of all men. And since further, having regard to sundry considerations, they did not consider an outsider as suitable, they cast the lot of this augury to the name of Bahá'u'lláh's brother Mírzá Yaḥyá.

'By the assistance and instruction of Bahá'u'lláh, therefore, they made him notorious and famous on the tongues of friends and foes, and wrote letters, ostensibly at his dictation, to the Báb. And since secret correspondences were in process, the Báb highly approved of this scheme. So Mírzá

Yaḥyá was concealed and hidden while mention of him was on the tongues and in the mouths of men. And this mighty plan was of wondrous efficacy, for Bahá'u'lláh, though He was known and seen, remained safe and secure, and this veil was the cause that no one outside (the sect) fathomed the matter or fell into the idea of molestation, until Bahá'u'lláh quitted Ṭihrán at the permission of the King and was permitted to withdraw to the Supreme Shrines.'

In a reference to this statement, Shoghi Effendi has explained the matter in *God Passes By*, pp. 28–29: 'A successor or vicegerent the Báb never named, an interpreter of His teachings He refrained from appointing. So transparently clear were His references to the Promised One, so brief was to be the duration of His own Dispensation, that neither the one nor the other was deemed necessary. All He did was, according to the testimony of 'Abdu'l-Bahá in *A Traveller's Narrative*, to nominate Mírzá Yaḥyá, on the advice of Bahá'u'lláh and of another disciple; he would act solely as a figure-head pending the manifestation of the Promised One, thus enabling Bahá'u'lláh to promote, in relative security, the Cause so dear to His heart.'

12 The Maid of Heaven

The Maid of Heaven is an image which appears recurrently in the Writings of Bahá'u'lláh. As in the Síyáh-Chál visions, there is no hint of the traditional ancient image of woman as only being symbolic of creativity, of the fertility of the earth and of mankind, and certainly there is nothing here of the implications of carnality. Rather, she is Spirit in womanly form, a female Messenger, but also she signals a distinct departure from the dominant androgenic figures featured in recent religious systems. Indeed, the absence of male images is itself conspicuous, although Bahá'u'lláh refers verbally to Gabriel in many passages; and He as the Bahá'í Manifestation forbids His own image to be duplicated, worshipped, idolized. Of course, there are echoes of the black-eyed maidens of paradise as portrayed in Islám in certain passages.

A notable later example of the image of the Maid of Heaven derives from days in 'Akká in what was then Syria. It is the transcendent female figure called forth in the Tablet of Ṭarázát (Ornaments), where she appears to the Manifestation in his Gardens of Riḍván (Paradise) as the symbol of a supreme virtue: '. . . *one of the Beauties of the Most Sublime Paradise, standing on a pillar of light, and calling aloud saying: ". . . By God, I am Trustworthiness and the revelation thereof, and the beauty thereof . . . I am the most great ornament of the people of Bahá, and the vesture of glory unto all who are in the kingdom of creation. I am the supreme instrument for the prosperity of the world, and the horizon of assurance unto all being."* ' (*Tablets of Bahá'u'lláh, p.* 38, the Fourth Taráz of the '*Tablet of Tarázat*'.)

In two later passages Bahá'u'lláh refers to the Maiden: '. . . *As bidden I waited expectant upon the hill of faithfulness, yet inhaled not from them that dwell on earth the fragrance of fidelity. Then summoned to return I beheld, and lo! certain doves of holiness were sore tried within the claws of the dogs of earth. Thereupon the Maid of Heaven hastened forth unveiled and resplendent from Her mystic mansion, and asked of their names, and all were told but one.'* (*Gleanings from the Writings of Bahá'u'lláh*, p. 91).

'Cry out before the gaze of the dwellers of heaven and of earth: I am the Maid of Heaven, the Offspring begotten by the Spirit of Bahá. My habitation is the Mansion of His Name, the All-Glorious. Before the Concourse on high I was adorned with the ornament of His names.' (*Gleanings from the Writings of Bahá'u'lláh*, p. 184.)

From His days in Baghdad comes the passage from the 'Prayer of the Maid of Heaven' (Munáját-i-Húríyyih) (see Balyuzi, *Bahá'u'lláh, The King of Glory*, p. 166.): '*Within this Paradise, and from the heights of its loftiest chambers, the Maids of Heaven have cried out and shouted: "Rejoice, ye dwellers of the realms above, for the fingers of Him Who is the Ancient of Days are ringing, in the name of the All-Glorious, the Most Great Bell, in the midmost heart of the heavens. The hands of bounty have borne round the cup of everlasting life. Approach, and quaff your fill. Drink with healthy relish, O ye that are the very incarnations of longing, ye who are the embodiments of vehement desire!"*' (*Gleanings from the Writings of Bahá'u'lláh*, p. 32.)

13 The Recognition of Mission

Other telling passages regarding His Voice of Recognition: '*I am the one, O my God, who lay fast asleep on his couch, when lo, the messengers of Thy manifold mercies were sent down upon me by Thee, and the gentle winds of Thy loving-kindness blew over me, and roused me up, and caused me to set my face towards the sanctuary of Thy knowledge, and to fix mine eyes upon the splendors of the light of Thy face.*' (*Prayers and Meditations of Bahá'u'lláh*, pp. 121–122.)

'God is My witness, O people! I was asleep on My couch, when lo, the Breeze of God wafting over Me roused Me from My slumber. His quickening Spirit revived Me, and My tongue was unloosed to voice His Call. Accuse Me not of having transgressed against God. Behold Me, not with your eyes but with Mine. Thus admonisheth you He Who is the Gracious, the All-Knowing. Think ye, O people, that I hold within My grasp the control of God's ultimate Will and Purpose? Far be it from Me to advance such claim. To this I testify before God, the Almighty, the Exalted, the All-Knowing, the All-Wise. Had the ultimate destiny of God's Faith been in Mine hands, I would have never consented, even though for one moment, to manifest Myself unto you, nor would I have allowed one word to fall from My lips. Of this God Himself is, verily, a witness.' (*Gleanings from the Writings of Bahá'u'lláh*, pp. 90–91.)

'Not of Mine own volition have I revealed Myself, but God, of His own choosing, hath manifested Me.' (*Epistle to the Son of the Wolf*, p. 11.)

'I was but a man like others, asleep upon My couch, when lo, the breezes of the All-Glorious were wafted over Me, and taught Me the knowledge of all that hath been. This thing is not from Me, but from One Who is Almighty and All-Knowing. And He bade Me lift up My voice between earth and heaven, and for this there befell

Me what hath caused the tears of every man of understanding to flow . . . This is but a leaf which the winds of the will of thy Lord, the Almighty, the All-Praised, have stirred, Can it be still when the tempestuous winds are blowing? Nay, by Him Who is the Lord of all Names and Attributes! They move it as they list. The evanescent is as nothing before Him Who is the Ever-Abiding. His all-compelling summons hath reached Me, and caused Me to speak His praise amidst all people. I was indeed as one dead when His behest was uttered. The hand of the will of thy Lord, the Compassionate, the Merciful, transformed Me.' (*Epistle to the Son of the Wolf*, pp. 11–12 and 39.)

'*The episode of Sinai hath been re-enacted in this Revelation and He Who conversed upon the Mount is calling aloud: Verily, the Desired One is come, seated upon the throne of certitude, could ye but perceive it.*' (*Tablets of Bahá'u'lláh*, p. 248.)

14 The Challenge of Ṭáhirih

In the Holy Spirit's bidding Bahá to break His silence, we are reminded that Ṭáhirih had challenged both Siyyid Yaḥyá and Bahá to break their silence and act on behalf of the Báb's Message. Siyyid Yaḥyá of Dáráb, Vahíd, had thereupon done so, to his great distinction as a man and a hero, and had become a martyr. But Jináb-i-Bahá, despite His obvious and proven courage and His clear leadership, and despite His brave attempt to join the besieged Bábís at Fort Shaykh Ṭabarsí, had knowingly awaited His great Godly summons of the fateful 'year nine', and thereafter the Great Call ten years later in Baghdad. Throughout this life of a Supreme Spirit there is a clear sense of the timeliness of key events. (See Shoghi Effendi, *God Passes By*, p. 103.)

15 The Garden of Eden

At Baghdad in Mesopotamia (now Iraq), the Tigris and the Euphrates Rivers come close together, then diverge downstream to form between them the fertile alluvial plain once called Eden, home of the mythical and symbolic Adam and Eve* of the Hebrew Bible. From the east into the Tigris River just above that plain flowed the Diyálá River out of the Zagros Mountains. In Eden stood Nippur of the terrible Sun-God El-Lil. Southward stood Ur of the Chaldees, mentioned in the Bible. All of this mixed mythology and social evolution of man is timed at vague dates from 4500 to 2500 BC.

What reverberates into modern times from this small segment of the earth's crust is the birth of ideas and religions mirrored by the stories in the

* Note that Adam in its original means 'earth' or 'soil', while Hava (Eve in translation) means 'living' or 'life'. Thus the names of the original couple mean 'soil and life'. (Hillel, *Out of the Earth*, p. 15.)

Biblical Genesis of Adam and Eve and their descendants, of the Flood and Noah with his sons, Shem, Ham and Japheth, giving their symbolic fatherhood to three great differing families of man.

The writer or reviser of the Biblical story in Genesis had probably never visited the far-off place of the legend, for he lived in Canaan or Judah. Had he done so, the line referring to Gihon might well have read: '. . . the river which went out of the Garden to water Eden', for Eden is now sited with some certainty in the lower Tigris-Euphrates valleys, and the river Diyala-Gihon (the Gusher) is east and just north of the plain of Eden.

16 Bahá'u'lláh's Recollections of the Bábí Tragedies

In other recollections of that time of great tragedy for the Bábís and for the Cause of God, Bahá summarized events in succinct fashion: '*The events that have happened in Persia during the early years have truly saddened the well-favored and sincere ones. Each year witnessed a fresh massacre, pillage, plunder, and shedding of blood. At one time there appeared in Zanján that which caused the greatest consternation; at another in Nayríz, and yet another in Ṭabarsí, and finally there occurred the episode of the Land of Ṭá* (Teheran). *From that time onwards this Wronged One, assisted by the One True God – exalted be His glory – acquainted this oppressed people with the things which beseemeth them. All have sanctified themselves from the things which they and others possess, and have clung unto, and fixed their eyes upon that which pertaineth unto God.*' (*Epistle to the Son of the Wolf*, pp. 88–89.) And again: '*Call thou to remembrance, O Land of Ṭá* (Teheran), *the former days in which thy Lord had made thee the seat of His throne, and had enveloped thee with the effulgence of His glory. How vast the number of those sanctified beings, those symbols of certitude, who, in their great love for thee, have laid down their lives and sacrificed their all for thy sake! Joy be to thee, and blissfulness to them that inhabit thee. I testify that out of thee, as every discerning heart knoweth, proceedeth the living breath of Him Who is the Desire of the world. In thee the Unseen hath been revealed, and out of thee hath gone forth that which lay hid from the eyes of men. Which one of the multitude of thy sincere lovers shall We remember, whose blood hath been shed within thy gates, and whose dust is now concealed beneath thy soil? The sweet savours of God have unceasingly been wafted, and shall everlastingly continue to be wafted upon thee. Our Pen is moved to commemorate thee, and to extol the victims of tyranny, those men and women that sleep beneath thy dust.*' (*Gleanings from the Writings of Bahá'u'lláh*, p. 109.)

Appendix I The Báb's Message to the Letters of the Living

O My beloved friends! You are the bearers of the name of God in this Day. You have been chosen as the repositories of His mystery. It behoves each one of you to manifest the attributes of God, and to exemplify by your deeds and words the signs of His righteousness, His power and glory. The very members of your body must bear witness to the loftiness of your purpose, the integrity of your life, the reality of your faith, and the exalted character of your devotion.

For verily I say, this is the Day spoken of by God in His Book: 'On that day will We set a seal upon their mouths; yet shall their hands speak unto Us, and their feet shall bear witness to that which they shall have done.'*

Ponder the words of Jesus addressed to His disciples, as He sent them forth to propagate the Cause of God. In words such as these, He bade them arise and fulfil their mission: 'Ye are even as the fire which in the darkness of the night has been kindled upon the mountain-top. Let your light shine before the eyes of men. Such must be the purity of your character and the degree of your renunciation, that the people of the earth may through you recognize and be drawn closer to the heavenly Father who is the Source of purity and grace. For none has seen the Father who is in heaven. You who are His spiritual children must by your deeds exemplify His virtues, and witness to His glory. You are the salt of the earth, but if the salt have lost its savor, wherewith shall it be salted? Such must be the degree of your detachment, that into whatever city you enter to proclaim and teach the Cause of God, you should in no wise expect either meat or reward from its people. Nay, when you depart out of that city, you should shake the dust from off your feet. As you have entered it pure and undefiled, so must you depart from that city. For verily, I say, the heavenly Father is ever with you and keeps watch over you. If you be faithful to Him, He will assuredly deliver into your hands all the treasures of the earth, and will exalt you above the rulers and kings of the world.'

O My Letters! Verily I say, immensely exalted is this Day above the days of the Apostles of old. Nay, immeasurable is the difference! You are the witnesses of the Dawn of the promised Day of God. You are partakers of the mystic chalice of His Revelation. Gird up the loins of endeavour, and be mindful of the words of God as revealed in His Book: 'Lo, the Lord thy God is come, and with Him is the*

---

* Quotations from the Qur'án.

company of His angels arrayed before Him!' Purge your hearts of worldly desires, and let angelic virtues be your adorning.

Strive that by your deeds you may bear witness to the truth of these words of God, and beware lest, by 'turning back', He may 'change you for another people', who 'shall not be your like', and who shall take from you the Kingdom of God. The days when idle worship was deemed sufficient are ended. The time is come when naught but the purest motive, supported by deeds of stainless purity, can ascend to the throne of the Most High and be acceptable unto Him. 'The good word riseth up unto Him, and the righteous deed will cause it to be exalted before Him.'

You are the lowly, of whom God has thus spoken in His Book: 'And We desire to show favor to those who were brought low in the land, and to make them spiritual leaders among men, and to make them Our heirs.' You have been called to this station; and will attain to it, only if you arise to trample beneath your feet every earthly desire, and endeavour to become those 'honored servants of His who speak not till He hath spoken, and who do His bidding.'

You are the first Letters that have been generated from the Primal Point, the first Springs that have welled out from the Source of this Revelation. Beseech the Lord your God to grant that no earthly entanglements, no worldly affections, no ephemeral pursuits, may tarnish the purity, or embitter the sweetness, of that grace which flows through you. I am preparing you for the advent of a mighty Day. Exert your utmost endeavour that, in the world to come, I, who am now instructing you, may, before the mercy-seat of God, rejoice in your deeds and glory in your achievements. The secret of the Day that is to come is now concealed. It can neither be divulged nor estimated. The newly born babe of that Day excels the wisest and most venerable men of this time, and the lowliest and most unlearned of that period shall surpass in understanding the most erudite and accomplished divines of this age.*

Scatter throughout the length and breadth of this land, and, with steadfast feet and sanctified hearts, prepare the way for His coming. Heed not your weaknesses and frailty; fix your gaze upon the invincible power of the Lord, your God, the Almighty. Has He not, in past days, caused Abraham, in spite of His seeming helplessness, to triumph over the forces of Nimrod? Has He not enabled Moses, whose staff was His only companion, to vanquish Pharaoh and his hosts? Has He not established the ascendancy of Jesus, poor and lowly as He was in the eyes of men, over the combined forces of the Jewish people? Has He not subjected the barbarous and militant tribes of Arabia to the holy and transforming discipline of Muḥammad, His Prophet?

Arise in His name, put your trust wholly in Him, and be assured of ultimate victory.†

Nabíl, *The Dawn-Breakers*, pp. 92–94

* One of the Báb's titles.

† The Báb refers to the Letters of the Living in the Persian Bayán in the following terms: '*All of these formed the name of the Living One, for these are the names that are nearest to God; the others are guided by their clear and significant actions, for God began the creation of the Bayán through them, and it is to them that the creation of the Bayán will again return. They are the lights which in the past have eternally prostrated themselves and will prostrate themselves eternally in the future, before the celestial throne.*' (*Le Bayán Persan*, vol. 1, pp. 24–5; English translation from *Translation of French Foot-Notes of the Dawn-Breakers*.)

Appendix II Poems of Ṭáhirih: A Taste of Her Genius

Another translation of the ode, composed possibly in reaction to the king's proposal, strengthens Ṭáhirih's feeling of the contrast between the worldly Sh͟áh and herself, woman of spirit:

Kingdom, wealth and ruling be for thee.
Wandering, becoming a poor dervish and calamity be for me.
If that station is good, let it be for thee,
And if this station is bad, I long for it; let it be for me!
(From *Ṭáhirih the Pure*, pp. 622–629)

A translation of the complete ghazal, or ode, is found in Browne, *Materials for the Study of the Bábí Religion*, pp. 348–349.

An ode of Ṭáhirih which may refer to the Báb is quoted in these excerpts to give a taste of her eloquent words and deep feeling:

I, longing to behold Your face,
upon the winds of grace have come,
breath of the Spirit blowing me apace.
To seek You out in every home
at every door, in every room,
in alley way and market place.

. . .

Your eyes like Royal falcons fell
upon the sparrow of my trembling heart
and hell and paradise were torn apart
as earth and heaven fought within my soul –
who could control that sudden, endless fall,
what wings recall the faculty of flight,
what eye distinguish in that moment day and night,
or tell how earth or sky, heaven and hell
were joined together as I fell
as life and death with one breath dwell within the womb.

. . .

and though I sing in wondrous tones
the praises of that loving Friend,
these pages bear no verses of my own,
and you may see if you but gaze thereon,
naught but the traces of His traceless pen.

(From M.S. Israeli, *A Golden Treasury of Persian Poetry*, p. 412)

Lamenting her grief at her failure ever to meet the Báb, Ṭáhirih addressed a short poem to Him:

I'd explain all my grief, dot by dot, point by point –
if heart to heart we talk and face to face we meet.

Wherefore, to catch a glimpse of thee, I am wandering
like the breeze, from house to house, door to door,
place to place and street to street.

With separation from thee, the blood of my heart
gushes out from my eyes, torrent after torrent, river
after river, stream after stream, sheet after sheet.

An aching heart has woven thy love with the pattern
of my soul, stitch by stitch, strand by strand, thread
by thread and pleat by pleat.

(ibid. p. 412)

Glossary

Word	*Literal Translation*	*Interpretative Meaning and/or Explanation*
Abad	Eternity	
Ábád	Developed, inhabited	Used in compound names
'Abbás	The lion, also stern-looking, formidable, stentorian	A name derived from 'abasa, originally meaning a furious lion, hence with a lion's characteristics.
'Abdu'l-Bahá	The Servant of Glory (of Bahá)	The title adopted by Bahá'u'lláh's eldest son and successor, 'Abbás Effendi.
'Ábidín	Worshippers	The plural of 'Ábid' – see as used in conjunction with Zayn.
Adíb	Learnèd, erudite	Superlative form of 'Aduba' (to learn).
Afchih or Afjih		A village northeast of Teheran in Lavásán District.
Aḥmad	More praised	Comparative form of 'hamida' (to praise).
Aḥsá		A town in northern Bahrain, birthplace of Shaykh Aḥmad.
'Akká		A city in Israel, near Haifa. Also known as Akko or Acre.
Alborz		Name of the principal mountain range in northern Iran.
Akbar	Greater, greatest	Compound name – comparative form of 'kabura' (to elevate).
Alláh	God	
'Alí	High, eminent	The first Imám who was also the fourth Caliph and son-in-law of Muḥammad.

Word	*Literal Translation*	*Interpretative Meaning and/or Explanation*
‘Amá	A light cloud, a cloud of light	Symbolizes the ‘First Invisible Substance’, The station of ‘The Hidden Treasure’.
Amín	Most faithful, loyal, trustee	Superlative form of ‘amuna’ (to trust).
Amír	Prince, commander, governor	
Ámul		A town in Mázindarán, near the Caspian Sea on the Haraz River.
Anís	Companion	Title of Muḥammad-‘Alí Zunúzí, the companion of the Báb in martyrdom.
Anṣárí	Related to Anṣár, the Helpers	The Medinites who rallied around Muḥammad after His flight from Mecca to Medina were called the Anṣár.
Anú<u>sh</u>írván		A Sásáníd king of Persia known for his just rule. The Prophet Muḥammad was born in Arabia at the time of his reign.
Áqá	Master, Sir; when affixed to a name means Mr	A male honorific – the title given by Bahá’u’lláh to ‘Abdu’l-Bahá, in which context it means ‘the Master’.
Áqásí		Turkish proper name.
Aqṣá	The Most Remote	The Aqṣá Mosque built on the Temple Mount at Jerusalem.
‘Arafih		The day before the festival of Immolation of ‘Ídu’l-Aḍḥá (vigil of the Feast of Sacrifice, when Mecca pilgrims proceed to Mount ‘Arafát. The ninth day of the month of <u>Dh</u>i’l-Ḥijjih).
Asadu’lláh	Lion of God	Compound proper name.
Asad	Lion	Masc. proper name.
Aṣ<u>gh</u>ar	Minor, smaller, younger	Comparative form of ‘sa<u>gh</u>íra’ (to belittle).
Ásíyih	Feminine form of Ásí (sad or sorrowful)	The given name of Bahá’u’lláh’s wife, entitled Navváb. Also the name of Pharoah’s daughter who rescued Moses.

Word	*Literal Translation*	*Interpretative Meaning and/or Explanation*
Asmá	Names	Symbols of all created things. 'The Lord of all names refers to God.'
'Aválim	Worlds	Plural of 'álam' (world).
'Ayn	Eye, spring	
Ayyúb	Job in Arabic	Name of the Hebrew minor prophet Job.
Azal	Eternity	Ṣubḥ-i-Azal is the title given by the Báb to Bahá'u'lláh's half-brother Yaḥyá.
A'ẓam	The Greater One	Comparative form of 'azuma' (to make great).
'Aẓím	The Great One	Superlative form of 'azuma'.
'Azíz	Strongest, most powerful	Superlative form of 'azza'.
Báb	Gate	Title of Siyyid 'Alí-Muḥammad, Founder of the Bábí Faith.
Bábí	Follower of the Báb	
Bábíyyih		Center in Mashhad for Bábí activities. The first house built in Mashhad for the gathering of the Bábís.
Badasht		The name of a village near Sháhrúd in Khurásán, venue of the first Bábí conference.
Bágh	Garden	
Bahá	Glory	Title taken by Mírzá Ḥusayn-'Alí at Badasht
Bahá'í	A follower of Bahá'u'lláh; a person of light, of enlightenment	
Bahá'u'lláh	The Glory of God	Title of Mírzá Ḥusayn-'Alí of Núr, Founder of the Bahá'í Faith.
Bahíyyih	Radiant, a derivative from Bahá	Daughter of Bahá'u'lláh.
Bahjí	Delight	Name of an area, and specifically a large garden northeast of the city of 'Akká in Israel.

Word	*Literal Translation*	*Interpretative Meaning and/or Explanation*
Bahman	Avalanche	The second month of the winter in Persian calendars.
Bakhtíyárí		Name of a nomadic tribe of western Iran.
Bálá	Up, above	
Baní-Háshim	Sons of, or children of, Háshim	The family from which Muḥammad descended, i.e. the people deriving from the quasi-mythical Shem, son of Noah.
Báqir	One who expands or breaks	Title of the fifth Shi'ite Imám.
Baráthá		A mosque situated on a highway between Baghdád and Kaẓímayn.
Bárfurúsh		A town in Mázindarán, presently known as Bábul.
Basṭámí		Basṭám, a town in Khurásán, home of Mullá 'Alí, the fourth Letter of Living.
Baṣír	Most insightful, discerning, endowed with insight	Superlative form of Baṣár (sight). See Siyyid Baṣír, the blind Indian Bábí.
Bayán	Utterance, exposition	Name of the primary Book of the Báb.
Begum	Great, a lady of rank, a princess	Fem. form of Beg or Big.
Big	Great, a lord or prince	
Burújird		Capital city of the province of Luristán, place of the governorship of Mírzá Buzurg.
Bushrúyih.		A town in Khurásán, birthplace of Mullá Ḥusayn, first disciple of the Báb.
Buzurg	Great	The title given by Fatḥ-'Alí Sháh to 'Abbás, Bahá'u'lláh's father.
Chál	Pit	Used in Síyáh-Chál, the Black Pit.
Chihríq		Fortress in Kurdish Ádhirbáyján, designated by the Báb as Jabal-i-Shadíd (the Grievous Mountain).

Word	*Literal Translation*	*Interpretative Meaning and/or Explanation*
Daoud	David	Hebrew masc. proper name.
Daoudis	Followers of David	Name of a small sect of Islam.
Dáráb		A town in Fárs, southern Persia, home of Vaḥíd's ancestors.
Dárkalá		A village in Núr in Mázindarán, a second ancestral home of Mírzá Ḥusayn-'Alí.
Dáru'l-funún	Center for arts and sciences	The first technical college of Iran in Teheran founded by Prime Minister Mírzá Taqí Khán.
Dín	Religion	Suffix in proper names, i.e. Salah-ed-Dín.
Diván	Court, tribunal; poetical works.	Used in titles, as in Amír-Diván, Head of the Court, or Prime Minister.
Effendi	Sir	An honorific used by Ottoman Turks. It designates a higher rank than Big.
Farmá	One who issues orders	From the infinitive 'Farmúdan' (to bid, to order), but never used alone, i.e. Farmán-Farmá, the one who establishes order; the Governor.
Farmán	Order, command	A royal decree
Fárs		A southern province of Iran, from which the name Persia derives.
Fatḥ-'Alí Sháh		Name of a Qájár king, father of Muḥammad Sháh.
Fatḥ'u'lláh	Victory of God	Compound proper name.
Fáṭimih	One who weans	Fem. of 'Fátim', daughter of the Prophet Muḥammad and wife of the Imám 'Alí.
Fatwá	A sentence	Sentence of judgment by a Muslim mufti (and court).
Firaydún		Name of an ancient Persian king.
Funún	Arts and technology	Plural of 'fan'.
Furútan	The humble	Masc. name
Gílán		A northern province of Iran on the Caspian Sea.

Word	*Literal Translation*	*Interpretative Meaning and/or Explanation*
Gird	Round circular	As in Kinár-Gird, a village where the Báb paused in His exile journey to Máh-kú.
Gurgin Khán		Nephew and successor of Governor Manúchihr Khán in Iṣfahán.
Guzal	The Pass	As in Ádí-Guzal, Sayyáh, the messenger.
Ḥadith	A tradition	Oral sayings of the Prophet Muḥammad and the Imáms.
Ḥáfiz		Persian mystic poet of Shíráz (1320–1390), author of odes in the ghazal form.
Ḥájí	A pilgrim	Muslim title, one who has made the pilgrimage to Mecca.
Hamadán		A town in Iran, originally Ecbatana of the ancient Medes.
Ḥamzih	The lion	Masc. proper name.
Ḥasan	Good	Name of the second Imám. Masc. proper name.
Háshim	Of Shem	The Baní-Háshim were Muḥammad's ancestors, a tribal group in southern Arabia. From 'hashama', one who smashes to pieces.
Ḥayát	Life, existence	
Ḥaydar	The lion	Masc. proper name.
Hejira	The Flight	Refers to Muḥammad's flight from Mecca to Medina in 622 AD.
Ḥisámu's-Salṭanih	Sword of the sovereign	Title of Prince Sulṭán Murád Mírzá, son of 'Abbás Mírzá.
Ḥiṣár	Fence, wall, fortification	A town in Khurásán province.
Ḥujjat	The proof	Title of Mullá Muḥammad-'Alí of Zanján.
Ḥusayn	Diminutive form of Ḥasan	Name of the third Imám, Ḥusayn.
Húshang	The first emanation, intelligence	Masc. proper name.

Word	*Literal Translation*	*Interpretative Meaning and/or Explanation*
Ḥusníyyih	Beauty	Fem. proper name.
Ibráhim	Abraham	Patriarch of the people of Israel.
Ílkhání	A tribal chief, a chieftain	Also the name of a garden outside Teheran where Ṭáhirih was martyred.
Imám	Leader	The title of Shi'ite successors of the Prophet Muḥammad.
Isfandíyár	Created holy and pure	Name of loyal servant of Bahá.
Ishráq	Illumination	Name of each chapter in the 'Tablet of Ishráqát' of Bahá'u'lláh.
Ismá'íl		Ishmael (in Hebrew), the son of Abraham and the Egyptian Hagar, who was considered to be the forerunner of the desert Arabs.
Jábir	One who uses coercion, despotic	Masc. proper name.
Ja'far		Name of the sixth Imám.
Jamál	Beauty	Masc. proper name.
Ján	Soul, life	
Jání	Devoted	Title of a merchant of Kashán, Ḥájí Mírzá Jání, early historian of the Bábí Cause and a martyr. Masc. proper name.
Javád	Generous, bountiful; also a race horse	Masc. proper name.
Jináb		Courtesy title sometimes translated as 'His Honor', or 'The Honorable'.
Jinnat	Paradise	
Jum'ih	The congregation	Used with Imám as Imám Jum'ih.
Ka'bih (Kaaba)	A cube, cube-like	A sanctuary believed to have been originally built by Ibráhím (Abraham) and Ismá'íl (Ishmael), and appointed by Muḥammad as the Qiblih (the Point of Adoration) to which people turn in prayer in Mecca.
Kabír	Greatest, biggest	Superlative form of 'kabura'.

Word	*Literal Translation*	*Interpretative Meaning and/or Explanation*
Kád-khudá	An alderman, bailiff	Head man of a village of a town, district or ward.
Káfí	Sufficient	
Kalantar	A mayor	
Kalím	He who engages in discourse	Title of Mírzá Músá, Bahá'u'lláh's faithful brother; also Áqáy-i-Kalím, Master of Discourse, his usual full title.
Kand		Village in the province of Teheran.
Karand		A town in western Persia, home of the 'Alíyu'lláhís (an Islamic sect, followers of the Imám 'Alí).
Karbilá		A Shí'ite holy city in Iraq where the Imám Ḥusayn was murdered and is buried.
Káshán		One of the oldest cities of Iran, located in north central Persia.
Katúráh		The name of the Patriarch Abraham's third wife.
Káẓim	One who suppresses his passion	The title of the Seventh Imám of the Shí'ites, masc. proper name.
Káẓimayn		A town near Baghdád, burial place of two Shí'ite Imáms.
Khadíjih		Name of Muḥammad's first wife; also the name of Ḥusayn-'Alí, Bahá'u'lláh's mother, and of the Báb's wife.
Khájih	Title of honor	Name of a fortress near the town of Nayríz.
Kháliq	The Creator	Used as a name, preceded by 'Abd (servant), ('of the Creator').
Khán	A noble gentleman	Title of nobility, Mongolian in origin.
Kháníqayn		A town in Iraq on the border of Iran near Baghdád.
Khánum	Lady, wife	Fem. form of Khán.
Khátún	Lady, matron	Title and fem. name, a prefix.
Khávarí	Of Khávar (east)	Persian family name.

Word	*Literal Translation*	*Interpretative Meaning and/or Explanation*
Khurásán (Khorasan)		A province in the northeastern part of Iran.
Khusraw (Khosrow)		Name of a Persian king.
Kinár-gird		A small fortress and village near Teheran.
Kirmánsháh		Name of a province and city in western Iran.
Kúchik	Small, young	Used as a proper name, masc. or fem.
Kúfih		A town in Iraq on the Euphrates River; the Imám 'Alí made it the center of his operations, and was murdered in its mosque.
Kuláh	Hat, cap	Worn by laymen of standing e.g. government officials.
Kulayn		A village southwest of Teheran.
Kulthúm	Plump-faced, chubby, good-looking	Fem. proper name.
Kumayl		Arabic proper name. Ibn-i-Ziyád-Nakha'í, of the Imám 'Alí's companions, was known as Kumayl. It is also the name of a prayer.
Lawḥ	Tablet	As in Lawḥ-i-Sabr, the Tablet of Job, of patience.
Lavásán		An eastern district in the province of Teheran.
Lur		Name of a warlike tribe living in Luristán.
Luristán		An area in western Iran in the Zagros Mountains.
Maḥbúb	Beloved	Masc. proper name.
Mashhad		The provincial capital of Khurásán (Khorasan).
Maḥallih	Location	See Garden of Murgh-Maḥallih, place of birds or chickens.

Word	*Literal Translation*	*Interpretative Meaning and/or Explanation*
Mahdí	The one guided	Title of the First Promised One expected by the Shi'ites.
Máh-kú		Four-towered fortress above the village of the same name in northwestern Ádhirbáyján (Azerbaijan).
Maḥmúd	Laudable, praiseworthy	Masc. proper name.
Majzúb, (Majdhúb)	Attracted	Masc. proper name.
Manúchihr		Masc. proper name.
Maryam	Mary	Fem. proper name.
Marzieh (Marḍíyyih)	Well-favored	Arabic fem. proper name.
Masíḥ	Messiah, the Anointed	From Meshiah (Hebrew).
Masjid	A mosque	
Mas'úd	Happy, prosperous	Masc. proper name.
Ma'ṣúm	Infallible, innocent	Masc. proper name, used as a suffix.
Maydán	A city square	
Mázindarán		A province in northern Iran, on the Caspian Sea.
Mihdí	One who guides aright	
Mílán		A town in Ádhirbáyján (Azerbaijan), northwestern Iran.
Mi'ráj	The ascent	Reference to Muḥammad's vision of His night journey to the outermost mosque and His ascent to the heavens on His steed Burak.
Mírzá		When following a name, a title of nobility and signifies a prince. Given to children of Amírs (Emirs) and to princes of royal families. When used before a name, a worthy person.
Momen	A believer	Used as a surname.
Mu'allim	A teacher or tutor	

Word	*Literal Translation*	*Interpretative Meaning and/or Explanation*
Mu'áwíyyáh		Omayyad caliph, establisher of the dynasty in Damascus.
Mubárak	One blessed	One title of Bahá'u'lláh: Jamál-i-Mubárak, the Blessed Beauty.
Muḥammad	The Praised One	Name of the Prophet of Islám.
Muḥarram	Forbidden	Name of the first month in the Muḥammadan calendar.
Mujtahid		Title of a doctor of Islamic law.
Mullá		A Muslim priest, a person versed in theology and sacred law.
Murád	A desire, wish, intention	Masc. proper name.
Murg͟h	Hen or bird	Name of a market in S͟hīráz, also of the garden Murg͟h-Maḥallih.
Músá	Moses	Bahá'u'lláh's faithful brother, known by his title as Áqáy-i-Kalím.
Muṣṭafá	Chosen	Arabic masc. proper name.
Nabát	A plant, sugar-candy	Fem. proper name.
Nabíl	Noble, excellent	Used as a title.
Nahr	River, stream, canal	Also used as suffix to a proper name suffix, i.e. Siyyid Muhammad-'Alíy-i-Nahrí, father of 'Abdu'l-Bahá's wife, Munírih K͟hánum.
Najaf		One of the Shi'ite holy cities in Iraq.
Nanih	A mother or grandmother	Fem. proper name, sometimes used in compound form as in K͟hán-Nanih.
Náṣir	A helper or defender	Masc. proper name.
Naṣr'u'lláh	Victory of God	Masc. compound proper name.
Naw-Rúz	New Day	The Bahá'í New Year's Day, which usually falls on March 21. If the vernal equinox falls after sunset, it is celebrated on March 22.

Word	*Literal Translation*	*Interpretative Meaning and/or Explanation*
Nayríz		A town in the province of Fárs, southeast of Shíráz.
Naẓar	Sight	Masc. proper name.
Nisá	Woman	Name of the younger sister of Bahá'u'lláh.
Nishapur		A town in northeast Persia west of Mashhad, famous for its emerald mines.
Níyálá		A village in Khurásán (Khorasan).
Niyávarán		A village in Shimírán District, north of Teheran.
Niẓám	Order, system	Used as a name or title in conjunction with another word, i.e. Niẓámu'l-'Ulamá, Niẓámu'l-Mulk, or Amír-Nizám.
Núr	Light	A district in Mázindarán province.
Nuṣayr	Victory, dimin. form of Nasr	Name of the founder of an Islamic sect.
Nuṣayrí	Related to Nuṣayr	People of victory, a small Islamic sect of western Iran.
Omar		The second Khalif in Islám. Masc. proper name.
Omayyad		An Islamic dynasty (caliphate) founded by Mu'áwíyyáh, with its capital in Damascus.
Pahlaví		Family name of the dynasty of Sháhs begun in 1925 by Riḍá Khán.
Páshá		Honorary title formerly given to officers of high rank in Turkey.
Qá'im	He Who shall Arise	Title designating the First Promised One of Islám.
Qájár		Name of a Turkoman tribe whose leaders reigned from 1795 to 1925 in Persia; the dynasty was begun by Áqá Muḥammad Khán.
Qanbar		Masc. proper name.
Qánitih		The attendant of Ṭáhirih at Badasht.

Word	*Literal Translation*	*Interpretative Meaning and/or Explanation*
Qará-Guhar	Big and heavy	One of the two chains of Bahá'u'lláh in the Black Pit of Teheran.
Qásim	Divider, distributor	Masc. proper name.
Qayyúm	Self-sufficient, Self-subsisting	Superlative of 'Qá'im', the Most Great One Who will arise.
Qazvín		Name of a town 160 kilometers (90 miles) from Teheran.
Qúch-Ḥiṣár	Fence or border	A village in the vicinity of Teheran.
Quddús	The Most Holy One	The title of Muḥammad-'Alí of Bárfurúsh, last of the 18 Letters of the Living, second only to the Báb in rank among the Bábís.
Qulí	Son of	Suffix to a masc. proper name, as in Muḥammad-Qulí.
Qur'án	The Reading, or that which ought to be read	The Holy Book of Islám revealed by Muḥammad.
Qurbán	Sacrifice, offering	The name of the father of Mírzá Taqí Khán.
Qurratu'l-'Ayn	Solace of the eyes	The title given by Siyyid Káẓim to Fáṭimih of Qazvín (Ṭáhirih).
Raḥim	Merciful	Masc. proper name.
Rashh-i-'Amá	Sprinklings from an effulgent light	First poem written by Bahá'u'lláh after His release from the Black Pit.
Rayy		Old city, south of Teheran, once capital of the Medes.
Riḍá	Good-pleasure	Masc. proper name.
Riḍván	Paradise	Name of two gardens significant in Bahá'í history.
Rúd	River	Used as a suffix with given name, as in Yálrúd.
Sa'ádat	Prosperity	Used in compound words, as in Sa'adat-Ábád, a developed place of prosperity.

Word	*Literal Translation*	*Interpretative Meaning and/or Explanation*
Sabzih-Maydán	Vegetable square	Name of a square in Teheran just outside the palace walls where martyrdoms of early Bábís took place.
Ṣádiq	Righteous	Masc. proper name
Ṣadr-i-A'zám	Prime Minister	One of the honorifics attached to the Chief Minister of the Sháh.
Ṣáḥibu'z-Zamán	Lord of the Age	A title of the Promised One of Islamic tradition.
Sakínih	Tranquil	One of the half-sisters of Bahá'u'lláh.
Salásil	Chains	Plural of 'silsilih', a chain.
Ṣálih	Righteous	Name of a Prophet sent to Thamúd, an old Arabian tribe. Masc. proper name.
Salím	Peaceable	Name of a famous Ottoman emperor. Masc. proper name.
Salṭanih	Sovereignty	Used in title, as in Ḍíyá'u's-Salṭanih, daughter of Fatḥ-'Alí Sháh.
Sanandaj		Provincial capital of Persian Kurdistán.
Sar-Galú		Place of the retirement of Bahá'u'lláh near Sulaymáníyyih, in Iraqi Kurdistán.
Sardár	A leader, a commander	Title of certain high officials, as Chief of Police.
Sárí		A town in eastern Mázindarán province.
Sárih	Sarah	Fem. proper name; Persian version of Hebrew name of the wife of the Patriarch Abraham.
Sayyáḥ	The traveler	Title given to Adí-Guzal of Maraghih, as 'Alíy-i-Sayyáh, the eminent traveler.
Shafí'	One who intercedes	Proper name, and title given to certain persons, i.e. Sháfí' Khán, Prime Minister Áqásí's adviser.
Sháh	King	Title of kings of Persia/Iran.

Word	*Literal Translation*	*Interpretative Meaning and/or Explanation*
S͟háh-rúd	King river	Name of a crossroad city northeast of Teheran.
S͟háhzádih	Prince or princess (child of the king)	Royal title.
S͟hayk͟h	Elder	Respectful title given to honored older persons.
Shi'ite (S͟hí'ih)		A major sect of Islám.
S͟hikastih	Broken	An elegant form of Persian writing.
S͟himírán		The name of a district north of Teheran at the foot of the Alborz Mountains.
Shoghi	Zeal, imbued with ardent desire	Masc. proper name, first name of the Guardian, great-grandson of Bahá'u'lláh.
S͟hukru'lláh	Praise of God (a proper name)	A kinsman of Bahá'u'lláh who accompanied Him on the first exile to Iraq.
Ṣiráṭ	Bridge	Symbolic bridge over which the believer must pass to reach heaven.
Síyáh-C͟hál	The Black Pit	Place of imprisonment of Jináb-i-Bahá in Teheran.
Siyyid	Master	A title given to descendants of the Prophet Muḥammad.
Ṣubḥ-i-Azal	Morning of eternity	Title of Yaḥyá, the half-brother of Bahá'u'lláh.
Ṣúfí	A mystic	A sect of Islám notable for its mystical teachings.
Sug͟hrá	Lesser, minor, smaller	One of the half-sisters of Bahá'u'lláh.
Sulaymán	Solomon	Persian version of Hebrew name.
Sulṭán	A sovereign	Title of Turkish rulers.
Sunná	Tradition, custom, law	The corpus of Islamic law and traditions.
Sunní	Of the sunná	The major sect of Islám, and the name of those who followed Abú-Bakr, first caliph; those who uphold the elective principle in the matter of succession to the Prophet Muḥammad.

Word	*Literal Translation*	*Interpretative Meaning and/or Explanation*
Súrih (Sura)	A chapter	Used particularly in reference to the Qur'án.
Ṭabarsí	Of Ṭabaristán	Shaykh Ṭabarsí, shrine of a local saint in Mázindarán near Bábul, and scene of the siege of the Bábís.
Ṭabíb	A physician	Masc. proper name.
Ṭáhir	The pure one	Masc. proper name
Ṭáhirih	The pure one	Title bestowed by Jináb-i-Bahá on Fáṭimih, Qurratu'l-'Ayn.
Táhirzádih	Son of the pure one.	Family name taken by a distinguished Bahá'í family of Yazd.
Takyih		A monastery-seminary, a religious establishment.
Tákur		A village in a division of the Núr district.
Ṭálib	A seeker	Masc. proper name.
Taqí	The virtuous, the pious one	Name of first Prime Minister of Náṣiri'd-Dín Sháh, Mírzá Taqí Khán.
Ṭarázát	Ornaments	Plural of 'ṭaráz', an ornament, the title of a Tablet of Bahá'u'lláh.
Turáb	Dust	Masc. proper name, used in conjunction as in Abú-Turáb.
Urúmíyyih		Present day Riḍá'íyyih, an ancient city in Azerbaijan on the shores of the lake of the same name. The purported birthplace of Zoroaster.
Vahháb	One who bestows	Superlative form of 'vahaba', to grant, to bestow.
Vahid	A unit, one	A 'unit' or section of the Bayán, the Book of the Báb.
Vaḥíd	Unique, single, matchless	Superlative form of 'vahada', to be alone.
Vakíl	A deputy, representative	From 'vakala', to appoint as a representative or agent.
Válí	Governor	Ottoman Turkish word.
Vazír	Minister, vizier of the government	From 'vazara' (to carry a heavy burden).

Word	*Literal Translation*	*Interpretative Meaning and/or Explanation*
Yaḥyá	John	Masc. proper name.
Yálrúd	Yál (name of a stream) and rúd (river)	A village in the Míyanrúd division of the Núr district and birthplace of Ásíyih, wife of Bahá'u'lláh.
Yazd		A province and city in central Iran, notable as the primary center of the Persian Zoroastrian population.
Yúsif	Joseph	Masc. proper name.
Zádih	Born of, son of, offspring	Suffix to family names, i.e. Ṭáhirzadih.
Zamán	Time, age	See Ṣáḥibu'z-Zamán, Lord of the Age.
Zanján		A town in the district of Khamsih between Qazvín and Tabríz, home of the redoubtable disciple Ḥujjat.
Zarand		A division of Sávih, district and village.
Zarrín-Táj	Crown of gold	One of the titles of Ṭáhirih.
Zarkandih (Zargandih)	Filled with gold	A small village in the Shimírán division of Teheran, site of the Russian legation in 1852.
Zaynu'l-'Ábidín	The worshipper's ornament	Title of a distinguished Bahá'í.
Zoroaster (Zartusht or Zardusht)		Founder of the Zoroastrian religion; also known as Zarathustra.
Zunúz		The name of the capital of Marand.

Bibliography

'Abdu'l-Bahá. *Memorials of the Faithful.* Translated and annotated by Marzieh Gail. Wilmette, Illinois: Bahá'í Publishing Trust, 1971.

— *A Traveller's Narrative Written to Illustrate the Episode of the Báb.* Trans. and notations by Edward G. Browne from the original Persian. New York: Bahá'í Publishing Committee, 1930. A new and corrected version, Wilmette, Illinois: Bahá'í Publishing Trust, 1980.

Abu'l-Faḍl, Mírzá. 'Encounter with a Missionary' published in '*Herald of the South*', Vol. 21, October-December 1989.

Afnan, Abu'l-Qásim. *Black Pearls.* Los Angeles: Kalimát Press, 1988.

Amánat, Abbas. *Resurrection and Renewal.* Ithaca, N.Y.: Cornell University Press, 1989.

Báb, The. *Selections from the Writings of the Báb.* Trans. by Habib Taherzadeh with the assistance of a Committee at the Bahá'í World Centre. Haifa: Bahá'í World Centre, 1976.

Bahá'u'lláh. *Epistle to the Son of the Wolf.* Trans. by Shoghi Effendi. Wilmette, Illinois: Bahá'í Publishing Committee, 1941.

— *Gleanings from the Writings of Bahá'u'lláh.* Trans. by Shoghi Effendi. Wilmette, Illinois: Bahá'í Publishing Trust, rev. edn. 1952.

— *Hidden Words, The.* Trans. by Shoghi Effendi. Wilmette, Illinois: Bahá'í Publishing Trust, 1979.

— *Kitáb-i-Íqán. The Book of Certitude.* Trans. by Shoghi Effendi. Wilmette, Illinois: Bahá'í Publishing Trust, 1950.

— *Prayers and Meditations by Bahá'u'lláh.* Trans. by Shoghi Effendi. Wilmette, Illinois: Bahá'í Publishing Committee, 1938.

— *Tablets of Bahá'u'lláh,* Trans. by Habib Taherzadeh with a Committee at the Bahá'í World Centre. Haifa: Bahá'í World Centre, 1978.

Bahá'í Revelation, The. A selection from the Bahá'í Holy Writings of Bahá'u'lláh and 'Abdu'l-Bahá. London: Bahá'í Publishing Trust, 1955.

Bahá'í Scriptures. Selections from the utterances of Bahá'u'lláh and 'Abdu'l-Bahá. Ed. by Horace Holley. New York. Brentano's, 1923.

Bahíyyih Khánum, The Greatest Holy Leaf. Compilation from Bahá'í sacred texts and writings of the Guardian of the Bahá'í Faith and Bahíyyih Khánum's own letters. The Research Department of the Bahá'í World Centre, Haifa: Bahá'í World Centre, 1982.

Balyuzi, H.M. *Bahá'u'lláh, The King of Glory.* Oxford: George Ronald, 1980.

— *Edward Granville Browne and the Bahá'í Faith.* London: George Ronald, 1970.

— *Muḥammad and the Course of Islám.* Oxford: George Ronald, 1976.

— *The Báb. The Herald of the Day of Days.* Oxford: George Ronald, 1973.

Bahá'í World, The. A Biennial International Record, 1930–1932, Vol. V. National Spiritual Assembly of the Baha'ís of the United States and Canada, 1933.

— *Vol. XIII,* 1954–1963.

Ben Dov, Meir. *In the Shadow of the Temple.* Jerusalem: Keter Publishing House, Ltd., 1982.

Bird, F.L. 'Modern Persia and its Capital.' National Geographic Magazine, April 1921, pp. 353–417.

Blomfield, Sara, Lady. *The Chosen Highway.* Wilmette: Bahá'í Publishing Trust, 1940, 1967.

Browne, E.G. *A Persian Anthology.* Methuen & Co., Ltd., 1927.

— *A Traveller's Narrative Written to Illustrate the Episode of the Báb* (see 'Abdu'l-Bahá above).

— *Materials for the Study of the Bábí Religion.* Compiled by E.G. Browne. Cambridge: University Press, 1918.

Curzon, Hon. George N. *Persia and the Persian Question.* Longmans, Green & Co., 1892.

Esslemont, J.E. *Bahá'u'lláh and the New Era. An Introduction to the Bahá'í Faith.* 3d rev. edn. Wilmette, Illinois: Bahá'í Publishing Trust, 1970.

Furútan, 'Alí-Akbar. *Stories of Bahá'u'lláh.* Trans. by Katayoon and Robert Crerar with the help of friends. Oxford: George Ronald, 1986.

Hasan, Hadi. *A Golden Treasury of a Persian Poetry.* Rev. edn. M.S. Israeli, Indian Council for Public Relations.

Ḥaydar-'Alí, Ḥájí Mírzá. *Stories from The Delight of Hearts. The Memoirs of Ḥájí Mírzá Ḥaydar-'Alí.* Trans. by A.Q. Faizi. Los Angeles: Kalimát Press, 1980.

Hillel, Daniel. *Out of the Earth: Civilization and the Life of the Soil.* New York: Free Press, Macmillan, 1991.

Holy Bible, The. King James Authorized Version. Philadelphia: John C. Winston Co., 1935.

Huseyn of Hamadán. *Tárikh-i-Jádid or New History of Mírzá 'Alí-Muhammad, the Báb.* Trans. with Introduction, Illustrations & Appendices by E.G. Browne. London: C.J. Clay and Sons, 1893.

Kazemzadeh, Firuz. *Russia and Britain in Persia 1864–1914 A Study in Imperialism.* Yale University Press, 1968.

Lambden, Stephen. 'Rashh-i-'Amá, Translation and analysis of poem of Bahá'u'lláh'. *Bahá'í Studies Bulletin,* September, 1984.

Maḥmúd (Zarqání, Mírzá Maḥmúd-i). *Kitáb-i-Badáyi'u'l-Áthár [Maḥmúd's Diary].* Diary of 'Abdu'l-Bahá's Travels in Europe and America, written by His secretary. Bombay: Vol. I, 1914; Vol. II, 1921.

Mehrabkhani, R. *Mullá Ḥusayn, Disciple at Dawn.* Los Angeles: Kalimát Press, 1987.

Momen, Moojan. *The Bábí and Bahá'í Religions, 1844–1944. Some Contemporary Western Accounts.* Oxford: George Ronald, 1981.

— 'The Trial of Mullá 'Alí Bastámí: A Combined Sunní-Shí'ite Fatwa Against the Báb.' *Iran*, XX, British Institute of Persian Studies, 1982.

— *Selections from the Writings of E.G. Browne on the Bábí and Bahá'í Religions.* Moojan Momen, Ed. Oxford: George Ronald, 1987.

Nabíl-i-A'zam (Mullá Muḥammad-i-Zarandí). *The Dawn-Breakers, Nabíl's Narrative of the Early Days of the Bahá'í Revelation.* Trans. and edited by Shoghi Effendi. New York: Bahá'í Publishing Committee, 1932.

Nietzsche, Fredrich. *Thus Spake Zarathustra.* Modern Library, 1982.

Phelps, Myron H. *The Master in 'Akká, Including Recollections of the Greatest Holy Leaf.* Los Angeles: Kalimát Press, 1985.

Qur'an, The. Trans. J.M. Rodwell. Everyman's Library. London and New York: Dent 1909, 1939.

Richards, Fred. *A Persian Journey. An Etcher's Impressions of the Middle East.* London: Jonathan Cape, 1931.

Root, Martha. *Ṭáhirih the Pure, Irán's Greatest Woman.* Rev. edn. Los Angeles: Kalimát Press, 1981.

Ruhe, David S. *Door of Hope. A Century of the Bahá'í Faith in the Holy Land.* Rev. edn. Oxford: George Ronald, 1986.

Seyhoun, Hushang. *Regards sur l'Iran. 100 Drawings with Commentary.* Paris: Editions La Deësse, 1974.

Shoghi Effendi. *God Passes By.* Wilmette: Bahá'í Publishing Trust, 1957.

— *The Promised Day is Come.* Wilmette: Bahá'í Publishing Trust, 1961.

Sohrab, Mírzá Ahmad. *'Abdu'l-Bahá in Egypt.* New History Foundation. J.H. Sears & Co., 1929.

Star of the West. A collection of the Bahá'í Magazine, 1910–1924. Reprinted Oxford: George Ronald, 1978, 1984.

Taherzadeh, Adib. *The Revelation of Bahá'u'lláh*, a four-volume study. Oxford: George Ronald, Vol. I, 1974; Vol. II, 1977; Vol. III, 1983; Vol. IV, 1988.

Townshend, George. *The Promise of All Ages.* London: George Ronald, 1948.

Ward, Allan L. *239 Days. 'Abdu'l-Bahá's Journey in America.* Wilmette: Bahá'í Publishing Trust, 1979.

Weston, Harold F. 'Persian Caravan Sketches.' Published in National Geographic Magazine, April 1921, pp. 417–468.

Universal House of Justice, The. *A Synopsis and Codification of the Kitáb-i-Aqdas, the Most Holy Book of Bahá'u'lláh.* Haifa: Bahá'í Word Centre, 1973.

References

INTRODUCTION: THE GREAT SOUL AND HIS HOUR

1. Bahá'u'lláh, *The Kitáb-i-Íqán*, p. 191.
2. Bahá'u'lláh, *Gleanings from the Writings of Bahá'u'lláh*, p. 81.
3. Bahá'u'lláh, *Epistle to the Son of the Wolf*, p. 34.
4. Bahá'u'lláh, *The Kitáb-i-Íqán*, p. 213.
5. Quoted by Shoghi Effendi, *God Passes By*, p. 220.
6. Bahá'u'lláh, *The Kitáb-i-Íqán*, pp. 192–193.
7. ibid. p. 43.

CHAPTER 1: FIRST GLIMMERINGS

1. Bahá'u'lláh, *The Kitáb-i-Íqán*, p. 65.
2. Nabíl, *The Dawn-Breakers*, p. 2.
3. ibid, pp. 4–5.
4. ibid, p. 8.
5. ibid, pp. 10–11.
6. ibid, p. 12.
7. Bahá'u'lláh, *Ayyám-i-Tis'ih*, unpublished. By permission of the Bahá'í World Centre.
8. ibid, pp. 17–18.
9. ibid, p. 16.
10. ibid, p. 17.
11. ibid, p. 25.
12. ibid, p. 27; Muḥammad, *The Qu'rán* 76:21.
13. Nabíl, *The Dawn-Breakers*, p. 27.
14. ibid, pp. 38, 40–42.
15. ibid, p. 42.
16. ibid, pp. 44–45.
17. ibid, p. 45.
18. ibid, p. 16.

CHAPTER 2: THE CELESTIAL TREE GROWS

1. Shoghi Effendi, *God Passes By*, p. 190.
2. Nabíl, *The Dawn-Breakers*, pp. 12–13; Balyuzi, *Bahá'u'lláh, The King of Glory*, p. 13.
3. The Universal House of Justice, *A Synopsis and Codification of the Kitáb-i-Aqdas*, p. 27.
4. Bahá'u'lláh, *Gleanings from the Writings of Bahá'u'lláh*, p. 111.
5. Mírzá Abu'l-Faḍl, *Star of the West*, Vol. 14, No. 10, p. 291 (January 1924).
6. Nabíl, *The Dawn-Breakers*, pp. liv-lvii.
7. Balyuzi, *Bahá'u'lláh, The King of Glory*, p. 13.
8. Furútan, *Stories of Bahá'u'lláh*, p. 1.
9. 'Abdu'l-Bahá, quoted in *Star of the West*, Vol. 3, No. 9, p. 3 (1912).
10. 'Abdu'l-Bahá, *A Traveler's Narrative to Illustrate the Episode of the Báb*, pp. 56–58.
11. *Bahá'í World*, Vol. XIII, p. 433.
12. *Star of the West*, Vol. 14, No. 10, p. 292; Balyuzi, *Bahá'u'lláh, The King of Glory*, pp. 19–20.
13. Nabíl, *The Dawn-Breakers*, pp. 119–120.
14. Balyuzi, *Bahá'u'lláh, The King of Glory*, p. 20; Furútan, *Stories of Bahá'u'lláh*, p. 2 (with attributions to Ishráq-Khávarí).
15. Bahá'u'lláh, *Epistle to the Son of the Wolf*, p. 129.
16. Bahá'u'lláh, *Epistle to the Son of the Wolf*, pp. 11, 39.
17. Esslemont, *Bahá'u'lláh and the New Era*, p. 37.
18. 'Abdu'l-Bahá, *A Traveler's Narrative*, p. 34 (paraphrase).
19. Balyuzi, *Bahá'u'lláh, The King of Glory*, p. 21.
20. Sohrab, *'Abdu'l-Bahá in Egypt*, p. 17.
21. Bahá'u'lláh, Tablet for 'Álí Páshá, by permission of the Bahá'í World Centre.
22. Bahá'u'lláh, *Gleanings from the Writings of Bahá'u'lláh*, p. 138.
23. Esslemont, *Bahá'u'lláh and the New Era*, p. 38.
24. Nabíl, *The Dawn-Breakers*, p. 111.
25. ibid, pp. 111–112.
26. ibid, p. 112.
27. Balyuzi, *Bahá'u'lláh, The King of Glory*, pp. 22.
28. Mírzá Abu'l-Faḍl, *Star of the West*, Vol. 14, No. 10, p. 292.
29. Bahá'u'lláh, *Gleanings from the Writings of Bahá'u'lláh*, pp. 320–321.

CHAPTER 3: FATHER OF THE POOR

1. Bahá'u'lláh, *Epistle to the Son of the Wolf*, p. 93.
2. Nabíl, *The Dawn-Breakers*, p. 109.
3. Balyuzi, *Bahá'u'lláh, The King of Glory*, pp. 14, 16–18.
4. ibid, p. 25.
5. ibid, p. 25.

6. Balyuzi, *Bahá'u'lláh, The King of Glory*, p. 23; Blomfield, *The Chosen Highway*, pp. 34–40; *The Bahá'í World*, Vol. V. p. 53.
7. Nabíl, *The Dawn-Breakers*, p. 109.
8. Furútan, *Stories of Bahá'u'lláh*, pp. 2–3 (from Dr Ḍíyá Baghdádí's Memoirs, unpublished.)
9. Bahá'u'lláh, *Epistle to the Son of the Wolf*, p. 170; Balyuzi, *Bahá'u'lláh, The King of Glory*, pp. 16–17.
10. Bahá'u'lláh, quoted by Nabíl, *The Dawn-Breakers*, pp. 110–111.
11. Esslemont, *Bahá'u'lláh and the New Era*, p. 38.
12. Nabil, *The Dawn-Breakers*, p. 121.
13. ibid, p. 122.
14. ibid, p. 122.
15. 'Abdu'l-Bahá, *A Traveler's Narrative*, p. 35.
16. Balyuzi, *Bahá'u'lláh, The King of Glory*, pp. 22–23.
17. Bahá'u'lláh, *Epistle to the Son of the Wolf*, pp. 14–15.
18. Bahá'u'lláh, *Gleanings from the Writings of Bahá'u'lláh*, p. 196.
19. Blomfield, *The Chosen Highway*, p. 40.
20. Furútan, *Stories of Bahá'u'lláh*, p. 5.
21. Blomfield, *The Chosen Highway*, p. 40.
22. Bahá'u'lláh, *Gleanings from the Writings of Bahá'u'lláh*, p. 79.

CHAPTER 4: THE FIRST HIGH PROPHET

1. Bahá'u'lláh, *Gleanings from the Writings of Bahá'u'lláh*, p. 77.
2. Nabíl, *The Dawn-Breakers*, p. 53.
3. Muḥammad, *Qur'án, p.* 57.
5. Muḥammad, *Qur'án*, Súrih XXII; Genesis 37:18–36.
6. Bahá'u'lláh, *The Kitáb-i-Íqán*, p. 223.
7. Shoghi Effendi, *God Passes By*, p. 23.
8. The Báb, *Selections from the Writings of the Báb*, p. 47.
9. The Báb, *Selections from the Writings of the Báb*, pp. 57–58; Bahá'u'lláh, *Tablets of Bahá'u'lláh*, p. 120.
10. The Báb, *Selections from the Writings of the Báb*. p. 59.
11. Nabíl, *The Dawn-Breakers*, pp. 67–79, 80–81.
12. ibid, pp. 92–94.
13. ibid, p. 87.
14. ibid, p. 96.
15. ibid, p. 86.
16. ibid, pp. 104–106.
17. ibid, p. 107.
18. ibid, p. 107.
19. ibid, p. 107–108.
20. ibid, p. 113.
21. ibid. footnote (Dr. T.K. Cheyne).
22. ibid, pp. 116–117.
23. ibid, p. 117.
24. Bahá'u'lláh, *Tablets of Bahá'u'lláh*, pp. 12, 44.

25. Nabíl, *The Dawn-Breakers*, p. 583.
26. ibid, pp. 130–141.
27. Balyuzi, *The Báb*, p. 98.
28. Bahá'u'lláh, *Prayers and Meditations*, pp. 84–85.

CHAPTER 5: EPICENTER OF THE BÁBÍ CAUSE

1. Bahá'u'lláh, *Prayers and Meditations*, p. 295.
2. Nabíl, *The Dawn-Breakers*, pp. 228–229.
3. ibid, p. 236.
4. 'Abdu'l-Bahá, *Memorials of the Faithful*, p. 190.
5. Nabíl, *The Dawn-Breakers*, p. 279.
6. ibid, p. 279.
7. ibid, p. 585 (paraphrase).
8. ibid, p. 284.
9. Browne, *A Persian Anthology*, p. 72.
10. Nabíl, *The Dawn-Breakers*, p. 286.
11. ibid, p. 460.
12. Mehrabkhani, *Mullá Ḥusayn*, pp. 136–187; Nabíl, *The Dawn Breakers*, p. 261.
13. Nabíl, *The Dawn-Breakers*, p. 287.
14. Browne, *New History [Tarikh-i-Jadíd]*, p. 64.
15. Momen, *The Bábí and Bahá'í Religions*, p. 91.
16. Nabíl, *The Dawn Breakers*, p. 294.
17. Shoghi Effendi, *God Passes By*, p. 32.
18. Nabíl, *The Dawn-Breakers*, pp. 460–461.
19. ibid, p. 295.
20. ibid, p. 295–296; Shoghi Effendi, *God Passes By*, p. 33.
21. Nabíl, *The Dawn-Breakers*, p. 296.
22. Balyuzi, *The Báb*, pp. 168–169; see also Nabíl, *The Dawn-Breakers*, fn. pp. 297–298 (Dr. T.K. Cheyne).
23. Nabíl, *The Dawn-Breakers*, p. 461.
24. ibid, p. 297.
25. ibid, p. 293.
26. ibid, p. 299.
27. ibid, p. 299.
28. ibid, p. 584.
29. Bahá'u'lláh, *Tablets of Bahá'u'lláh*, pp. 57–58.

CHAPTER 6: CLASH: THE BÁBÍS AND REFORM OF SHI'ITE ISLÁM

1. Nabíl, *The Dawn-Breakers*, title page; Bahá'u'lláh, *The Kitáb-i-Íqán*, p. 252.
2. Nabíl, *The Dawn-Breakers*, pp. 315–316.

3. ibid, p. 319.
4. ibid, fn. p. 321.
5. ibid, p. 323.
6. Mehrabkhani, *Mullá Ḥusayn*, p. 183.
7. ibid, pp. 171–182.
8. ibid, pp. 212–215.
9. Nabíl, *The Dawn-Breakers*, p. 349.
10. ibid, p. 349.
11. ibid, p. 349.
12. ibid, pp. 583–584.
13. ibid, p. 461.
14. ibid, p. 370.
15. ibid, p. 461.
16. ibid, p. 371.
17. ibid, p. 372.
18. ibid, p. 273.
19. ibid, p. 375.
20. ibid, p. 375.
21. ibid, p. 584.
22. Bahá'u'lláh, *The Hidden Words*, No. 45, Arabic.
23. ibid, No. 47, Arabic.
24. Israeli, *A Golden Treasury of Persian Poetry*; Browne, *Materials for the Study of the Bábí Religion*, pp. 348–349. See Appendix 2.
25. Nabíl, *The Dawn-Breakers*, p. 432.
26. ibid, fn.2, p. 285.
27. ibid, fn.1, p. 465.
28. Bahá'u'lláh, *The Kitáb-i-Aqdas*, para. 00.
29. Bahá'u'lláh, *The Tablet of Patience [Súriy-i-Ṣabr]*, also known as the Tablet of Job [Ayyúb], unpublished.
30. ibid.
31. ibid.
32. ibid.
33. Nabíl, *The Dawn-Breakers*, pp. 501–502, paraphrase.
34. ibid, pp. 504–505; Browne, *A Traveler's Narrative to Illustrate the Episode of the Báb*, pp. 41–42.
35. Mehrabkhani, *Mullá Ḥusayn*, p. 158.
36. Nabíl, *The Dawn-Breakers*, pp. 508–514.
37. Bahá'u'lláh, unpublished Tablet, by permission of the Bahá'í World Centre.

CHAPTER 7: BANISHMENT AND FIRST RECOGNITION

1. Bahá'u'lláh, *Gleanings from the Writings of Bahá'u'lláh*, p. 222.
2. Browne, *New History (Tarikh-i-Jadíd)*, pp. 310–311.
3. Nabíl, *The Dawn-Breakers*, pp. 518–520; Browne, *A Traveller's Narrative to Illustrate the Episode of the Báb*, fn. p. 46; Balyuzi, *Bahá'u'lláh, The*

King of Glory, p. 65; Browne, *New History (Tarikh-i-Jadíd*, pp. 309–312, 330–331.
4. Nabíl, *The Dawn-Breakers*, p. 521.
5. ibid, p. 522.
6. ibid, p. 522.
7. ibid, p. 523.
8. Furútan, *Stories of Bahá'u'lláh*, pp. 7–8; Muḥammad, *The Qur'án*, 19:18.
9. Furútan, *Stories of Bahá'u'lláh*, pp. 7–8; Muḥammad, *The Qur'án*, 3:179.
10. Shoghi Effendi, *God Passes By*, pp. 68, 125.
11. Browne, *A Traveller's Narrative to Illustrate the Episode of the Báb*, pp. 62–63 (from the Lawḥ-i-Siraj).
12. Ḥaydar-'Alí, *Stories from the Delight of Hearts*, pp. 10–11.
13. Shoghi Effendi, *God Passes By*, p. 82; Balyuzi, *Bahá'u'lláh, The King of Glory*, p. 66.
14. Nabíl, *The Dawn-Breakers*, p. 588.
15. Balyuzi, *Bahá'u'lláh, The King of Glory*, pp. 96–97.
16. Nabíl, *The Dawn-Breakers*, p. 188.
17. ibid, pp. 31–32.
18. ibid, pp. 32–33.
19. ibid, pp. 595–598.
20. Unknown Persian poet cited in Browne, *A Persian Anthology*, p. 40.

CHAPTER 8: THE TORRENT AND THE MAIDEN

1. Bahá'u'lláh, *Gleanings from the Writings of Bahá'u'lláh*, p. 90.
2. Nabíl, *The Dawn-Breakers*, p. 598.
3. ibid, p. 599.
4. ibid, pp. 599–600.
5. Bahá'u'lláh, *Epistle to the Son of the Wolf*, p. 20.
6. Nabíl, *The Dawn Breakers*, p. 602.
7. ibid, p. 603.
8. ibid, p. 603.
9. ibid, p. 604.
10. ibid, fn. p. 609; see also Bahá'u'lláh, *Epistle to the Son of the Wolf*, p. 20, Nabíl, *The Dawn-Breakers*, pp. 607–608; Balyuzi, *Bahá'u'lláh, The King of Glory*, p. 77.
11. Nabíl, *The Dawn-Breakers*, pp. 607–608; Balyuzi, *Bahá'u'lláh, The King of Glory*, p. 78.
12. Bahá'u'lláh, *Epistle to the Son of the Wolf*, p. 20.
13. Bahá'u'lláh, *Epistle to the Son of the Wolf*, pp. 20–21; Balyuzi, *Bahá'u'l-láh, The King of Glory*, p. 78.
14. Bahá'u'lláh, *Epistle to the Son of the Wolf*, p. 77; Balyuzi, *Bahá'u'lláh, The King of Glory*, p. 79.
15. Nabíl, *The Dawn-Breakers*, p. 616.
16. Blomfield, *The Chosen Highway*, pp. 40–43.
17. Mírzá Maḥmúd-i-Zarqání, *Maḥmúd's Diary (Kitáb-i-Badáyi'u-Áthar)*, unpublished.

18. *Bahíyyih Khánum*, p. 33.
19. Furútan, *Stories of Baha'u'lláh*, pp. 13–14; Balyuzi, *'Abdu'l-Bahá*, pp. 11–12.
20. Ward, *239 Days: Remembrances of 'Abdu'l-Bahá*, p. 207; Mírzá Maḥmúd-i-Zarqání, *Maḥmúd's Diary*, Vol. 2, p. 206.
21. Nabíl, *The Dawn-Breakers*, pp. 631–633.
22. ibid, p. 613; footnote.
23. ibid, p. xxviii.
24. ibid, p. 613.
25. Shoghi Effendi, *God Passes By*, p. 80.
26. Bahá'u'lláh, *Tablets of Bahá'u'lláh*, p. 90.
27. ibid, p. 85.
28. Bahá'u'lláh, *Gleanings from the Writings of Bahá'u'lláh*, p. 72.
29. Balyuzi, *Bahá'u'lláh, The King of Glory*, p. 90.
30. Shoghi Effendi, *The Promised Day is Come*, p. 68.
31. Bahá'u'lláh, *Epistle to the Son of the Wolf*, p. 74.
32. Nabíl, *The Dawn-Breakers*, pp. 637–641.
33. ibid, pp. 642–645.
34. ibid, pp. 622–629.
35. Shoghi Effendi, *God Passes By*, p. 75.
36. Nabíl, *The Dawn-Breakers*, pp. 80–81.
37. Bahá'u'lláh, *The Tablet of Patience [Súriy-i-Ṣabr]*, unpublished.
38. Shoghi Effendi, *God Passes By*, p. 104; Nabíl, *The Dawn-Breakers*, p. 636.
39. Nabíl, *The Dawn-Breakers*, pp. 636–637.
40. Bahá'u'lláh, *Gleanings from the Writings of Bahá'u'lláh*, p. 222.
41. ibid, p. 99.
42. Bahá'u'lláh, *Epistle to the Son of the Wolf*, p. 21.
43. ibid, p. 22.
44. Shoghi Effendi, *God Passes By*, pp. 101–102.
45. Bahá'u'lláh, *Gleanings from the Writings of Bahá'u'lláh*, p. 284.
46. ibid, p. 282.
47. Bahá'u'lláh, *Prayers and Meditations*, p. 21.
48. Bahá'u'lláh, *Epistle to the Son of the Wolf*, pp. 11–12.
49. Bahá'u'lláh, *Gleanings from the Writings of Bahá'u'lláh*, p. 103.
50. Bahá'u'lláh, *Tablets of Bahá'u'lláh*, p. 66.
51. Bahá'u'lláh, *Prayers and Meditations*, p. 306.

CHAPTER 9: EXILE AND EXPATRIATE

1. Bahá'u'lláh, *Tablets of Bahá'u'lláh*, p. 66.
2. Bahá'u'lláh, *Epistle to the Son of the Wolf*, p. 141.
3. Shoghi Effendi, *God Passes By*, p. 92.
4. ibid, p. 29.
5. ibid, p. 25.
6. Bahá'u'lláh, *Epistle to the Son of the Wolf*, p. 142.
7. Shoghi Effendi, *Citadel of Faith*, p. 101.

8. Bahá'u'lláh, *Epistle to the Son of the Wolf*, p. 20.
9. Blomfield, *The Chosen Highway*, pp. 43–44.
10. 'Abdu'l-Bahá, *A Traveler's Narrative*, p. 31.
11. Nabíl, *The Dawn-Breakers*, pp. 648–650.
12. Bahá'u'lláh, *Epistle to the Son of the Wolf*, p. 57.
13. Shoghi Effendi, *God Passes By*, p. 106.
14. 'Abdu'l-Bahá, *A Traveler's Narrative*, p. 31.
15. Job 1:21 (the Nevium [Prophets]).
16. Bahá'u'lláh, *The Tablet of Patience [Súriy-i-Ṣabr]*, unpublished.
17. Blomfield, *The Chosen Highway*, p. 45.
18. Bahá'u'lláh, *Epistle to the Son of the Wolf*, p. 169.
19. Bahá'u'lláh, *Prayers and Meditations*, p. 34.
20. The Universal House of Justice, *A Synopsis and Codification of the Kitáb-i-Aqdas*, pp. 21–22.
21. Bahá'u'lláh, *Epistle to the Son of the Wolf*, pp. 21–22.
22. Bahá'u'lláh, *Gleanings from the Writings of Bahá'u'lláh*, p. 228.
23. Shoghi Effendi, *God Passes By*, p. 109.
24. Bahá'u'lláh, *Tablets of Bahá'u'lláh*, p. 40.
24. Bahá'u'lláh, *Gleanings from the Writings of Bahá'u'lláh*, p. 98.
26. Genesis 2:20 (The Torah [The Law]).
27. Blomfield, *The Chosen Highway*, p. 46.
28. Bahá'u'lláh, *Gleanings from the Writings of Bahá'u'lláh*, p. 109.
29. ibid, p. 121.
30. Bahá'u'lláh, *The Tablet of Patience [Súriy-i-Ṣabr]*, unpublished.

Index

This index is arranged letter by letter, ignoring connectives. Thus 'Abdu'lláh follows 'Abdu'l-Karím and precedes 'Abdu'l-Vahháb.

By the same author

Door of Hope
A Century of the Bahá'í Faith in the Holy Land

Since its first publication in 1983, **Door of Hope** has proved to be an indispensable guide to the history and sites of pilgrimage of the Bahá'í Faith in the Holy Land. The author lived at the Bahá'í World Centre for twenty-five years, and used this opportunity to make the subject of this book his special study. He has methodically examined the geography, archaeology and history of all that relates to the Bahá'í Faith, as well as the results of Jewish, Christian and Bahá'í scholarship.

The text is enriched by a unique collection of photographs and drawings, of great value for Bahá'í pilgrims and visitors, as well as those who have not had the opportunity of visiting the Holy Land.

The book is arranged in four sections: an **Introduction** giving an overview of the significance of the Holy Land and Bahá'u'lláh's arrival there in exile: **'Akká**, from ancient times until now, including the places and events, closely associated with Bahá'u'lláh, 'Abdu'l-Bahá and their followers; **the 'Akká area** including Mazra'ih, the Riḍván Garden, Bahjí and other sites related to the Bahá'í Faith; and **Haifa**, describing the developments on Mount Carmel from the arrival of the Templers in the 1860s to the completion of the Seat of the Universal House of Justice in 1982. The text is completed by informative Appendices, a chronology of key Bahá'í events in the Holy Land, notes, bibliography and index.

Paperback edition reprinted 1989
ISBN 0–85398–150–7
George Ronald, Publisher

MÁH-KÚ
TABRÍZ
URÚMÍYYIH
ZANJÁN
QAZVÍN
ÁMUL
SÁRÍ
BÁRFURÚSH
TÁKUR
TEHERAN
KULAYN
HAMADÁN
KHANIQAYN
KARAND
KIRMÁNSHÁH
KÁSHÁN
BAGHDAD
TO KARBILA
IṢFAHÁN
ABADIH
BAṢRA
PERSEPOLIS
SHÍRÁZ
BÚSHIHR
C A S P I A N
S E A
84 feet below the level of the Black Sea
P E R S
Route of the Báb
Route of Bahá'u'lláh